Volume 22 I0028099

TALKING ABOUT WELFARE

TALKING ABOUT WELFARE

Readings in Philosophy and
Social Policy

Edited by
NOEL TIMMS AND DAVID WATSON

Routledge
Taylor & Francis Group
LONDON AND NEW YORK

First published in 1976 by Routledge & Kegan Paul Ltd

This edition first published in 2019
by Routledge
2 Park Square, Milton Park, Abingdon, Oxon OX14 4RN

and by Routledge
711 Third Avenue, New York, NY 10017

Routledge is an imprint of the Taylor & Francis Group, an informa business

British Library Cataloguing in Publication Data
A catalogue record for this book is available from the British Library

ISBN: 978-1-138-61373-7 (Set)
ISBN: 978-0-429-45813-2 (Set) (ebk)
ISBN: 978-1-138-61153-5 (Volume 22) (hbk)
ISBN: 978-1-138-61158-0 (Volume 22) (pbk)
ISBN: 978-0-429-46532-1 (Volume 22) (ebk)

Publisher's Note
The publisher has gone to great lengths to ensure the quality of this reprint but points out that some imperfections in the original copies may be apparent.

Disclaimer
The publisher has made every effort to trace copyright holders and would welcome correspondence from those they have been unable to trace.

Talking
about welfare

readings in philosophy
and social policy

Edited by

Noel Timms

*Professor of Social Work
University of Newcastle upon Tyne*

and

David Watson

*Department of Moral Philosophy
University of Glasgow*

Routledge & Kegan Paul
London, Henley and Boston

First published in 1976
by Routledge & Kegan Paul Ltd
39 Store Street,
London WC1E 7DD,
Broadway House,
Newtown Road,
Henley-on-Thames,
Oxon RG9 1EN and
9 Park Street,
Boston, Mass. 02108, USA
Manuscript typed by Jacqueline Bayes
Printed in Great Britain by
Redwood Burn Limited
Trowbridge & Esher

ISBN 0 7100 8382 3 (c)
ISBN 0 7100 8383 1 (p)

As is the case with social policy in any State . . . the student must eventually make up his own mind and act on his own convictions. Even if the term 'Welfare State' were to pass out of common usage he would still find himself discussing 'The Good Society', for the debate is in fact about the meaning and conditions of the good life, always to be sought, never finally to be attained. Kathleen M. Slack, 'Social Administration and The Citizen', p.74.

A name is worthless without a backing of descriptions which can be produced on demand to explain its application. P. F. Strawson, 'Individuals', p.20.

Contents

Talking
about welfare
readings in philosophy
and social policy

Notes on the contributors

T.H. MARSHALL is Professor Emeritus of Sociology at the University of London. Among his many publications are 'Sociology at the Crossroads and other Essays', 1963 and 'Social Policy', 1965.

RICHARD B. BRANDT is Professor of Philosophy at Yale University. His publications include 'Ethical Theory', 1959 and, as editor, 'Social Justice', 1962.

G.H. VON WRIGHT is Research Professor in the Academy of Finland and Andrew D. White Professor-at-Large, Cornell Univeristy. His publications include 'Norm and Action', 1963 and 'Explanation and Understanding', 1971.

KAI NIELSEN is Professor of Philosophy at the University of Calgary. His publications include 'Scepticism', 1973.

MAURICE CRANSTON is Professor of Political Science at the University of London. Among his many publications are a biography of John Locke and 'What are Human Rights?', 1973.

R.M. TITMUSS was Professor of Social Administration at the London School of Economics until his death in 1973. His publications include 'Essays on the Welfare State', 2nd edn, 1963, and 'Commitment to Welfare', 1968.

R.S. DOWNIE is Professor of Moral Philosophy at the University of Glasgow. His publications include 'Roles and Values', 1971. He was chairman of the Working Party on The Teaching of Values in Social Work, set up by the Central Council for Education and Training in Social Work, whose Report was published in 1976.
xi

ELIZABETH TELFER is Senior Lecturer in Moral Philosophy
at the University of Glasgow.   Among her publications
are 'Education and Personal Relationships', 1974, with
R.S. Downie and Eileen M. Loudfoot.

DAVID DONNISON is Director of the Centre for Envrion-
mental Studies at the University of London.   His
publications include 'Social Policy and Administration',
1965 and 'The Government of Housing', 1967.

JOHN BENSON is Professor of Philosophy at the University
of Lancaster.

PETER LEONARD is Professor of Applied Social Studies,
University of Warwick.   Among his publications are
'Sociology in Social Work', 1966.

ALAN KEITH-LUCAS, educator and social worker, is
Professor at the University of North Carolina.   His
publications include 'Some Casework Concepts for the
Public Welfare Worker', 1957 and 'Giving and Taking
Help', 1972.

DOROTHY WALSH is Professor of Philosophy at Smith
College.

IAN T. RAMSEY was Nolloth Professor of the Philosophy of
the Christian Religion at Oxford until 1966.   He was
Bishop of Durham from 1966 until his death in 1972.
His publications include 'Christian Ethics and Contemporary Philosophy', 1966.

Acknowledgments

We gladly acknowledge the assistance of Professor P.F.
Strawson, Professor R.S. Downie, Vernon Pratt, Rita
Timms and Rosemary Watson by way of comment on earlier
drafts of the Introduction, and of Beverley Symes,
Anne Valentine and Wilma White by way of typing.

All the essays printed here, except that by Professor
Leonard, have been published before and details of previous publication are given below.   We thank the
authors, editors and publishers concerned for permission.   We reprint T.H. Marshall, The Right to Welfare
from 'Sociological Review', 1965, pp. 261-72;   Richard
B. Brandt, The Concept of Welfare, from Sherman Roy
Krupp, ed., 'The Structure of Economic Science: Essays
on Methodology', (c) 1966, reprinted by permission of
Prentice-Hall, Inc., Englewood Cliffs, New Jersey,
pp. 257-76; G.H. Von Wright, The Good of Man, ch. 5
of 'The Varieties of Goodness', London, Routledge &
Kegan Paul and New York, Humanities Press, Inc., 1963;
Kai Nielsen, Alienation and Self-Realisation, from
'Philosophy', vol. 48, 1973; Maurice Cranston, Human
Rights, Real and Supposed, ch. 4 in D.D. Raphael, ed.,
'Political Theory and the Rights of Man', London,
Macmillan, 1967; R.M. Titmuss, Welfare State and Wel-
fare Society, ch. 11, of 'Commitment to Welfare',
London, George Allen & Unwin and New York, Random
House, Inc., 1968; R.S. Downie and Elizabeth Telfer,
Respect for Persons and Public Morality, ch. 2 of
'Respect for Persons', London, George Allen & Unwin,
and New York, reprinted by permission of Schocken
Books, Inc., 1969; David Donnison, Liberty, Equality
and Fraternity, reprinted from 'The Three Banks Review',
no. 88, December 1970, published by the National and
Commercial Banking Group Ltd, pp. 3-23; R.M. Titmuss,
Who is my Stranger?, ch. 13 of 'The Gift Relationship',

London, George Allen & Unwin, and New York, Random House, Inc., 1970; John Benson, The Concept of Community, from L. Bright and S. Clements, eds, 'The Committed Church', London, Darton, Longman & Todd, 1966; Alan Keith-Lucas, The Art and Science of Helping, from 'Case Conference', vol. 13, 1966; Dorothy Walsh, Knowing by Living Through, from 'Philosophy and Phenomenological Research', vol. 31, no. 2, 1970-71; Ian T. Ramsey, On not being Judgmental, from 'Contact', no. 30, 1970, pp. 2-16.

Introduction

Noel Timms and David Watson

This introduction does not consist of abbreviated
versions of the essays and extracts which follow.   Our
main purpose is to bring a particular philosophical
perspective to bear on 'welfare talk', and in our view,
such a purpose can best be realised through a substantive introduction concentrating on a major theme - in
this case, identification.   In using this book it is
important to keep in mind that all the readings, and
our introductory essay, should be examined carefully
and critically.
Our introductory essay falls into two sections, A
and B.   Section A is divided as follows:
1 Conceptual clarification
2 Talk and welfare talk
3 Identification
4 Explanation
5 Identification and explanation in welfare
The first part of Section A explains our conception
of the role of conceptual analysis and the contribution
it might make to discussion of welfare, where technical,
would-be technical, and everyday terms are somewhat
haphazardly used and insufficient attention is given,
for example, to the distinction and connections between
evaluative and descriptive meaning.   In the second
part we introduce the main general argument of this
section that (i) every subject of welfare discussion
must be capable of a certain sort of description, and
that (ii) every welfare activity must be capable of a
certain sort of explanation.   Questions of identity
and explanation are first considered in terms of
everyday examples.   A philosophical theory of identification is then introduced, in part three, largely
through the work of Professor P.F. Strawson.   This
particular part may seem too abstract at a first

1

reading, but it has an important role in our argument
for it provides detailed justification of point (i)
above and declares our conception of adequate identification. We see conceptual analysis as an important
means to the adequate identification of subjects of
welfare discourse.

The value of conceptual analysis for welfare discourse may be questioned on the grounds that there are
countless cases in which we understand a word perfectly
well *without* being able to give a philosophical account
of it. However, some of these words, and in particular
those which are key words in discussions of welfare,
are taken out of their normal setting and put to use
in accounts of new activities, relationships, social
policies, administrative structures, and so on. We
may know perfectly well how to employ these words for
everyday tasks, but be less happy when we employ them
on special duties. No doubt sometimes special uses
simply call for technical or legal stipulative definition. But it seems to us that this is not always the
case. There are occasions on which discussion of
welfare would be best advanced by conceptual analysis,
by an examination of, for example, the nature of
welfare, respect, dignity, indifference, interests and
charity.

In part four of this section we introduce, but do
not develop, the related theme of explanation. In part
five we consider the implications of the accounts of
identification and explanation using examples of
welfare talk taken from some well-known texts.

The second section of our introduction uses the
essay by Professor T.H. Marshall to trace some connect-
ing themes to be found in the readings. These include
questions concerning welfare, the right to welfare, a
welfare society, possible moral foundations of a
welfare society and community. Identifying these,
being able to say what these things are, will clearly
be an important contribution to talk about welfare.

A

1 Conceptual clarification

Discussion of welfare has reached sufficient proportions
to enable us to identify a field of discourse, though
it can be indicated only in outline. This introduction, and the essays and extracts it introduces are
concerned with a preliminary exploration of certain

general and certain specific problems that arise in
discussions of welfare.
Our interest in this collection centres on general
questions of identification - what is welfare, what
sort of a right is a right to welfare and so on. The
following quotations from welfare writing indicate the
persistence of problems of identification in welfare
talk. How, we may ask, is it possible to identify
an activity from the following (italics added);
The basis of public relief *is* partly the race
instinct of sympathy, partly reasoned benevolence,
religious belief and ethical philosophy, partly a
deliberate measure of social protection, partly a
socialized form of mutual insurance against misfortune and accidental misery, to whose fund all
citizens contribute, and by which all who need are
entitled to profit (Henderson, 1902).
The care of the poor, sick, and abnormal members
of human society *is* part of politics with a social
orientation (Hnik, 1938).
Social services *represent* a compromise between
compassion and indifference, just as they reflect
our dispositions both to remember and to forget
our social obligations (Pinker, 1971).
We believe that now is an opportune time to try to
bring into collaboration the methods and insights of
contemporary analytical philosophy and the whole
business of talking about welfare. Of course, conceptual analysis is not the whole of philosophy, and
though we concentrate on it we do not want to suggest
that other philosophical methods and insights can make
no contribution to welfare discourse. The methods of
phenomenological philosophy might contribute to accounts
of inter-personal relationships, for example.
We have collected essays, some by professional
philosophers and others not, covering a range of concepts and beliefs which figure prominently in discussions about welfare. In this way we hope to draw
attention to an area of common interest to students of
social administration, social work and social policy;
and students of social and moral philosophy. The
essays and even sections of our Introduction may be
found to vary in level of difficulty according to the
reader's academic background. Students of social
administration and social policy will be more familiar
with the essays say, by T.H. Marshall, R.M. Titmuss
and David Donnison. They may be less sure of the
relevance for their own study of the essays say, by
G.H. Von Wright, Maurice Cranston, R.S. Downie and

Elizabeth Telfer, John Benson and part 3 of our Introduction. Students of social and moral philosophy will, no doubt, be more at home using the latter essays and less so using the former. However, both groups of students may take heart from the fact that the essays and extracts have been chosen as contributing to philosophical discussion of welfare in a serious but *readable* manner.

Discussions of welfare (a welfare state, a welfare society, even the welfare lady), the descriptions and evaluations of formal and informal help, contain far more conceptual and theoretical problems than is commonly realised, even by the more sophisticated of the welfare talkers. Philosophical analysis, we shall argue, is more richly effective, even in the realm of practice, than, for example, the common and dismissive charge of an exclusive and therefore sterile concern with 'mere words' suggests. We would argue that this view is misguided as follows.

It is very difficult to imagine an exclusive concern merely with *words*. The novelist and the poet, and indeed writers in general, cannot truly be said to have such a concern, even though they give words much of their attention. Neither may the grammarian, studying the sounds, inflexions, and constructions used in a language, nor the philologist studying the structure and development of language may be seriously so accused. A language is more than words. Perhaps the man whose researches show that there are four hundred four-letter words in the English language might with some truth be said to have had an exclusive concern with words, but thus occupied in compiling lists of words, he is not engaged in philosophical analysis.

Contemporary analytical philosophy in general aims at the clarification of concepts. Since the examination of concepts can only be carried out by considering the use of words, the contemporary analytical philosopher *may* be said to be concerned with *the use of words*, though not with words merely.

We may think of concepts very roughly, and thus debatably, as expressed by the uses of general words or descriptions, words or descriptions used to refer to a number of things. For example, such words or descriptions as 'horse', 'colour', 'tribe', 'rainbow', 'rational being', 'social service' and 'rapacious monster with the face and body of a woman and the wings and claws of a bird'. To clarify a particular concept is to understand better what it is to be a

thing referred to by the use of a general word or
description (words or descriptions), to be a thing of
that sort.   You may know enough about the use of the
word 'therapist', say, to know that, for example,
Jungian analytical psychologists are therapists, but
not know enough about the use of the word, 'therapist'
to say, for example, whether or not the word is
correctly used to refer to social workers.   In so far
as your concept of a therapist is unclear, you do not
know how the word 'therapist' is used, and, we may say,
thus far you do not know what a therapist is.   And,
of course, if you do not know what a therapist is, you
do not know who or what is a therapist.   In our
illustration, you do not know whether social workers
are therapists.   Clarification of the concept of a
therapist might provide you with grounds for denying
that social workers are therapists, and thus you would
better understand what it is to be a thing referred to
by the use of a general word or description (words or
descriptions), to be a thing of that sort.

We said that we may think of a concept as the uses
of general words or descriptions, but it is important
to remember that more than one general word or description may have the same use.

The *same* concept may be expressed by the uses of
different words, or descriptions.   Let us suppose
that 'therapist' is used to refer to 'a person providing a curative service'.   Because the same concept
may be expressed by the uses of different words or
descriptions, it does not follow from the fact that
someone does not know how a particular word or description is used that he does not have a clear concept
of whatever is in question.   He might know the use
of another general word or description which expresses
that concept.   His ignorance of the use of a particular word does not justify the conclusion that he does
not know what it is to be a thing of that sort, that
he does not know what are, and what are not, things
of that sort.   Suppose, for example, I say to you of
a mutual acquaintance, 'Pevsner is a marvellous
therapist', and you reply 'I don't know about that,
but he certainly provides a first class curative
service.'   In this case you do not know the use of
the word 'therapist', but you do nevertheless know what
it is to be a thing of that sort.   You refer to things
of that sort using the description 'person providing a
curative service'.   In such cases conceptual clarification is not required.   It may be that we need to see
and say some such thing as 'Ah, you use "therapist" as

I use "provider of a curative service",' but otherwise,
no difficulty arises concerning the identification of
things of the sort in question.

We said that in cases in which the same concept
may be expressed by the use of more than one word or
description, it does not follow from the fact that
someone does not know how a particular word or description is used either that he has an unclear conception
of whatever is in question, or that he does not know
what it is to be a thing of that sort. However,
where the person does not know how *any* general word
or description used to signify things of the sort in
question is used, the person does not merely have an
unclear conception of whatever is in question, he has
none; nor does he know what it is to be a thing of
that sort.   In our immediately preceding illustration
the thing in question could be identified only because
one person in the dialogue, though not knowing how the
particular word 'therapist' is used, knew at least how
some general word or description used to signify
things of the sort in question is used. We shall
later use some of the work in Professor P.F. Strawson,
to emphasise the importance of their being, for every
thing, *some* general word or description used to signify
things of that sort, and shall consider the implications, in a given case, of there being no such general
word or description.

We can distinguish three kinds of difficulty in
connection with general words or descriptions used to
signify a subject: (i) there is some general word or
description used to signify things of the sort in
question, but the use of that general word or description is unclear to at least one, but not both,
parties to the discussion; (ii) there is some general
word or description used to signify things of the sort
in question, but its use is unclear to *both* parties
to the discussion; (iii) the kind of case in which
the use of no general word or description to signify
things of a sort purported to be in question is clear
to anyone. In the first two kinds of case, conceptual unclarity and difficulty in identifying things
of the sort in question, go hand in hand. In the
third kind of case conceptual unclarity, we shall later
argue, goes hand in hand with impossibility of identifying things of the sort in question, goes hand in hand
with there being no sort of things in question.

In practice it is difficult to distinguish these
kinds of case. Listening to, or reading, a discussion
of a certain idea we often suspect a case of the first

kind, where the use of the general word or description
used to signify the item in question is unclear to at
least one party to the discussion - ourselves.   That
this is a case of the first kind and not of either of
the other kinds is indicated when another party to the
discussion is able to clarify the use of the general
word or description.   Thus the use of the word
'therapist' might be clarified for someone uncertain
of its use within a staff conference.   A case is of
the second and not of the third kind where the use of
the general word or description, though initially
unclear to both parties to a particular discussion,
may become clear to both for example, by their being
referred to other discussions in which the general
word or description in question is used.   For example,
members of a Local Authority Social Services Committee
might, in discussion of local community care provision,
discover themselves unclear about the technical use
of the general term 'community care'.   Their problem,
however, may be resolved by an examination of policy
statements by Central Government.   Where this general
kind of procedure is not efficatious, we may have a
case of the third kind.   In all three kinds of case,
discussion in a sense can proceed, with clarification
unconsidered or not attempted.   Discussion can continue in the sense that people can go on talking.
In another and more important sense, in all three
kinds of case, discussion cannot proceed: we have not
begun and cannot begin to communicate with others
about the subject of our discussion, for we have not
identified any item as the subject of our discussion.
All three kinds of case are common in discussions of
welfare.   In our Introduction and in the essays
collected, attention is focused upon conceptual clarification in relation to identification, and so upon
important philosophical problems concerning communication in discussion of welfare.

    Of course, conceptual clarification is not achieved,
like the age of 18, once and for all.   A notion of
adequate conceptual clarification, however, will allow
room for the varying needs to be clear and to identify
things as of a certain sort.   The adequacy of a conceptual clarification, like the adequacy of a legacy,
must be judged relative to the demands made of it.
A certain legacy might be adequate for the purpose of
buying a hamper, but not for buying a house.   Similarly the degree of conceptual clarity necessary in
praying for 'the aged' may be less than is necessary
in discussion of pensions for 'the aged'.   This idea

of adequacy of clarification will be taken up later.
At this point we simply stress the relation between
conceptual clarification and identification.   This
relation makes philosophical investigation of this
kind important in the realm of practice.

Alan Keith-Lucas (1953) makes the following point
in connection with social work.

As social work becomes increasingly professionalised,
the theories of social needs and goals developed by
the profession become more and more esoteric, and
consequently less easily understood and less suscep-
tible to the control of public opinion.   Because
the practice of social work has increasingly become
a governmental function affecting the lives and
rights of millions of individuals, because the client
group is increasingly in the hands of highly trained
specialists whose theories are not easily understood
or checked by public opinion, it has become more
important than ever to examine critically the presuppositions underlying modern social work practice -
if only to bring them to the light of day, where
those concerned with the rights of people may be
aware of the issues involved.

Keith-Lucas's concern to discover the implications
for human rights contained in social work practice,
and, we might add, a concern to discover the implications for human rights contained in *theories* offering
accounts of social work practice, a welfare state, a
welfare society etc., supports our view that philosophical investigations of this kind are important in
the realm of practice.   In general, where the presuppositions of a social theory are not already understood, they may be exposed through conceptual clarification of that theory.

General words and descriptions often appear, of
course, within statements which we not only want to
understand, but whose truth or falsity we wish to
determine.   But, as Professor David Raphael, (1970)
says,

in order to know whether a belief is tenable, and
in particular whether it involves any inconsistencies, either within itself or between it and
other accepted beliefs, it is necessary to understand just what the belief is and what it implies.
We need to know clearly what is meant by the terms
used in it.

Thus, an understanding of the uses of words, and in
particular, we have argued and shall argue further,
the uses of general words or descriptions is necessary

before we can say a belief is *tenable*, i.e. could be true, let alone is true.   This general point, which applies to beliefs of all kinds, is a further ground for asserting that the methods and insights of contemporary analytical philosophy will be usefully employed in talking about welfare.   The distinctions drawn in philosophical analysis may be more or less complex, but without them, as Professor Raphael has said, 'we are likely to talk and act confusedly in social and political affairs and are liable to follow blind alleys in social and political science' (1970, p. 17).

Raphael (1970) points out that the clarification of concepts has three related purposes, analysis, synthesis, and improvement of concepts.

By analysis of a concept I mean specifying its elements, often by way of definition; for example, one can analyse or define sovereignty as supreme legal authority, specifying the three essential elements which make up the concept.   By synthesis of concepts I mean showing the logical relationships whereby one concept implies or is implied by another; for example, one can show a logical relationship between the concept of a right and that of an obligation by pointing out that whenever A has a right against B, that implies that B has an obligation.   By improvement of a concept I mean recommending a definition or use that will assist clarity or coherence; for example, one can recommend, as I do, that the concept of sovereignty should be used *only* of the legal authority, and not of the coercive power, of a State (pp. 12-13).

The purposes of analysis, synthesis, and improvement go together and constitute the general aim of clarification of concepts which we have argued is the main focus of a form of philosophy which should play an important part in discussions of welfare.

In the chapter cited, Raphael suggests that in the main tradition of Western philosophy the clarification of concepts was pursued until very recently only as a necessary aid to another aim, *the critical evaluation of beliefs*.   Conceptual clarification, as we have seen, may help us determine the tenability of a belief and its consistency within itself and between it and other accepted beliefs, but though unclarity and inconsistency are grounds for not adopting a belief, necessary truths apart, clarity and consistency are not grounds for positively *adopting* a belief.   Until very recently, says Raphael, philosophy has been thought of as contributing not only to our understanding

of a belief, but also to the debate leading to our
adoption or rejection of a belief.   According to
Raphael, the philosophical activity of the critical
evaluation of beliefs is the attempt to give rational
grounds for accepting or rejecting beliefs which we
normally take for granted without justification.
There seems to be no reason why critical evaluation
of beliefs might not extend also to the examination of
the rationality of grounds given for accepting or
rejecting beliefs not normally taken for granted.   We
hope to indicate, later in this introductory essay
and in our selection of the essays and extracts which
follow, that both the philosophical activity of the
clarification of concepts and that of the critical
evaluation of beliefs have an important place in talking
about welfare.

On the account given, conceptual clarification is
required in connection with a belief or set of beliefs
expressed in the terms (words or phrases) of a field
of discourse.   We are concerned with the field of
social welfare discourse which contains technical,
would-be technical and 'everyday' terms.   Conceptual
clarification is required when, for example, the would-
be technical terms of that belief or set of beliefs
are explained in a way which does not permit us to
know whether it is tenable, and in particular whether
it involves any inconsistencies, either within itself
or between it and other accepted beliefs.   Conceptual
clarification is also required if it is left unclear
precisely which of the terms of the belief or set of
beliefs are intended to be technical.   These conditions may themselves go unnoticed because the terms
in question, would-be technical or otherwise, have a
familiar everyday use or uses.   This familiarity may
be retained when a term is transferred to or employed
within a more (or less) precise field of discourse,
but when such a transfer occurs we may forget the
important task of explaining changes in use.   And,
of course, difficulties may arise even in connection
with terms transferred to the more restricted field
of discourse which suffer no change in use but continue
to have their everyday use.   The everyday uses of
such terms may themselves require conceptual
clarification.

These difficulties of language can easily be illus-
trated from the field of welfare if we begin to list
some of the terms frequently used within its discussions
- stigma, rights, community, love, integration, need,
help, self-determination, second class citizen, welfare,

community.   As R.B. Brandt, for example, states in his
essay (the second in the present collection): 'The term
"welfare" seems to carry a meaning, in ordinary talk
about the welfare of individuals, different from what
it carries in many recent discussions in which it
appears in the expression "social welfare"'.   Or
again, in the case of rights, Maurice Cranston, in an
essay re-printed here, argues that the journey from
the relatively well-defined territory of traditional
human rights (to life, liberty and a fair trial) to the
new land of universal social and economic rights (such
as the right to unemployment insurance, old age
pensions, medical services, and holidays with pay,) is
a journey from sense to nonsense.   Moreover, it is,
in his view, dangerous nonsense since the circulation
of a confused notion of human rights hinders the
effective protection of what are correctly seen as
human rights.   With these and other terms we uncon-
sciously move between technical, would-be technical
and everyday usage, neglecting the fact that each of
these perspectives offers its own way of elucidating
the term in question.   John Benson in an essay in
this collection identifies three senses of the word
'community'.   These senses
     even if not very clear, are pretty clearly different.
     Of course, their areas of application overlap, but
     this is just where the danger lies, for though the
     word may apply in two or all of its senses to the
     same thing, it does so by virtue of different
     criteria and says very different things depending
     on the criteria which are held to justify the
     application.
     Another particularly acute problem for discourse in
social welfare is that the terms of the discourse
commonly have both descriptive and evaluative meaning:
where the term is both used to name or describe some
object or state of affairs *and* to evaluate it.
Professor R.M. Hare, in his book 'The Language of
Morals', has developed this distinction between descriptive and evaluative sorts of remark, using simple
examples to highlight the logical point.   'Examples
of the first sort of remark are "This strawberry is
sweet", and "This strawberry is large, red, and
juicy".   Examples of the second sort of remark are
"This is a good strawberry" and "This strawberry is
just as strawberries ought to be"' (1952, p. 111).
Both sorts of remark, says Hare, can be, and often
are, used for conveying information of a purely
factual or descriptive character.   This may be less

obvious about an evaluative remark, but, using Hare's
example, if our hearer knows what sorts of strawberries
we are accustomed to call 'good' (knows what is the
accepted standard of goodness in strawberries), as
Hare says, he undoubtedly receives information from
our evaluative remark.   He will complain that we have
misled him if he subsequently discovers the strawberry
to be small, green, and hard rather than juicy (cf.
pp. 112-13).

However, an evaluative remark can be used to express
a thought which a descriptive remark cannot be used to
express.   'It is a thought which has something to do
with choosing or being inclined to choose' (p. 105).
An evaluative remark has a commendatory force which a
descriptive remark does not possess.   Thus, to say,
'This strawberry is just as strawberries ought to be',
is to commend and express an inclination to choose
this strawberry, while to say 'This strawberry is
sweet' is not.

The similarity and difference between these two
sorts of remark may now be brought together.   We
commend and are inclined to choose this strawberry,
say, precisely because this strawberry comes up to our
standard of goodness in strawberries, it satisfies the
description we would give of a good object of this
sort.   Thus an evaluative remark may both commend and
supply information about the object in question: it
has both evaluative and descriptive meaning.

The fact that a person, or set of people, commend,
are inclined to choose, or perhaps 'behave preferen-
tially' towards a certain member of a class 'is not in
itself a necessary or sufficient condition for saying
that it is a good member of the class; it is only
the most important of the many things that might make
us want to say that they *think* that it is a good
member' (p. 109).   Evaluative remarks express the
speakers conventional or unconventional evaluations,
and, of course, different speakers may commend or be
inclined to choose different members of a class.
Hare points out, in connection with the word 'good'
that

the evaluative meaning is constant for every class
of object for which the word is used.   When we
call a motor car or a chronometer or a cricket bat
or a picture good, we are commending all of them.
But because we are commending all of them for
different reasons, the descriptive meaning is
different in all cases (p. 118).

The description which a motor car must satisfy before

we shall be inclined to choose it, is quite different
from what a cricket bat must satisfy for us to be
inclined to choose it. And, we might add that the
associated descriptive meaning may not only be
different in relation to objects in different classes,
it may also be different for different people or
groups of people in relation to objects in *the same*
class. Thus, your criteria for a good holiday or a
good lecture may not be ours.

Evaluative remarks are thus often controversial.
Further, since the criteria of application employed by
the speaker may differ from those which the hearer
would employ in making the evaluative remark in question, evaluative remarks commonly require conceptual
clarification. The descriptive meaning of the evaluative remark may need to be made explicit. It is
arguable that the terms listed as frequently used
within discussions of welfare: stigma, rights,
community, love, integration, need, and so on, all
have evaluative as well as descriptive meaning, and
thus may figure in evaluative remarks about welfare.
The fact that the term 'social work' commonly has both
evaluative, and descriptive force, is one of the
serious complications in any attempts to evaluate the
activity: 'this is social work' and 'this is good
social work' are characteristically interchangeable.
In any case, evaluative remarks form a significant
segment of controversial discussions of welfare.
Their discrimination, and making explicit the descriptive meaning in each case where this is required, are
important philosophical contributions to be made to
discussions of welfare. And, as Keith-Lucas reminded
us, so also is the exposure and critical evaluation
of the principles of evaluation implied by evaluative
remarks.

In this collection of readings we approach such
discussions through the published work of academic
theorists. This is not to suggest that social
administrators, etc., have no views on their professional activities different from those discussed by
academics in this field. Conceptual clarification
may very well be required over a far larger set of
beliefs than arise in published academic discussion
for there are almost as many professional social
administrators, policy-makers and social workers as
there are amateur philosophers! However, our *introduction* is effected through academic discussion first,
because such discussion may be expected to be more
rigorous, leaving us less mileage to cover to the goal

of conceptual clarification, and second, because the
beliefs of professional social administrators, etc.,
in the absence of published academic empirical work
on the subject, do not form a discernible set to which
students of social and moral philosophy might be
introduced, as is the case with published academic
beliefs. Of course, there is a third party whose
views might very well be worthy of philosophical
attention: those whose welfare is in question,
patients, clients, or service users. However, like
the beliefs of welfare administrators and workers, the
beliefs of those whose welfare is in question, in
general do not yet constitute a discernible set from
which philosophical analysis can begin. (1)

Raphael draws the following analogy which we might
use to indicate what might be expected from the collaboration we hope to encourage.

> The clarification of concepts is like cleaning the
> house. When you have cleaned the house, there is
> not much to be seen for your work. You have not
> acquired any new possessions, though you will have
> thrown out some things that are not wanted and are
> just a nuisance. What you have at the end of it
> is a tidier house, in which you can move around
> more easily and in which you can find things when
> you need them (1970, p. 16).

For those who weary of conceptual clarification the
news is bad. As Raphael adds, 'the analogy is apt
in another respect also. Cleaning the house is not
a job that can be done once and for all'. Old
questions recur and new questions arise because
society is a living thing. We have argued that the
consequent scope for regular conceptual clarification
raises what are not matters of 'mere words' and, for
our field of interest, matters which constitute the
basic stuff of welfare.

Some of the difficulties that arise in consideration of these conceptual matters have, as we shall
note later, been acknowledged in the published work
of academic social administrators, but the significance of these difficulties, as we shall also argue,
has not been sufficiently appreciated. First, however, it is necessary to review some philosophical
considerations that arise in any attempt to talk,
which includes, of course, any attempt to talk about
welfare, welfare activities, and in general all items
which are subjects in welfare discussion. We shall
also review some philosophical considerations that
arise in any attempt to describe any such items as
human activities.

2   Talk and welfare talk

We shall argue that every subject of welfare discussion
must be capable of a certain sort of description, and
that every human welfare activity must be capable of a
certain sort of explanation.   Discerning these
necessities very usefully structures the philosophical
tasks already delineated.   They are the goals of conceptual clarification.   We shall begin with a general
review of some of the complexities in description and
explanation, using simple illustrations.   We shall
then re-trace this ground using a philosophical theory
of identification as a means of establishing why in
general terms description and explanation are of
central importance.

We may ask of any item 'What is it?'   We may ask
anyone engaged in any activity 'What are you doing?'
In each case we are seeking a general name or description which distinguishes the subject as the thing it
is.   But it is no good using a name for something
unless one knows who or what is referred to by the
use of the name.   What Professor P.F. Strawson has
said of proper names is also true of general names,
'a name is worthless without a backing of descriptions
to explain its application' (1959, p. 20).   When we
ask the questions 'What is it?' and 'What are you
doing?', we are seeking a *description* which distinguishes the subject as the thing it is.   Such a description may be more or less detailed, and, if the
item is an activity, may include a description of
the method adopted in carrying on or carrying out
the activity.   Thus, in answer to our first question,
'What is it?', a man in The Plough and Harrow might
say, for example, 'It is a cribbage board', or
perhaps, if this answer was not enlightening, 'It is a
board used to keep the points score, in the card game
cribbage, by placing pegs in certain holes in the
board.'   In answer to our question, 'What are you
doing?' the same man might offer any one of a range of
types of possible answers.   He might say, 'I am
drinking', or perhaps 'I am raising my glass to my
mouth', or again, 'I am drinking by raising my glass
to my mouth.'

We may also ask anyone engaged in any activity the
question, 'Why are you doing what you are doing?'
seeking a purposive explanation of the activity.   An
activity may be explained in this way by reference to
something beyond itself: an activity may be a means
to an end distinct from the activity itself.   Thus,

indifferent to snooker, one might play to keep fit,
and explain one's playing snooker by referring to
this end. But activities need not be thus explained.
An activity might be what we call 'an end in itself'.
One might play snooker for its own sake, and explain
one's playing simply by saying 'snooker's got everything!' The man in The Plough and Harrow might
drink for its own sake, but carry out preliminary
activities merely as means to an end distinct from
the preliminary activities themselves. Thus in
answer to our question he might say 'Try it and you'll
understand', or perhaps, 'I adopt the method of raising my glass to my mouth because I have found it
promotes drinking rather better than the method of
lowering my mouth to the glass.'
    It is important to note in connection with human
activities that the questions 'What are you doing?'
and 'Why are you doing what you are doing?' are distinct, but also that the answers to these questions are
not entirely independent. It may be granted that
knowing what I am doing may not put you in a position
to say why I am doing it. For example, knowing that
I am saving money does not tell you that I plan to
buy a house. You might guess my plan, but you might
equally have guessed, in this case mistakenly, that
I plan to go on holiday. It may also be granted that
knowing why I am doing what I am doing may not put
you in a position to say what I am doing. For
example, knowing that I am doing what I am doing in
order to buy a house does not tell you that I am
robbing banks. Again, you might guess my method,
but you might equally have guessed mistakenly that I
am saving from my salary. Cases like these, and
there are many of them, arise because what I am doing
is often a means to more than one end, and why I am
doing what I am doing, my end, is often attainable by
more than one means. Nevertheless, the answers to
our two questions are not entirely independent, for
what I am doing is not in fact a means to *every* end,
but only to some ends, and why I am doing what I am
doing, my end, is not in fact attainable by *every*
means (to some end) but only by some. Thus, for
example, knowing that I am saving money could not
lead you reasonably to suppose that I plan to go to
bed early tonight, but might lead you reasonably to
suppose that I plan to buy a car. And this is
because saving money is not a means to the former end,
but is a means to the latter end. Similarly, knowing
that I plan to buy a house could not lead you reasonably

to suppose that I am watching a football match, but
might lead you reasonably to suppose that I am taking
out endowment insurance. And this is because the
former is not a means to the end of buying a house,
while the latter is. Problems of description and
explanation, then, are related.

To say that every subject of welfare discussion must
be capable of a certain sort of description, and that
every human welfare activity must be capable of a
certain sort of explanation is not to deny, of course,
that descriptions and explanations of these sorts
(which we have not yet specified) are subject to many
other kinds of appraisal. Descriptions and explanations may be unacceptable on various grounds. Some
descriptions don't fit; some explanations aren't
convincing. We do not want to deny the possibility
of offering a description of the sort in question or
an explanation of the sort in question which is
unacceptable on *some* criteria of appraisal. We wish
simply to make two assertions. First, it must be
possible, for every subject of welfare discussion, to
supply a description satisfying certain specifiable
criteria of appraisal, and second, it must be possible,
for every human activity (and so for every welfare
activity), to supply an explanation satisfying certain
specifiable criteria of appraisal. Both assertions
must be supported by specifying the criteria to which
we refer, by specifying the type of description and
the type of explanation we have in mind. We shall
do this in support of the first assertion by using
some of the work of Professor P.F. Strawson. We
have so far characterised descriptions of the sort in
question simply as 'a description which distinguishes
the subject as the thing it is'. To put it formally
we shall now set our first assertion in its descriptive metaphysics. Naturally, we have attempted to
put forward the general criteria to which we refer,
as clearly as possible, but the views introduced in
this discussion may also be usefully considered in
the context of their original homes, references to
which are supplied. Technical terms assumed in the
original work to be understood, and not explained
here, are explained in 'The Encyclopedia of Philosophy',
editor-in-chief Paul Edwards (Macmillan, 1967).

3   Identification

We set our first assertion in its descriptive metaphysics because we are concerned with descriptions as
means of identification.   Through the detailed
introduction of a theory of identification, we examine
the conditions of the possibility of identification.
We are then provided with criteria by which to assess
terms employed in talking about welfare *as* means of
identification.   To admit that problems of identification arise in our welfare talk and to urge greater
care with our means of identification, leaving a
theory of identification aside, is not enough - for
without a theory of identification we are not in a
position to say that these terms are means of
identification.
    We have said that the development of means of
identification of the sort in question is one of the
goals of conceptual analysis.   Our inclusion of this
piece of descriptive metaphysics reflects our view
that this goal should be presented as fully as possible,
so that it might be better understood.   We thus provide non-philosophers with an opportunity to consider
theoretical problems concerning descriptions and
explanations with which they are familiar, at a more
general level.   We return to the familiar descriptions
and explanations in part five of section A, but the
theory of the present section is also explicitly
related to pieces of welfare discourse.
    The subjects of welfare discussion are what
Strawson has called 'individuals'.   'An individual is
anything whatever; i.e. anything which can in
principle, in any way whatever, be distinguished, as
the single thing it is, from all other items under
different presentations or descriptions or in different manifestations' (Strawson, 1971, p. 199).
Usually when we talk about *individuals* we are talking
about single human beings, as opposed perhaps to
their societies or their families.   The word 'individual' is being used in this way, for example, when
it is argued that private markets in welfare erode
the freedom of the 'individual' (Titmuss, 1948).   It
is important to notice, particularly in a discussion
of welfare, that Strawson is using the word 'individual' in a way which recognises as *individuals* rather
more than individual human beings.   For Strawson an
individual is *anything whatever,* so that not only is
Aunt Fanny an individual, but so is her colouring, her
living-room carpet, the fly on the end of her nose,

etc., etc., so is anything whatever. Further, it
should be remembered that when Strawson says 'An
individual is anything whatever; *i.e.*, anything
which can in principle, in any way whatever, be
distinguished, as the single thing it is, from all
other items under different presentations or descriptions or in different manifestations' (italics ours),
what follows the 'i.e.' is not a *qualification* of his
first statement, but an *explication* of it, making the
same point more explicit by adding more detail.   He
is not allowing that there might *be* some thing which
cannot in principle, in any way whatever, be distinguished, as the single thing it is, from all other
items under different presentations or descriptions
or in different manifestations.   An individual is
anything whatever, and everything is an individual;
everything can in principle, in some way or other, be
distinguished as the single thing it is, from all
other items ... and so on.   On Strawson's account,
to *be* an individual is to be something in principle
in some way or other, distinguishable as the single
thing it is, from all other items ... etc.   On this
account the *existence* of an individual is neither
more nor less than its discriminability and identifiability as the single thing it is, from all other
items under different presentations or descriptions
or in different manifestations (cf. Strawson, 1971,
p. 200).   On this account, discriminability and
identifiability is a necessary and sufficient
condition (2) of existence as an individual, of being
something.
    Discrimination and identification are possible only
within a language; we cannot, for example, discriminate or identify anything without signifying the
sort of thing it is, and this we do, and must do,
within a language.   Suppose, for example, that I
want to pick out my pencil in order that you might
pass it to me.   I can only do this within a language,
picking out what is of interest by specifying, perhaps
amongst other things, what sort of thing it is.   I
might say, for example, 'Pass me the *pencil* by your
left hand.'   Thus, on this account we may say that
an individual *owes* its existence to its being specifiable within a language in a way which discriminates
and identifies it.   Following Strawson, we may say
that individuals owe their existence to a *style of
specification* the terms of which embody or imply in
their meaning principles for distinguishing, counting
and identifying individuals (cf. Strawson, 1971,

p. 195, p. 200).   In the example just given, in which
the individual in question was designated by the use
of the description 'the pencil by your left hand', the
individual is specified in a style the terms of which
embody in their meaning a principle or method for
distinguishing, counting, and identifying individuals.
The term 'pencil' embodies in its meaning just such a
principle; if we know what 'pencil' means, then we
know one method for distinguishing, counting and
identifying individuals.

If I said 'Pass me the *thing* by your left hand', the
individual in question, if any, is designated by the
use of the description 'the thing by your left hand'.
In this case the individual, if any, is specified in
a style the terms of which do *not* embody in their
meaning a principle or method for distinguishing,
counting, and identifying individuals.   The term
'thing' does not embody in its meaning any such
principle.   Everything is a thing, so the term 'thing'
distinguishes nothing.   To know what 'thing' means is
not thereby to know at least one method for distinguishing, counting, and identifying individuals.   In this
case, so far as it has been specified, my request
cannot be satisfied, you cannot pass to me what I
want you to pass to me because I have not specified
any individual in the required style; I have not
picked out anything which you might pass to me.   This
is why, from the point of view of the hearer of the
request, we said, 'the individual in question, *if
any*'; because the style of specification does not
embody in its meaning any principle or method for
distinguishing, counting, and identifying individuals,
the hearer is in no position to know that an individual *is* in question.

Suppose at a public meeting I stand up and say
'Scotland will receive no special benefits and may
suffer severe coastal pollution as a result of the
discovery of oil under the North Sea'.   In this
example, the individual in question is designated by
the use of the proper name 'Scotland'.   The individual is *not* specified in a style the terms of which
embody in their meaning a principle or method for
distinguishing, counting, and identifying individuals.
However, the individual in question *is* specified in
a style the terms of which *imply* in their meaning
just such a principle or method.

As Strawson says, two linguistic means of identification are available.   We can use descriptions or
names or both.   But, to repeat, it is no good using a

name for an individual unless one knows who or what is
referred to by the use of the name; a name is worthless without a backing of descriptions which can be
produced on demand to explain its application (cf.
1959, p. 20). In our example, the name 'Scotland'
would not succeed in picking out an individual if the
audience did not know some such description as 'the
most northerly country in the United Kingdom', which
they might use to pick out a certain individual. And
they use this description to pick out a certain individual because it is a description the terms of which
embody in their meaning a principle or method for
distinguishing, counting, and identifying individuals;
if we know what 'country' means, then we know one
method for distinguishing, counting, and identifying
individuals - individuals of the sort of which that
named 'Scotland' is an example. Thus, the identification of an individual by the use of a proper name
is possible if and only if the speaker and hearer know
some description of the individual the terms of which
embody in their meaning a principle or method for
distinguishing, counting, and identifying individuals.
When this condition is satisfied, the speaker can use
a proper name to pick out the individual in question
and the hearer can identify the individual picked out.
Our earlier example of a case in which the individual,
if any, is specified in a style the terms of which do
not embody in their meaning a principle for distinguishing, counting, and identifying individuals, the case
in which I say 'Pass me the thing by your left hand',
may also serve as an example of a case in which the
individual, if any, is specified in a style the terms
of which do not *imply* a principle or method of the
required sort.

  Examples of styles of specification the terms of
which embody or imply in their meaning principles for
distinguishing, counting, and identifying individuals
can, of course, also be found in welfare discourse.
When we talk about rent rebates, nuclear families,
meals on wheels, presenting problems and methods of
referral, the individual in question is specified in a
style the terms of which embody in their meaning a
principle or method for distinguishing, counting, and
identifying individuals. If we know what 'rent
rebate' means, for example, then we know one method
for identifying individuals. Suppose at another
public meeting I say 'Shelter must become politically
aggressive.' In this example the individual in
question is designated by the use of the proper name

'Shelter'.   The individual is *not* specified in a style
the terms of which embody in their meaning a principle
for identifying individuals, but *is* specified in a
style the terms of which *imply* in their meaning just
such a principle or method.   The name 'Shelter' would
not succeed in picking out an individual if the
audience did not know some such description as 'the
voluntary organisation devoted to providing accommodation for the homeless', which they might use to pick
out a certain individual because it is a description
the terms of which embody in their meaning a principle
of the required sort.   The term 'voluntary organisation' embodies such a principle in its meaning.

Examples of styles of specification the terms of
which neither embody nor *imply* in their meaning a
principle or method for distinguishing, counting, or
identifying individuals are more controversial.   Sayings such as 'things will improve substantially if we
are returned to office', where 'things' purportedly
functions as a name, might be suggested.   For, if
this is all that has been said, it may well be the
case that the speaker and hearers do not know some
description the terms of which embody in their meaning
a principle of the required sort, which can be produced on demand to explain the application of the name.
They may not know *what* it is that it is being claimed
will improve substantially.   Of course, it may be
that the speaker is using the name with a backing of
one description of the required sort and the hearers
mistakenly assume he is using the name with a backing
of a different description of the required sort.   But
it may also be the case that the name is being used
with *no* backing description of the required sort.   In
that case we do seem to have an example of a style of
specification the terms of which neither embody nor
imply in their meaning a principle or method for
distinguishing, counting, and identifying individuals.
An example from welfare talk can be found in Beales's
attempt (1945) to describe 'the branches of social
policy': 'They are *positive elements* in a world of
public as well as private enterprise' (italics ours).

We might also suggest as examples of styles of
specification of the kind at present in question,
sayings such as 'The needy will receive special priority
in future', where 'the needy' purportedly functions as
a name.   But in this case it would not be true to say
that the speaker and hearers do not know *some* description the terms of which embody or imply in their
meaning a principle of the required sort.   'The needy'

is elliptical. It is an incomplete expression which
requires completion, here clearly in the form of the
noun 'people', yielding 'needy people' or 'persons in
need'. Both the speaker and hearers know that the
individuals in question are people, and the term
'person' embodies in its meaning a principle of the
required sort - we do know how to count and identify
people. On the other hand, knowing how to identify
the *candidates* for neediness, we still don't know *which*
people are to count as needy because the word 'needy'
and the phrase 'in need' lack exact and rigid criteria
of application; these expressions are *vague*.

It is important to bear in mind, then, that in the
case of some styles of specification, it may not be
enough, from the point of view of individuation, that
the terms of the style of specification embody or imply
in their meaning a principle for distinguishing,
counting, and identifying individuals. Satisfaction
of this latter condition may not be enough if we want
to know *which* individuals are in question as opposed to
what sort. If the expression used to ascribe a distinguishing characteristic to an individual of a known
sort is vague, then though we know what sort of individual is in question; we shall not know which. We
might therefore distinguish the following as two issues
which may arise in connection with any style of specification of an individual. (i) Do its terms embody or
imply in their meaning a principle for distinguishing,
counting, and identifying individuals? (ii) Are any
of its terms vague? We might go on to argue that
both issues arise in connection with styles of specification employed within, as well as outside, the
field of welfare. We might also argue that *both* are
philosophical issues which should be of interest to
anyone talking about welfare.

However, it might be suggested that these are not
two distinct difficulties which might arise in connection with a style of specification, but one difficulty
under different descriptions. In other words it
might be suggested that for the terms of a style of
specification neither to embody nor to imply in their
meaning a principle of identification etc., is for
those terms to be vague. Similarly, it might be
suggested that terms which are vague fail to embody or
imply in their meaning a principle of identification,
etc. Consider our earlier examples of each type of
case. In the case in which it was said that 'Things
will improve substantially if we are returned to
office', we have an example of a style of specification

the terms of which neither embody nor imply in their
meaning a principle for distinguishing, counting, and
identifying individuals. 'Things' may also be said
to be vague in the extreme; to say the least, it
lacks precise criteria of application. In the case
in which it was said (completing the incomplete
expression used in the original example) that 'People
in need will receive special priority in future', we
have an example of a style of specification one of
the terms of which embodies in its meaning a principle
of identification etc., and another of the terms of
which is vague: 'people' and 'in need' respectively.
'People' may also be said not to be vague, but to
possess precise criteria of application; 'in need'
may also be said neither to embody nor to imply in its
meaning a principle of identification etc.

Against the view that there are here two distinct
difficulties which might arise in connection with a
style of specification, it might thus be suggested
that we have here just one difficulty under two descriptions: for the terms of a style of specification
not to embody or imply in their meaning a principle
of identification, etc. *is* for its terms to be vague,
to lack precise criteria of application. This
rather complex problem needs more philosophical work.
It is a significant problem for those of us talking
about welfare, for if there are two distinct difficulties which might arise in connection with our
styles of specification, then we need to be able to
distinguish and identify examples as they arise.
However, in this context the problem perhaps serves
best as an example of an issue deep within philosophical territory which is nevertheless an issue which
is an important consideration in talking about welfare.
Whether there be one issue or two here, our present
interest is in distinguishing styles of specification
which supply a principle of identification, etc.,
from those which do not. The problem is relevant to
our present interest, but we shall take it no further
here.

We mentioned earlier another issue which might.
arise in discussion of any style of specification of
an individual: are any of its terms evaluative? It
is worth noting at this point that both terms which
may be used to evaluate and terms which may not, may
be more or less vague, or indeed not vague at all.
The exactness or looseness of their criteria of
application does absolutely nothing to distinguish
evaluative from non-evaluative terms. As Hare says,

Words in both classes may be descriptively loose or exact, according to how rigidly the criteria have been laid down by custom or convention. It certainly is not true that value-words are distinguished from descriptive words in that the former are looser descriptively, than the latter. There are loose and rigid examples of both sorts of word. Words like 'red' can be extremely loose, without becoming to the least degree evaluative; and expressions like 'good sewage effluent' can be the subject of very rigid criteria, without in the least ceasing to be evaluative (1952, p. 115).

The discrimination of evaluative uses of general words or descriptions, as we stressed earlier, is an important task for the philosophy of welfare. However, evaluation must always be evaluation of something, of an individual, or individuals; the evaluative use of a general word or description must always be associated with some descriptive meaning. One can evaluate strawberries, sewage and social relationships, but one cannot simply evaluate. The identification of individuals is thus as important for the evaluative use of general words or descriptions as it is for the non-evaluative use. For this reason, then, our present interest lies in distinguishing styles of specification the terms of which embody or imply in their meaning a principle for distinguishing, counting, and identifying individuals, from those the terms of which do not. The essays we have brought together may be seen as contributions to the development of styles of specification of the required sort for a range of purported subjects of welfare discussion.

Adapting what Strawson has said elsewhere (1959) we may say that it is not merely a happy accident that we are often able, as speakers and hearers, to identify the individuals which enter into our discourse. That it should be possible to identify individuals of a given type seems a necessary condition of the inclusion of that type in our ontology (very roughly, by 'our ontology' we mean 'what our talk commits us to the existence of'). For what could we mean by claiming to acknowledge the existence of a class of individuals and to talk to each other about members of this class, if we qualified the claim by adding that it was in principle impossible for any one of us to make any other of us understand which member or members, of this class he was at any time talking about?

We may say, then, that every individual owes its

existence to a style of specification the terms of
which embody or imply in their meaning principles
for distinguishing and identifying individuals.   Let
us say, again following a suggestion put forward by
Strawson, that an individual is specified in the
required style when it is specified by an *adequately
identifying designation*.

It will be recalled that Strawson's work was introduced as supporting and clarifying our assertion that
it must be possible, for every subject of welfare
discussion, to supply a description satisfying certain
specifiable criteria of appraisal.   Let us summarise
our account so far.   Given (i) that for every individual, that is, for everything, being specifiable by
an adequately identifying designation is a necessary
and sufficient condition of its being something, then
(ii) being something entails being specifiable by an
adequately identifying deisgnation;   (iii) every
subject of welfare discussion is something;   therefore
(iv) if our descriptive metaphysics is sound, every
subject of welfare discussion must be specifiable by
an adequately identifying designation.

Earlier we stressed the relation between conceptual
clarification and, since the examination of concepts
can only be carried out by considering the use of
words, between clarification of the uses of words,
general words, or descriptions, and the identification
of things.   What has just been presented is an
account of the relation between the identification of
individuals and the use of general words or descriptions the terms of which embody or imply in their
meaning principles for distinguishing and identifying
individuals.   It is all very well, of course, to
label as an 'adequately identifying designation' a
style of specification the terms of which embody or
imply in their meaning principles for distinguishing
and identifying individuals, and to offer a clarifica-
cation of this explanation.   This still tells us very
little about what we might call the 'mechanics' of
distinguishing and identifying individuals;   for the
purpose of answering the question 'How do adequately
identifying designations *in general* succeed in
adequately identifying an individual?', the account
so far given is inadequate.   However, for our
purposes, entry into such a discussion seems unnecessary.   The account given is adequate for the purpose
of distinguishing this style of specification.   For
our purposes we may simply draw attention to the fact
that, as Strawson has pointed out, there are many

general terms under which individuals fall which embody
or imply in their meaning

> principles for distinguishing or picking out indi-
> viduals which fall under them from other things,
> for counting or enumerating such individuals
> (though perhaps only under favourable circum-
> stances) and for identifying such an individual
> encountered in one connexion or referred to under
> one description as the same item as one encountered
> in another connexion or referred to under another
> description (1971, pp. 195-6).

For individuals in general such general terms as fish,
shoe, postcard, book, gazumping and cooking and such
descriptions as raising one's glass, breaking and
entering and turning over a new leaf, embody in their
meaning principles for identifying individuals. Such
terms as Atlantis and Tricky Dicky imply in their
meaning principles for identifying individuals. For
individuals which are the subjects of welfare discourse we have mentioned such general terms as rent
rebate, nuclear family, and method of referral and
might mention such descriptions as admitting into care
and doing a domiciliary visit, as embodying in their
meaning principles for identifying individuals. Such
terms as Shelter and Oxfam imply in their meaning
principles for identifying individuals.

Strawson, we can now note, regards the requirement
that an adequately identifying designation should at
least embody or imply a general term of the kind
described as too stringent. He says

> Let us call terms which clearly satisfy that des-
> cription 'clearly individuating terms'. There
> are other terms which, in one way or another fall
> short of being clearly individuating, yet are
> such that if a designation of an individual
> brings that individual under one of these terms,
> that designation is to count as adequately
> identifying (1971, pp. 196-7).

One example of a term falling short of being clearly
individuating, says Strawson, is the kind of case in
which the criteria of identity to be associated with
the term are in dispute.

> This does not mean that there are no such criteria;
> only that the criteria are, so to speak, adjustable,
> depending on the purposes for which we wish to use
> the notion or the place we wish to give it in our
> theories. What we have here is the case where the
> meaning of the term is unsettled or disputed, but
> where any settlement of it would yield a clearly
> individuating term (1971, p. 197).

Strawson names the class of terms which fall short of being clearly individuating yet may be adequately identifying 'the class of variably individuating terms'.   Admitting the existence of this class of variably individuating terms and that they are to count as adequately identifying, means that point (ii) in our summary given earlier (p. 26) must now be interpreted as the view that being something entails being specifiable by a clearly individuating term. For individuals which are often, though not exclusively, the subject-matter of welfare discussion, we may suggest as examples of variably individuating terms of the kind described charity, poverty, need, community and welfare.   Of course, there will be cases where the criteria of identity to be associated with a term come to be disputed when we *change* the purposes for which we wish to use the notion or the place we wish to give to it in our theories.   In other cases, such as a dispute may arise even though there are no such changes.   The criteria of identity commonly associated with the term may be argued to make it unsuitable for the purposes for which we wish to use the notion or the place we wish to give it in our theories.   If the term is to be retained in effect the criteria of identity to be associated with the term are in dispute. ‐ In each case the meaning of the term is unsettled or disputed, but any settlement of it, we assume, would yield a clearly individuating term.   It is a central aim of the series of which this collection is a member, to provide a forum for discussion of the variably individuating terms we employ, sometimes fatally insensitive to the fact that they are variably individuating, in talking about welfare.   Strawson defines individuating terms in general as the logical sum of clearly individuating terms and variably individuating terms (1971, p. 198). We shall follow Strawson (cf. 1971, pp. 198-9) and say that any specification of an individual which embodies or implies an individuating term under which the item is presented as falling, is an adequately identifying designation.

We have now given a more precise account of the sort of description which we asserted earlier it must be possible to supply for every subject of welfare discourse: it must be possible to supply an adequately identifying designation for every subject of welfare discourse.

4   Explanation

Our second assertion, that it must be possible for every
human activity (and so for every welfare activity) to
supply an explanation satisfying certain specifiable
criteria of appraisal, must now be substantiated.
Having introduced the work of P.F. Strawson in supporting our first assertion, we shall introduce some of
the work of Professor R.S. Peters in supporting our
second assertion.   For a fuller treatment of points
used here, chapter I of his book (1958) should be read.
We have so far characterised explanations of the sort
in question simply as 'a purposive explanation of the
activity'.   This characterisation must now be
amplified.

As Peters says,
the general question 'Why did Jones do that?' is
capable of being asked and answered in a variety
of different ways.   The particular formula employed
in asking the question usually dictates the sort of
answer which is expected and which counts as an
explanation.   The paradigm case of a human action
is when something is done in order to bring about
an end.   So the usual way of explaining action is
to describe it as an action of a certain sort by
indicating the end which Jones had in mind.   We
ask what was his *reason* for doing that or what was
the *point* of it, what *end* he had in mind.   If we
ask why Jones walked across the road, the obvious
answer will be something like 'To buy tobacco....'
Even in this simple sort of explanation in terms
of a man's reason for doing something there are,
as a matter of fact, concealed assumptions.   We
assume, for instance, that walking across the street
is an efficient way of getting to the tobacconist.
This counts as an explanation not simply because
Jones envisaged walking across the street as a
means to getting the tobacco, but because it really
is a means to getting it.   We assume, too, that
a man who has this information will act on it if
he wants some tobacco.   We assume that men are
rational in that they will take means which lead to
ends if they have the information and want the
ends (1958, pp. 3-4).

He goes on,
but it is not only norms of efficiency and consistency that are implicit in the concept of 'his
reason'.   There are also norms or standards of
social appropriateness.   After all, Jones might

have crawled or run across the road.   But 'to get
some tobacco' would be a very odd answer to the
question 'Why did Jones *run* across?'   Yet running
would be quite an efficient way of getting across
the road.   It would, however, be socially odd as
a way of crossing the road to get some tobacco.
Man is a rule-following animal.   His actions are
not simply directed towards ends; they also conform to social standards and conventions, and
unlike a calculating machine he acts because of his
knowledge of rules and objectives (1958, p. 5).

This purposive, rule-following, model of human actions,
as Peters says, is the model in terms of which most of
our explanations of human actions are couched and our
predictions of people's behaviour presuppose it.   It
is this sort of explanation which we claim may be
offered for every human action; every human activity
may be accommodated within this purposive rule-
following explanatory framework.

To make this claim is not to deny that people sometimes invent reasons for actions or that people sometimes delude themselves into thinking that the reasons
they offer for their actions are operative reasons.
As Peters says, we draw a distinction between *his*
reason for doing so-and-so, and *the* reason why he did
it (1958, pp. 8-9).   And in some cases to offer an
explanation in which *the* reason is opposed to *his*
reason is to offer an explanation of a different sort
from the purposive rule-following sort of explanation
distinguished.   In some cases, to give *the* reason
why a person does something is to give a *causal*
explanation.   More generally, causal explanations are
offered

when there is some kind of *deviation* from the
purposive rule-following model....   In such cases
it is as if the man suffers something rather than
does something.   It is because things seem to be
happening to him that it is appropriate to ask
what made, drove, or possessed him to do that.
The appropriate answer in such cases may be in
terms of a causal theory (1958, p. 10).

Drawing this distinction between cases of doing something and cases of suffering something regarding only
the former as cases of genuine action, we may concede
that the latter sort of cases may be sufficiently
explained in terms of causes, but argue that the
former sort of cases may not.   A *sufficient* explanation, of genuine action, can only be given in terms of
the rule-following purposive model.   Again, this is

not to deny that there will be many causes in the sense
of *necessary* conditions, but these do not add up to a
sufficient explanation in the case of a genuine
action. (5)   Our second assertion may thus be
expressed as the assertion that it must be possible to
accommodate every genuine human activity within the
purposive rule-following explanatory framework.
Within the field of welfare, it must be possible to
accommodate the genuine activities of, for example,
policy-makers, executives, and the clientele, within
the purposive rule-following explanatory framework.

We may sum up the preceding discussion by repeating
our two assertions: (i) it must be possible, for
every subject of welfare discussion, to supply an
adequately identifying designation of that subject;
(ii) it must be possible, for every human activity
(and so for every welfare activity) to supply an
explanation accommodating it within the purposive rule-
following explanatory framework.   We have supported the
former assertion in greater detail.   We do not want to
suggest either that problems of explanation are less
significant than problems of identification, or that
they can be dealt with quite separately.   It may be
true in general that adequate explanations presuppose
the adequate identification of those whose purposes
they are and of whatever is to be explained, but the
identification of some individuals may involve reference to their purposes or use (e.g. a social policy,
a medical social worker, a reader, buying, tuning and
sieving).   The emphasis in our exposition upon problems of identification simply reflects our current
interest.

5   Identification and explanation in welfare

Our collection of essays is designed to facilitate an
examination of the adequacy, as identifying designations, of descriptions and definitions so far put
forward of activities which are the subject-matter of
welfare discourse.   We also wish to facilitate
consideration of the accommodation of the activities
in question within a purposive rule-following explanatory framework by an examination of the adequacy of
current designations of the objectives of the activities in question.   Neither the essays collected here
nor our introduction to them put forward final
adequately identifying designations of the activities
and objectives of interest, nor are these activities

finally accommodated within a purposive explanatory
framework.   Our aim is not at this point to settle
issues, even if we could, but to emphasise a number
of underrated issues from the discussion of which
both students of social administration, social policy
and social work, and students of social and moral
philosophy may benefit.   We have collected together
essays which may be regarded as undertaking the first
essential step towards such designations and such an
accommodation, the clarification of the use of terms
of our field of discourse, and in particular of the
terms in which current designations and accommodations
are couched. (6)

The collection also facilitates an examination of
what might be called 'justifications' in welfare discourse.   Earlier, following Raphael, we suggested
that the philosophical activity of the critical
evaluation of beliefs has an important place in
talking about welfare.   Raphael (1970, p. 4) links
critical evaluation to justification, adding that, 'I
use the word "justification" to mean the giving of
rational or justifying grounds either for accepting a
belief or for rejecting it'.   As Raphael uses
'justification' it might include examining purposive
explanations of human activities as grounds for
accepting or rejecting a belief about what some individual or group is doing.   But it is important to
stress that it might also include examining the moral
principles to which a belief commits one.   Welfare
talk, often explicitly but also sometimes implicitly
involves commitment to moral principles.   These
essays contribute to our consciousness of implicit
moral commitment and to the examination of the
principles to which we might be committed.

We are now in a position to consider further the
implications of our assertions that it must be
possible, for every subject of welfare discussion, to
supply an adequately identifying designation of that
subject, and that it must be possible, for every
human activity (and so for every welfare activity) to
supply an explanation accommodating it within the
purposive rule-following explanatory framework.   In
the discussion which follows we shall deal specifically with activities, but it should be remembered
that our first assertion applies to more than
activities.   It applies, for example, to those acting,
persons or things acted upon, the context or setting
of activity, and so on.

We recognised earlier that the same concept might be
expressed by the uses of different words or descriptions.   We may now recognise that the same item might
be designated by more than one adequately identifying
designation. Suppose the item in question is an
activity.   It is not a condition of doing (as opposed
to suffering) something that one can supply *every*
adequately identifying designation of what one is
doing or one's method of doing it.   One can imagine,
say, a sausage-linker asked by a neighbour 'What do
you do for a living?' unable to supply *every* possible
specification in the required style either of the
activity or of the method he adopts to carry it out
daily.   Such inability might be explained in various
ways.   The man might lack the necessary vocabulary,
for example.   Nor is it a condition of doing something that one can supply *every* possible accommodation
of what one is doing within the purposive rule-
following explanatory framework.   Our sausage-linker
might be as weak on such explanations as he was
supposed to be on adequately identifying designations,
and his weakness might be similarly explained.   The
fact that individual activities owe their existence
to the possibility of their being signified by an
adequately identifying designation is quite consistent
with its being true that a man might both engage in
an activity and be unable to supply *every* adequately
identifying designation of it, and, we added, be
unable to supply every accommodation of it within the
purposive rule-following explanatory framework.   And
this latter is as true of men engaged in activities
concerned with welfare as it is of sausage-linkers.
It doesn't follow from the fact than an individual
social worker, for example, is unable to supply every
specification of the required sort for social work
or for his way of doing social work, that he cannot
do his job.
    However, the fact that it must be possible, for
every subject of welfare discussion, to supply an
adequately identifying designation of that subject,
entails that *some* such designation of it can be given
by anyone for whom it is a subject.   This is *not*
consistent with its being true that a man might both
engage in an activity (the activity thereby being a
subject for him, the subject of his attention say)
and be unable to supply *some* adequately identifying
designation of it.   A man cannot engage in an activity
he is unable to identify. (7)   And if no adequately
identifying designation can be supplied by anyone,

then no man might engage in the putative activity, for there is no activity in question.   Again the fact that it must be possible, for every human activity, to supply an explanation accommodating it within the purposive rule-following explanatory framework, entails that *some* such explanation of it can be given by anyone for whom it is an activity.   This is *not* consistent with its being true that a man might both engage in an activity and be unable to supply *some* purposive explanation of it.   A man cannot engage in, actively take part in, what is not, for him, a genuine activity.   And if no purposive rule-following explanation can be supplied by anyone, then no man might engage in the putative activity, for there is no genuine activity in question.

In connection with our first assertion then, the important implication is that if an activity cannot be described in the required manner, then it is not something, and hence not something a man might do. Lack of an explanation of the required sort compounds the felony.   Not only is the putative activity not *something* a man might do, it is not something a man might *do*.   As regards activities concerned with welfare in particular, we may, therefore, say that if no descriptions or explanations of the required sorts can be supplied by anyone, then the putative activities (8) concerned with welfare are neither possible activities, nor possible human activities. Expressed in relation to every putative subject of welfare discussion, the important implication is that if a putative subject cannot be described in the required manner, then it is not something, it is no more than a putative subject.   We are not talking about anything and there is nothing to say.

Since a vast number of people and agencies are regularly *said* to be engaged in activities concerned with welfare, one might assume that adequately identifying designations and purposive explanations of their activities have been given, adequate in the context of the political, moral, or perhaps professional discussions in which these things are said. As we suggested earlier, an examination of current literature on activities concerned with welfare at the very least exposes the innocence of the assumptions that such designations and explanations have been *clearly* given. (9)   An examination of current literature makes the same point as regards putative subjects of welfare discussion which are not activities.

Writers on welfare have, naturally, noted both that
these are difficult matters and that they are unre-
solved.   These points have usually been made in
connection with activities, activities described by
Kathleen Slack, in a way which has a touch of irony
in the present connection, as aiming 'to advance and
secure the welfare and well-being of the citizen in
particular and general respects' (1966, pp. 73-4).
That is, in connection with welfare activities designated by such phrases as 'social service' and
'welfare state'.   Professor David Marsh states
(1970, p. 1) that 'even now, in the 1970's, there
seems to be no real consensus of opinion as to what
is a welfare state and what are the principles and
practices of a state which entitles it to be given
this label.'
Moreover, says Marsh, 'in Britain it would seem
that most people believe we have a welfare state
because we have a wide range of social services, yet
if one asked the man-in-the-street to define what he
means by the social services, he would probably find
great difficulty in giving an adequate definition'
(1970, p. 1).   Marsh, unfortunately, does not clarify
his use of the phrase 'an adequate definition', but
his remarks support our case if we assume that as
regards human activities, including socially organised
activities, an adequate definition is provided when
an adequately identifying designation and a purposive
rule-following explanation are given.
Those writers who have noted the absence of descriptions and explanations of the required sort for
such activities or organisations specifically concerned with individuals as are signified by such
phrases as 'social services' and 'welfare state'
have, in general, not gone on to offer the perspicuous
and consistent descriptions and explanations required.
Marsh, for example, concludes his discussion of the
evolution of the concept of a welfare state by
asserting a welfare state to be 'one in which there
are conscious and deliberate policies for ensuring at
least a minimum standard of life at all times for
everyone, and, as far as possible, equality of
opportunity for everyone to achieve the best out of
life, commensurate with aptitude and ability' (1970,
p. 21).   This 'definition' is inadequate, we would
argue, because it fails to put us in a position to
distinguish such individuals and fails to accommodate
them within a purposive rule-following explanatory
framework.   Too much is unsaid.   What criteria do

we or ought we to employ in assessing the standard of
life in a state?   How do we or ought we to distinguish
impaired opportunities from missed opportunities?   Are
conscious and deliberate government policies *ensuring*
my opportunity to achieve all that is best out of
life consistent with my achieving all that is best out
of life, in particular the development of self-
determination?   On what grounds and on what kind of
grounds does or ought the state to act in relation to
a man's opportunities?   Are all aptitudes and
abilities to be encouraged equally?   Do all aptitudes
and abilities contribute equally to 'the best in
life'?   And, of course, amongst the many remaining
questions, what is welfare?   Other sections of
Marsh's book do something towards satisfying the need
to accommodate social services and welfare within a
purposive rule-following explanatory framework, but
the requirement of an adequately identifying designation remains unsatisfied.

Penelope Hall noted (1952, p. 3) that the term
'social service' is 'relatively modern, having come
into general use with the multiplication of public
and voluntary provisions to further the well-being of
members of the community which is one of the outstanding characteristics of our times', it is a term which
is 'sometimes used rather vaguely, and universal
agreement has not yet been reached as to which services should be classified as "Social"'.   However,
Miss Hall suggested that if there is not universal
agreement, there is at least *general* agreement in the
description of welfare activities labelled 'social
service'.   'The generally accepted hall-mark of
social service is that of direct concern with the
personal well-being of the individual' (1952, p. 3).
More optimistic than Marsh, Miss Hall nevertheless
provided a description of social services which is
not perspicuous enough to be an adequately identifying
designation.   Again, too much is unsaid.   What
constitutes 'direct concern'?   What is personal well-
being?   Nor does her account accommodate social
services within a purposive explanatory framework.
What implications, for example, does 'direct concern'
have for the liberty of the individual, which is often
held to be a part of personal well-being?

Kathleen Slack provides a very useful survey of
descriptions and explanations of a welfare state in
Concepts of the Welfare State (1966, ch. 4), many
of which are, as adequately identifying designations
and purposive rule-following explanations, unsatis-

factory.   As she says, a major problem in discussions
of a welfare state is that

> like the social services, there is not consensus of
> opinion about its precise aims, or characteristics.
> It is clear that antagonist and protagonist have
> not the same concept in mind.   The Welfare State
> means or conveys different things to different
> people.   In these circumstances agreement about
> the value or disvalue of the Welfare State cannot
> easily, if ever be reached.   The student can but
> examine what has been said and done and make up
> his own mind (1966, p. 62).

If the situation with regard to these key terms is
as Kathleen Slack describes it, we have two cases of
variably individuating terms and so of adequately
identifying terms.   If matters were worse, the
student would not be in a position to follow Miss
Slack's advice.   The student may make up his own mind
about the value or disvalue of the welfare state only
when the subject of his value-judgment is signified
by an adequately identifying designation and accommodated within a purposive rule-following explanatory
framework.

In the essay The Subject of Social Administration
(1968, p. 21) Titmuss says

> the study of welfare objectives and of social
> policy ... lies at the centre of our focus of
> vision.   We may bring to this focus, singly or in
> combination, the methods, techniques and insights
> of the historian, the economist, the statistician,
> the sociologist, or, on occasion, some of the
> perspectives of the philosopher.

In our view the occasion for some of the perspectives
of the philosopher is when there is no consensus of
opinion about the characteristics or aims of an
activity, for one source of such a lack of consensus
is, as we said earlier, inadequate clarification of
descriptions and explanations of our subject-matter.
Until each of two men can offer an adequately
identifying designation of the item which is his
subject, it makes no sense to say either that they are
talking about the same thing or that they are not.
Until each can also offer a purposive rule-following
explanation of the item which is his subject it makes
no sense to say either that they are talking about
the same human activity or that they are not.   The
root of a lack of consensus about the characteristics
and aims of an activity may lie in inadequate identifying designation and purposive rule-following explanation of that activity.

In the pursuit of adequately identifying designation and perspicuous purposive rule-following explanation we must bear in mind the following point made by Aristotle in connection with the pursuit of clarity in offering an account of 'the good and the chief good' of human activities.

> Our discussion will be adequate if it has as much clearness as the subject-matter admits of, for precision is not to be sought for alike in all discussions, any more than in all of the crafts. Now fine and just actions, which political science investigates, admit of much variety and fluctuation of opinion, so that they may be thought to exist only by convention, and not by nature. And goods also give rise to a similar fluctuation because they bring harm to many people; for before now men have been undone by reason of their wealth, and others by reason of their courage. We must be content then, in speaking of such subjects and with such premisses to indicate the truth roughly and in outline, and in speaking about things which are only for the most part true and with premisses of the same kind, to reach conclusions that are no better. In the same spirit, therefore, should each type of statement be received; for it is the mark of an educated man to look for precision in each class of things just so far as the nature of the subject admits; it is evidently equally foolish to accept probable reasoning from a mathematician and to demand from a rhetorician scientific proofs ('The Nicomachean Ethics', Book 1, Chapter 3, 1094b11-27, trans. Ross, 1925).

As Penelope Hall puts it, 'some vagueness is inevitable, and may even be desirable, in a sphere in which growth and change are continually taking place' (1952, p. 3). Bearing these points in mind, adequately identifying designations and clear purposive rule-following explanations should nevertheless be pursued, for in their pursuit we may discover how much clearness is as much clearness as the subject-matter admits of and, in a sphere in which growth and change are continually taking place, in what way our subject-matter grows and changes.

B

This section of our essay introduces the works that follow partly through a critical review of the first

essay we reprint, Professor T.H. Marshall's The Right
to Welfare. Marshall's essay is chosen not because
its key concepts or beliefs 'stand in greater need of
clarification or critical evaluation than those of
any other essay.   Rather, Marshall's is an essay in
which a writer on welfare does not merely recommend
the perspectives of the philosopher, but adopts them
and offers a philosophical analysis.

In The Right to Welfare Marshall at least touches
upon most of the areas of discussion represented by
other essays. As well as being a useful vehicle for
the introduction of other contributions, the essay is
a contribution in its own right.

We now proceed to draw in some of the lines which
link the areas of interest represented by the essays
and extracts for, as we shall see, we are presented
with a cluster of problems.   To use another analogy,
what we have here is a problem family most easily
seen to be a problem family, and not just a number of
individual problems, by their being gathered together.
We also believe that the problem family in question is
more likely to be understood when it is considered as
a family.   A collection is a setting in which family
relationships and problems can be respectively clarified and, hopefully, resolved.

From the point of view of clarification, Marshall
begins his essay with salutary intentions.

Let me say first, by way of definition, that I am
using the word 'welfare' in the broad sense given
to it in the term 'Welfare State', and not with
the more specialised meaning of the services provided by Welfare Departments.
This method of distinguishing different senses of a
word requires comment.   Marshall's distinction between
the 'broad sense' and a 'more specialised meaning'
suggests his point to be that welfare takes many forms
and that there is a use of 'welfare' which signifies
all or most of those forms and another use which
signifies only some of them, those catered for by
Welfare Department services.   We would not deny
either that welfare takes many forms or indeed that
Welfare Department services do not cater for all of
these forms, but what is questionable is that it
follows that 'welfare' has more than one sense.   To
use the agreed facts as a method of distinguishing
different senses of the word 'welfare' is to assume
this case to fall under the general rule that if there
is more than one sort of X, then there is more than one
sense of 'X'.   This general rule and its application

in this particular case stand in need of support.
There is more than one sort of laughter and satirical
magazines do not cater for all of these sorts, but we
would surely not want to say that 'laughter' has more
than one sense.   We may object more strongly to the
rule and so to its application in any case along the
following lines.   We must distinguish the use of the
phrase 'there is more than one sort of X' from the
use of the phrase 'there is more than one sort of
thing called "X"'.   Use of the latter phrase allows
the possibility of more than one sense for 'X'.   Thus
we might say 'there is more than one sort of thing
called "tall"': men and stories. (10)   Use of the
former phrase does not allow the possibility of more
than one sense for X since every different sort of X
is an X and may be distinguished as such using the
same adequately identifying designation.   It follows
from the fact that there is more than one sort of X
that there is some adequately identifying designation
which distinguishes every different sort of X.   This
does not follow from the fact that there is more than
one sort of thing called X.   Every sort of laughter
is a sort of laughter, but not every sort of thing
called 'bank' is a sort of establishment for the
custody of money, some things called 'bank' are a
sort of sloping margin.

Another and independent objection may be developed
against Marshall's method in practice.   This objection may be most clearly developed in connection
with the use of the word 'welfare' in the phrase
'the welfare services', used to refer to the services
provided by Welfare Departments.   In this use 'welfare' has the grammatical role of adjective qualifying the noun 'services' so that services of a certain
sort are mentioned.   The suggestion is that we may
say quite precisely what services are provided by
Welfare Departments.   On this assumption, and the
assumption that welfare services in this sense of
'welfare' are all and only those services provided by
Welfare Departments, we may say quite precisely what
services are welfare services in this sense of 'welfare'; we may draw up a list.   But in doing this we
shall have done no more than clarify a use of 'welfare
services' as a noun-phrase: to name those services
provided by Welfare Departments; we shall not have
clarified the use of the adjective 'welfare' in that
noun-phrase, for we shall not have said what sort of
services the services provided by Welfare Departments
are.

Similarly, one might try to list state welfare provisions and claim to have given an account of the
sense of 'welfare' in or associated with the name
'Welfare State'. But the claim would be ill-founded.
One would do better to offer the criterion or range
of criteria by which one selected the provisions in
question, an adequately identifying designation of
welfare provision in a state given this label.

The essays The Concept of Welfare by R.B. Brandt,
The Good of Man by G.H. Von Wright and Alienation and
Self-Realisation by Kai Nielsen, reprinted in this
collection, discuss criteria of personal and social
welfare. One very common conception of personal
welfare is that on which personal welfare implies
realising one's potential, developing one's capacities
to the full. Kai Nielsen examines this 'murky doctrine'. Marshall's attempt to isolate the use of
'welfare' in which he is interested assumes that we
already know how 'welfare' is used in referring to
the services provided by Welfare Departments and in
labelling a Welfare State. Far from himself distinguishing two uses of 'welfare' Marshall assumes
the existence of two distinct uses and our ability to
distinguish them. We have suggested that the rule
supporting Marshall's assumption about the existence
of two distinct uses is dubious, and, as Marsh and
Hall noted, our ability to distinguish uses may also
be reasonably doubted. Brandt and Von Wright attempt
to distinguish uses of 'welfare' systematically, and
this is the essential groundwork preliminary to
adequately identifying designations of a welfare service and a Welfare State.

Marshall continues the preliminaries: 'When I
speak of rights, I include everything from legal
rights, through social rights to moral rights, though
I shall be concerned chiefly with the first two'.
We naturally feel the absence of an account of how
these three sorts of rights are to be distinguished,
and in particular, we should like to know where
rights to welfare fall.

> Any legal right there may be in the context of
> welfare must have an indirect or mediate character,
> being a right to those benefits which may be expec-
> ted to produce welfare and which, on the average,
> will do so.

In the context of welfare, 'The ultimate object' of
legislators and courts of law 'is something beyond the
scope of legislative or judicial action'. Marshall
conceives of welfare as an end to which legislation

can supply only what is, on the average, the means to
it.   Rights to welfare which are legal rights are,
says Marshall, rights to means rather than to welfare
itself.   At this point welfare is akin to happiness
for Marshall, both are ends beyond the scope of
legislative or judicial action.   One 'could not
give the citizen a legal right to sue for damages on
the grounds that he was ... unhappy', though one
might well give him a legal right to what was, on
the average, the means to it.   Discussions of happiness as an end and of the relation between welfare
and happiness are taken up by Von Wright and by
Nielsen.

On the other hand, says Marshall, 'it has been
consistently argued that there can be no legal right
in the fullest sense to a benefit the award of which
is subject to discretion'.   So it may be suggested
that there cannot be a legal right even to the means
of welfare, for as Marshall says,

> almost any benefit or service that is really
> designed to satisfy a particular individual need
> must include an element of discretion.   For the
> assessment of needs in an individual case, and of
> the measures that are best suited to meet it,
> involves an act of personal judgment.

This view stands in need of development.

Prima facie an element of discretion would not
seem to prevent a right from being a legal right,
and to suggest that this is so would seem to be to
adopt too simple and mechanical a view of the operation of the law.   Discretion introduces a flexi-
bility which Marshall seems to equate with an
uncertainty which is foreign to legal response.
Discretion

> as positive, personal and beneficent can only be
> fully realised in a 'welfare society', that is to
> say a society that recognises its collective res-
> ponsibility to seek to achieve welfare, and not
> only to relieve destitution and eradicate penury.

In such a society an element of discretion does not
undermine the certainty of benefit.   In a 'welfare
society' sanctions which are not legal sanctions
effectively sustain rights that are not enforceable
by litigation, for in such a society 'the public,
the politicians, and the administration fully accept
the legitimacy of the claims, take them seriously and
give them a high degree of priority'.   Against this
'background of welfare-consciousness' welfare benefits, even if we accept that they are not a legal

right, are awarded as a right, rather than as a favour.

Two other issues connected with **welfare rights** discussed by Marshall are taken up by **essays** which are included in this collection. We may introduce the essay Human Rights, Real and Supposed, by Maurice Cranston, by examining a criticism made by Marshall of the Beveridge plan 'for universal, unconditional benefits attached to compulsory contributory insurance'. Beveridge

> did not see that national social insurance is no longer a system for fulfilling obligations derived from 'impulses of common humanity' by meeting a need that is common to all human beings, the need for the means of subsistence. It is a fiscal arrangement devised by the citizens of a particular society to adjust the distribution of the income of that society in a manner considered most conducive to the welfare of all. It is a mutual benefit arrangement of a special kind, which to some extent favours the weaker at the expense of the stronger, and the rights it confers are not rights rooted in the nature of man as a human being, but rights created by the community itself and attached to the status of its citizenship.

Marshall does not explain what sort of rights and obligations may be said to be 'derived from impulses of common humanity'. Nor does he give an account of what it is for a right to be 'rooted in the nature of man as a human being'. It seems to us that Marshall is here referring to what have traditionally been called 'human rights' and Cranston's essay provides a useful systematic introduction to this notion in the context of a distinction between legal and moral rights which Marshall uses and Cranston draws.

We said earlier that Marshall does not give an account of his distinction between legal, moral, and social rights. Rights 'derived from impulses of common humanity' are, it seems, what Marshall would call moral rights. He says later in connection with welfare services for old people and the mentally handicapped, 'the motive that inspires the services rendered to these people is compassion rather than interest', so that these rights to welfare are each 'bound to be more dependent ... for its driving and sustaining force on the fact that it is a moral right'. Sympathy would seem to be the source of morality according to Marshall. Moreover, he thus allows that welfare rights may be legal rights and

that they may be moral rights.   The notion of a social
right is not explained but 'a right created by the
community itself and attached to the status of its
citizenship' would seem to be a reasonable suggestion.
Since Marshall describes the right to national social
insurance as a right of this kind, if this account is
accepted, then Marshall also allows that welfare
rights may be social rights.   As we said earlier, it
has not been shown that these are exclusive categories
of rights.   Reference to welfare rights as rights
created by the community itself and attached to the
status of its citizenship sets welfare rights once
more within the context of a welfare society.   The
essays mentioned earlier in this connection discuss
social rights based upon public morality and the concept of a community within which such rights are
sustained.

The instruments of state welfare policies such as
health regulations, health visitors and health education are, says Marshall,

> there to promote welfare by stressing a duty even
> more than a right, for your body is part of the
> national capital, and must be looked after, and
> sickness causes a loss of national income, in
> addition to being liable to spread.

It might be argued that to justify welfare rights on
grounds referring to the economic interests of the
nation, or of oneself, is to confuse economic exchange
with what Titmuss (1970) has called 'the gift relationship'.   It is at least to suggest that welfare
rights and duties may also be economic rights and
duties.   Throughout the essay, rights are conceived
as serving interests.   This perspective may be
enriched if we bear in mind that public morality may
take into account more than a principle of maximisa-
tion of welfare, and particularly economic welfare.
We might regard extreme inequality, for example, as
morally unjustified even if it promotes economic
welfare.   The chapter Respect for Persons and Public
Morality by R.S. Downie and Elizabeth Telfer sets a
Utilitarian outlook in the context of a public
morality which recognises the demands of equality,
liberty and fraternity.   Downie and Miss Telfer go
on to argue that 'the importance attached to the
three principles of utility, equality and liberty can
be explained only if we say that the principle of
respect for persons is assumed'.

Marshall's discussion of a 'background of welfare-
consciousness' sheds a little light on the distinction

between a welfare state and a welfare society.   The
implication is that in a welfare state there is what
might loosely be described as an official background
of welfare-consciousness, there are welfare policies
and machinery to administer those policies.   In a
welfare society, welfare-consciousness extends beyond
the official domain, to the public at large.   The
essay Welfare State and Welfare Society by Professor
R.M. Titmuss, which we include, is an attempt to
illuminate this important distinction.

   If welfare rights are not, or are not only legal
rights, but are moral or social rights too, it will
be useful to consider the concept of welfare in relation to moral and social principles.   Such a consideration will itself contribute to the elucidation of the
notion of 'a welfare society'.   In the welfare society
described by Marshall, which has developed 'socially
acceptable selective services aiming to discriminate
positively, with the minimum risk of stigma, in favour
of those whose needs are greatest' (Titmuss, op. cit.)
the principle of respect for persons may be expected
to be of some considerable significance.   It seems to
us that the notion of a welfare society is a rather
overworked and undereluciated one which might fruitfully be developed in this context.

   There is a serious danger, in our discussion of the
notions of a Welfare State and a Welfare Society, of
suggesting that the public morality which supports
such social arrangements is straightforwardly Utilitarian.   We are in danger of saying that a Welfare
State and a Welfare Society aim at the greatest
happiness for the greatest number or that actions are
right in proportion as they tend to promote happiness,
wrong as they tend to produce the reverse of happiness, or some other version of a Utilitarian morality.
Again, Professor R.S. Downie and Elizabeth Telfer, in
Respect for Persons and Public Morality, remind us
that the Welfare State and the Welfare Society may be
conceived within a public morality which supports
other principles as well as the principle of Utility.

   The principle of respect for persons is often
explicitly and crucially used in discussions of the
ways in which clients of social services should be
treated.   Professor W.G. Maclagan (1960) has argued
that an understanding of the principle may be gained
through an examination of the concept of friendship:
an examination of this concept offers a better route
to an adequate characterisation of the principle than
an examination of the concept of justice.   Now

'friendship' also features, in its own right as it were, both amongst the possible models for social work practice and amongst more general descriptions and even explanations of social policy.   It is not without significance, for example, that one of the chapters on social policy we reprint here is entitled 'Who is my Stranger?'   In this chapter Titmuss suggests that the lag of supply behind demand in blood-giving can be seen, in the words of Professor M. Mauss, as a 'refusal of friendship'.   The notion of friendship is left relatively undeveloped by Titmuss, and its necessary development, in our view, requires the kind of treatment attempted by Maclagan.

The concept of friendship seems to be closely related to those of fellowship, neighbourliness, and fraternity mentioned by David Donnison in his 'Liberty, Equality and Fraternity' which we reprint.   Donnison attempts to invigorate both discussion of social policy and some 'traditional' political theory by a judicious mixture of the two.   He distinguishes, however, only certain kinds of fraternity, and his view that

> A free world will be full of conflict: it cannot be a fellowship of friends, ruled by love, because the search for friends soon degenerates into the exclusion of enemies, the suppression of conflict and, ultimately, rule by hate,

alerts us to the importance of distinguishing matters of fact (here, actual tendencies) from matters of logic (here, the logic of the concept of a fellowship of friends, ruled by love).   The degeneration of a fellowship of friends may in fact always have taken place, along the lines described, but no such degeneration is implied by the concept and so a free world might conceivably be without conflict, a fellowship of friends ruled by love.   Indeed it might be argued by some that a fellowship of friends, guided by the principle of respect for persons, would be well equipped to resist degeneration to the point of the exclusion of enemies, for enemies (ignoring other animals, viruses, etc.) are persons.   The principle of respect for persons is set in the context of public morality in general and of the values of equality, liberty and fraternity in particular, in Professor R.S. Downie and Elizabeth Telfer's Respect for Persons and Public Morality.   In this chapter Downie and Telfer, but also elsewhere Downie, discusses the relation between fraternity and the concept of community. Downie (1971, p. 44) draws our attention to F. Tönnies

distinction between a *Gesellschaft* and a *Gemeinschaft*.
The distinction, says Downie, can be explained if we
translate it

> as one between an organisation or an association,
> such as a business or other commercial or official
> enterprise, and a community, such as may be found
> in a country district which has traditional ties
> with the soil.   In a commercial association the
> individuals involved have nothing in common other
> than their interest in a specific commercial aim.
> If that aim is once achieved then there is nothing
> left holding the group together.   A community, by
> contrast, is held together by many bonds, which are
> likely to be deep and complex.
>
>   But any organisation, however commercially orien-
> tated, is always liable to become more than a mere
> association of persons for a specific objective.
> The members will tend to have a single meeting-
> place, to adjourn for coffee after their discussions,
> to have an annual party, to have a small library,
> to give their surplus funds to a certain charity,
> etc.   All these additional interests are liable to
> be added almost imperceptibly to the basic commer-
> cial objective, and they all constitute growing
> points for a *Gemeinschaft*.

Thus Downie identifies through a concept of community that aspect of social morality he wishes to
identify by means of the concept of fraternity.
R.M. Titmuss's Who is my Stranger? provides discussion
and evidence of this kind of community.   Professor
John Benson's essay The Concept of Community details
different senses of 'community' and attempts to answer
the question what is it that makes a relationship a
human social relationship, what is it for a collection
of individuals to have a 'common life'.   His answer,
suggesting that we think of society as a network of
roles and that men share a 'common life' in so far as
there exists among them a consensus about the various
roles that individuals can occupy, leads him to
comments which put Tönnies distinction in a new light:
the sharp dichotomy can be misleading.   Amongst other
things, says Benson, 'we may be persuaded to think of
any large-scale society as a mechanical contrivance,
hostile or at best indifferent to human values, and
having nothing to do with genuine human relationships'
    Welfare provision is delivered in the context of a
community in the sense of a collection of individuals
having a 'common life'.   It is not necessarily only
delivered when such a community is a *Gemeinschaft*.

In The Function of Social Work in Society Peter
Leonard reminds us of the range of possible conceptions of social relationships, social work and society.
It may be that the consensus model of society, in
which society is conceived as 'a system of interacting
parts which are cemented together by a common set of
values' fits poorly the actual context in which we
deliver welfare provision through social work agencies.
    Alan Keith-Lucas's The Art and Science of Helping
makes interesting reading, particularly following
Leonard's discussion. We have all confidently said
that social work, amongst others, is a helping profession. The conjunction of these two papers helps
us to see that what constitutes helping depends upon
one's conception of social relationships and society.
Leonard shows us a range of conceptions which have
different implications for what it is to help a
client. Keith-Lucas develops an account of helping
which is not offered as one among many and which can
be read as an attempt to marry more than one conception
of social relationships and society.   At one point
Keith-Lucas reminds us that many clients 'refuse to
admit their real need ... demand help from us on their
own terms ... find ways of neutralising our help',
suggesting both that client's and social worker's
perceptions of what Leonard calls 'social reality'
are in conflict, and that really, which hopefully the
client will in time have the courage to recognise,
there is consensus. A helping profession, it seems,
can give its clients what they want and at the same
time impose on them what they don't want.
    Keith-Lucas includes an account of empathy. It
is 'an act of compassionate understanding. It says
"I can understand how you feel, and feel it with you
in a limited way, but I don't feel that way myself."'
In Knowing by Living Through, Dorothy Walsh discusses
in more detail the nature of self-knowledge and understanding others. In On not being Judgmental Ian T.
Ramsey takes up another theme introduced by Keith-
Lucas. According to Keith-Lucas 'the helping relationship must be one in which negative feelings can be
expressed without fear of blame, anger, sorrow or loss
of face'. Ramsay provides us with a careful analysis
of such 'acceptance' through consideration of what a
'judgmental' attitude may involve. (11)

NOTES

1   Social workers' views appear in, amongst others, the
    journal of The British Association of Social
    Workers, 'Social Work Today'.   The views of some
    of those whose welfare is in question are recorded
    in John E. Mayer and Noel Timms 'The Client Speaks',
    London, Routledge & Kegan Paul, 1970.
2   A brief explanation of the terms 'necessary condi-
    tion' and 'sufficient condition' is provided by
    G. Wallace and A.D.M. Walker at the foot of p. 2 in
    their collection 'The Definition of Morality',
    London, Methuen, 1970.
3   That there may be two distinct issues here was sug-
    gested to us by Professor Strawson.
4   Those who feel deprived by the omission of a dis-
    cussion of what we called the 'mechanics' of
    successful designation might usefully read the
    Introduction to Wallace and Walker's 'The Defini-
    tion of Morality' (especially pp. 1-4), and
    Strawson (1970) especially pp. 194-9.
5   Peters's *argument* for the insufficiency of causal
    explanations as explanations of genuine action
    should be examined.
6   See Slack (1966), ch. 4.
7   This is of course a logical rather than a psycho-
    logical point.   Our sausage-linker might very well
    engage in the activity of sausage-linking and be
    unable, because too embarrassed, to identify that
    activity for someone else.   Our point is that it
    must be the case that he is able to identify it,
    even if, in particular circumstances, he can't
    bring himself to do it.
8   Since an item lacking an adequately identifying
    designation cannot be identified, when we talk in
    such circumstances of 'the activity', 'activities',
    'it', or of 'the item', we are not signifying an
    individual, but are rather signifying what is, as
    it were, a would-be individual, a putative indi-
    vidual.   Talk of putative individuals does not
    commit us to their existence, i.e. their discrim-
    inability and identifiability.
9   It seems fair to say that in the context of theory
    construction in this field, adequately identifying
    designations and purposive rule-following explana-
    tions cannot reasonably be expected to be *clearly*
    given.   This may be our aim, but descriptions and
    explanations of the required sorts must first be
    developed.   However, we would argue that a

distinctly philosophical contribution might be made
to their development, by way of conceptual clarification and critical evaluation of the set of beliefs
which constitute the theory.   Further, while descriptions and explanations of the required sorts
are still in the process of development, what we
possess is not a theory about certain individuals
within the field of welfare, but merely a theory *in
the course of construction* about putative individuals.

10   On the other hand, use of this phrase does not pre-
clude the possibility of just one sense for X.
Thus we might say 'there is more than one sort of
thing called "popular": music and mother's cooking', but not mean to suggest that 'popular' has
more than one sense.

11   Many of the articles are taken from books and contain references to other parts of their original:
e.g. chapters by Von Wright and Cranston.   These
then are not references to other parts of this
collection.   They remain to give the reader access
to extended and related discussion in the original
sources.

1   The right to welfare

T. H. Marshall

Twenty years ago the Welfare State was a novelty, and
there was much that could be said, in general terms,
about the genesis and the nature of the rights to which
it gave effect.   Today all this can be taken for granted, and anybody who is bold enough to broach the subject afresh will be expected to try to dig deeper and
to look more closely into the details of the picture.
It is difficult for him to say anything that is worth
saying without getting involved in matters that are
either technical or controversial, or both, and these
are apt to demand more space for their proper treatment
than I have at my disposal here.   So I shall be content to concentrate on the highlights of the scene, as
I see it, and to indicate the paths along which one's
thoughts would travel, if one were to pursue the subject further.

Let me say first, by way of definition, that I am
using the word 'welfare' in the broad sense given to
it in the term 'Welfare State', and not with the more
specialised meaning of the services provided by Welfare
Departments.   And when I speak of rights, I include
everything from legal rights, through social rights to
moral rights, though I shall be concerned chiefly with
the first two.

It is tempting to dismiss at once the idea that
there can be a legal right to anything as nebulous, as
subjective and as personal as welfare.   My dictionary,
having made the obvious remark that it means the
'state of faring or doing well', can find nothing
better to add to this than 'freedom from calamity, etc.:
enjoyment of health, etc.:   prosperity', and one cannot
have a legal right to et cetera's, or even, for that
matter, to prosperity.   Welfare, as I have suggested
elsewhere, is a compound of material means and

51

immaterial ends; it is located somewhere on the axis
which runs between the poles of wealth and happiness.
Now it may well be that the wealth of nations and the
greatest happiness of the greatest number are the
proper preoccupations of social scientists and politicians, but you could not give the citizen a legal
right to sue for damages on the grounds that he was
one of the greatest number but was nevertheless unhappy.   Any legal right there may be in the context
of welfare must have an indirect or mediate character,
being a right to those benefits which may be expected
to produce welfare and which, on the average, will do
so.   But we still have to ask whether there can be
rights *of some kind* to the thing itself - to welfare,
and how the concept of such rights may influence social
policy.   For it is beyond question that it has influenced and does influence policy.   As we watch legislators framing statutes and courts of law pronouncing
judgments, all in a perfectly proper and practical way,
we can see that what they are doing is deeply coloured
by the knowledge that their ultimate object is something lying beyond the scope of legislative or judicial
action.   The constitution of one of the States of the
American Union contains a clause to the effect that
the Counties within the State 'shall provide as may be
prescribed by law for those inhabitants who, by reason
of old age, infirmity, or other misfortune, may have
claims upon the sympathy and aid of society. (1)
That expresses the dilemma very neatly.   Somehow the
law has got to prescribe to what acts our sympathy is
to move us.

The dilemma became apparent when the poor laws
gave statutory force to the obligation of society to
look after its destitute members.   An eminent American
judge defined this obligation when he said in 1873,
perhaps a trifle over-optimistically, that 'the relief
of the poor, the care of those who are unable to care
for themselves, is among the unqualified objects of
public duty.   In obedience to the impulses of common
humanity, it is everywhere recognised. (2)   But did
the duty to care for the poor, even when 'unqualified',
imply a right of the poor to be cared for?   In England
the answer was an equally unqualified 'No'.   The
pauper was a person deprived of rights, not invested
with them.   The duty to relieve him was admitted, but
its source did not lie in any rights possessed by the
person relieved.   He was the *object* of the action
taken, just as he had previously been the *object* of
charity.   The 'impulses of common humanity', one could

say, were considered to be a matter between the people
and their conscience, just as the impulses of charity
belonged to the moral welfare of the charitable.   And
this was reflected in the legal doctrine.   The duty
to relieve the poor, says Sir Ivor Jennings (writing
about the Poor Law of 1930), was 'a duty owed to the
public and not to the poor person himself'.   Consequently no action could be brought by the poor person
to whom relief was denied, and any negligence of an
official in his treatment of the poor was an offence,
not against the pauper, but against the public who
employed him to look after paupers. (3)

    In some other countries, notably in Scandinavia
and the United States, there was evident a desire to
recognise the pauper as something more than an object,
and to regard him, in fact, rather as the *subject* in
the case, that is to say as a person who could be a
source of rights and therefore of obligations.   And
this led, at times, to the very brink of an admission
that the poor had a legal right to receive what the
society had a legal obligation to give them.   In a
survey of the social services of the Northern Countries
published in 1953 the chapter on Assistance opens with
the statement that 'Assistance from the community as a
legal right of the citizen in need is barely a century
old.'   And it appears that the term 'legal right' did
appear for a period in Norwegian legislation, but was
rather quickly dropped.   It was replaced early in the
present century both in Norway and in Sweden by a
classification of basic minimum relief as 'mandatory
assistance', and anything given over and above that as
'optional assistance'.   This meant, in effect, that
the poor person had an undeniable right to 'mandatory
assistance', for it was expressly stated that relief
was 'mandatory' whatever the cause of the need.   But
technically the right was not a legal one, because no
legal remedy was attached to it; the pauper could not
sue for his relief, he could only appeal. (4)   The
difference is that a legal remedy takes the matter to
an independent court which judges the issue strictly
in terms of the law; an appeal normally takes the
matter to a higher level in the same system of authority, where it is decided by somebody who acts, not
judicially, but administratively.

    Edith Abbott (1940) summed up the position in the
United States by saying that 'every American poor law
for the past century and a half has given the person
who is in need a "right to relief"'.   The quotation
marks indicate that special significance was given to

the phrase, and she goes on to explain that there was much discussion of the issue whether the right was 'legal' or not.   The verdict, it seems, was that it was not.   This is so, in spite of the fact that the existence and nature of the right were a constant subject of litigation.   The Courts were asked to decide who the poor were, which of their needs could and should be relieved and, of course, in which local government area their right was effective.   The so-called 'seed and feed' cases illustrate this.   In one of the American States crops had been destroyed by locusts. The farmers were facing destitution.   The local authorities decided to provide them with means to get food to eat and corn to sow.   They were taken to Court for this and the judge decided that it was legitimate to provide corn to eat, but not to provide corn to sow. Lack of seed-corn was not destitution.   This judgment was subsequently reversed, on the grounds that, without seed-corn, they would have become destitute next year, and that prevention was better than cure.   More generally, it was a matter of dispute whether a man could be a pauper if he still possessed land, even if the land was producing nothing.   Another case raised issues both of settlement and of redress for negligence. A man was suffering from frozen feet, and applied for care.   The County pushed him out, disputing his settlement.   He was chivied along until eventually both his feet had to be amputated.   He wanted to sue the original County for damages, but was denied the right to do so.   And the County which treated him wanted to sue it for expenses, but, though it was warmly praised for saving the man's life, it could not recover from the local authority which had defaulted, and which was hotly rebuked for doing so. (5)

What one notices about the Court cases cited in profusion by Edith Abbott is that they are nearly all negative in character.   They are initiated by a local authority or by one or more tax-paying citizens in order to prove that, in this particular case, there is no obligation to give relief and no right to receive it.   When action has been taken with the opposite end in view - to assert a right or to condemn a violation of it, this has been done on the initiative of private citizens or voluntary bodies who, as Elizabeth Wickenden put it, 'were crusading for social justice in the highest tradition of the law'. (6) The number of such cases has increased in recent years, as the 'war on poverty' has gathered strength. This does not mean, however, that the poor are on the

way to winning a legal right to relief.   For, it has
been consistently argued, there can be no legal right
in the fullest sense to a benefit the award of which is
subject to discretion.   In support of this one may
quote high American and British authority. The
American so-called 'Ruling Case Law' on the subject
held that 'the extent of relief, and its character, as
well as the necessity therefor, are left to the discretion and judgment of the officers charged with the
care of the poor', (7) and that precludes a legal
claim by the beneficiary.   And Beveridge, in his book
'Insurance for All and Everything' (1924), insisted
that a benefit must be classed as assistance rather
than insurance if its receipt 'depends in any way upon
the discretion of some authority', and it is therefore
'given not as a right but as a favour'. (8)   The point
is clear and the distinction just, but its significance
requires closer examination.   This will lead us to
consider two things, the concept of need and the relation of rights to duties.

The question is whether discretionary aid deserves
the inferior status that has generally been ascribed
to it.   It has, I think, earned this reputation
largely owing to its association with various forms of
'means test'.   This has encouraged the view that the
essence of discretion is that it gives somebody the
power to refuse or to reduce the benefit.   But this
is quite false.   In the first place a means test is
not usually discretionary in Beveridge's sense,
because it is applied by the officials concerned
according to a schedule set out in regulations based
on a statute.   This was true, for example, of non-
contributory Old Age Pensions.   It was true to a
less degree of unemployment assistance between the
wars.   According to Ronald Davison, 'no attempt was
made to enforce rigid uniformity' on the Public
Assistance Committees.   But approximate uniformity
was achieved except in ten or a dozen places, with
Labour Committees, where the instructions for calculating private income were ignored.   He describes these
as 'rebellious areas'; their rebellion consisted in
using more discretion than was permitted.   When subsequently the Unemployment Assistance Board was set
up, it actually encouraged in its officers 'a generous
interpretation of the regulations and a use of their
discretionary powers which seemed to be beyond anything revealed in the original plan'.   And it is
significant that the Board also made the most of its
discretionary powers in another direction, namely to

develop its welfare services. (9)   It would almost
seem that in the course of these few years the idea
of discretion as a brake on generosity and a safeguard
against extravagance had yielded place to a conception
of it as a positive, not a negative, instrument of
policy, to be used to increase the services rendered
to those whose need for them was most pressing.

The truth is that almost any benefit or service
that is really designed to satisfy a particular individual need must include an element of discretion.
For the assessment of needs in an individual case, and
of the measures that are best suited to meet it,
involves an act of personal judgment.   This is true
not only of the decision how much cash income a
family requires to satisfy its right to welfare, or
of the organization of care for the aged, but also of
the provision of an education suited to the talents
of a student and of the doctor's diagnosis of an illness and his prescription of treatment.   That is why
the right to such benefits and services cannot be
fully legal.   You may sue a doctor for gross negligence, but not simply for refusing to prescribe the
treatment you asked for, nor can you take legal action
against an examining body for giving you lower marks
than you consider you were entitled to.   But discretion exercised in this way does not make a right
inferior in quality to other rights.   On the contrary, it is from some points of view superior,
because the question asked in each case is not 'What
do the regulations say must be done?', but 'What
action is most likely to produce the desired result?'
The 'means test' is transformed into a 'needs test',
and the desired result becomes identifiable with
'welfare'.   No doubt many Poor Law Guardians in the
old days would have claimed that they used their
discretionary powers in this spirit, but the claim
could not be generally sustained for a moment.   It
would be nearer the truth to say that this notion of
discretion as positive, personal and beneficent can
only be fully realised in a 'welfare society', that
is to say a society that recognises its collective
responsibility to seek to achieve welfare, and not
only to relieve destitution or eradicate penury.

The inferiority of discretionary assistance was
emphasised in the Beveridge plan for universal, unconditional benefits attached to compulsory contributory
insurance.   He insisted that insurance benefits were
given 'as of right' whereas assistance was not, and
that assistance, therefore, 'must be felt to be some-

thing less desirable'. (10)   His argument bred confusion in the public mind. For his aim was to
guarantee to everybody a 'national minimum', or
subsistence income at a flat rate.   Now a guaranteed
subsistence income is one way of meeting the obligation accepted by all societies to satisfy the basic
needs of their members, an obligation arising, as the
American judge said, from 'impulses of common
humanity'.   But Beveridge's plan took no account of
needs at all, chiefly because to do so would involve
applying a means test and this, he thought, would
impair the right.   He did not see that the right to
'mandatory assistance' can be made quite firm, even
if it is not strictly speaking legal or, in his sense,
unconditional.   More important, he did not see that
national social insurance is no longer a system for
fulfilling obligations derived from 'impulses of
common humanity' by meeting a need that is common to
all human beings, the need for the means of subsistence.   It is a fiscal arrangement devised by the
citizens of a particular society to adjust the distribution of the income of that society in a manner
considered most conducive to the welfare of all.   It
is a mutual benefit arrangement of a special kind,
which to some extent favours the weaker at the expense
of the stronger, and the rights it confers are not
rights rooted in the nature of man as a human being,
but rights created by the community itself and
attached to the status of its citizenship.   The plan
adopted, therefore, takes account, not only of the
national income and the demands made upon it, but
also of the structure of the society and the position
of the individual in it; so it is now customary for
benefits to be related in some measure to individual
earnings.   To speak of modern social insurance as a
means of waging war on want is misleading.   It is
better described as an apparatus by which the income
of workers is spread over the periods when they can
no longer work.   This increases the total sum of
welfare enjoyed in a life-time, and the social right
to this welfare is converted into a legal right to
the maintenance of income at whatever level the
society may determine, after considering what is fair
and appropriate in relation to the general standard
of living attainable with its collective income.
    I have referred several times to the difference
between rights that are legal and rights that are
less than legal.   There is no doubt at all that in
the past this difference mattered a lot; but does it

matter now?   In other words, granted that, in the
strict legal sense, 'there can be no right without a
remedy', can there, in another sense, be a remedy
without a right?   Are there other sanctions that can
equally effectively sustain the rights - or claims -
that are not enforceable by litigation?   Once again,
as in the case of the positive, personal and beneficent use of discretionary powers, the answer is, I
think, that such a remedy can exist in a 'welfare
society'.   It can exist if the public, the politicians and the administration fully accept the legitimacy of the claims, take them seriously and give them
a high degree of priority.   Against this background
operate various forces, latent and manifest, which
constrain all those on whom the implementation of the
claims depends to carry out their duties honestly,
impartially, consistently and in accordance with the
intentions of the legislation on which the service is
based.   In addition to the ever-growing latent force
of tradition, there is the manifest force of rules and
principles, sustained by publicity, accountability,
supervision and, finally, the right of appeal.   This
right has been recognised in all the countries to
which I have referred.   It invokes, as I said, not
the judicial decision of a court of law, but generally
an over-ruling decision by a higher instance in the
administrative structure, or by some special tribunal
set up for the purpose.   Such is the Appeal Tribunal
established by the National Assistance Act, and in
recent years it was hearing an average of some eleven
or twelve thousand appeals annually.   The number is
very small in proportion to the total volume of cases
dealt with under the National Assistance Board, but
it helps to keep alive the idea that the granting of
assistance is not an act of grace, but the satisfaction of a right, even if not strictly a legal right.
   But the right of appeal is of little use if the
background of welfare-consciousness is not present,
as is apparent if one looks at what has been happening
in many parts of the United States.   Elizabeth
Wickenden cites several cases to illustrate the
arbitrary way in which some of the administrators of
public assistance behave, such as the imprisonment of
five recipients of relief for failure to cut brush in
eight feet of snow, the claim made by a caseworker
that she could decide 'whether a legal resident of New
York would be "better off" in North Carolina', the
decision to treat a woman who has an illegitimate
child while on relief as automatically guilty of child

neglect, and so forth.   The theme of her paper was that use should be made of every possible opportunity of invoking the law in defence of the rights of the poor, and it is clear that this was necessary precisely because the other kinds of sanctions which guarantee the enjoyment of social rights were not fully operative. (11)

Another reason for making the award of benefits discretionary lies in the relation between rights and duties.   The point is a very simple one.   If you concede to a poor person an absolute, unconditional right to relief, the question then arises how to deny him the right to become poor if he so wishes.   The obligation of the community to relieve destitution must somehow be matched by a duty of the individual not to become destitute, if he can help it.   That is why the emphasis in the early poor laws was on the punishment of idle vagabonds and on setting the poor, both adults and children, to work.   As it became increasingly difficult to do either of these things, an easy substitute was found in reliance on the deterrent character of relief to keep the undeserving away.   In conditions of full employment and a rising standard of living the temptation to indulge in voluntary penury has lost any force it ever had, and, though difficult cases may still sometimes arise, the problem is not one of real importance.

I have been speaking so far of the relief of poverty and of social insurance, and I have left myself little space to discuss the social and welfare services.   So I must confine myself strictly to the highlights, as I see them.   First, then, we find that here there is a much more intimate blending of rights and duties, and that it takes a different form.   It is not that the discharge of a duty - the duty to work - gives entitlement to the right, but that the exercise of the right is at the same time a duty.   This is most obvious in the case of education. For education is not only something to which every citizen has a right;   it is a process by which citizens are made.   As such it is something that every society must promote in its own interest, and every society that can afford to do so, and can produce the necessary teachers, makes education up to a certain level compulsory.   For the individual, education at this level is simply a part of the social environment into which he is born and by which he is absorbed. Even above that level, right up to the university, education is of such vital importance for the health and prosperity of a nation, that it is regarded as something of which the individual has a duty to avail himself, to the extent that his natural abilities warrant. So the government is as much concerned to persuade children to stay at school, to take examinations, and to go on to technical colleges and universities, because society needs them, as it is to provide additional educational facilities because young people want them and claim that they have a right to them.

It is just as important for a society to have a healthy population as to have an educated one, so the right to health, like the right to education, is blended with duties. Public health is in large measure a form of public discipline, and the element of obligation spreads from environmental to personal health, from one's duty to one's neighbours to one's duty to one's dependants and one's duty to oneself. Health regulations, health visitors and health education are there to promote welfare by stressing a duty even more than a right, for your body is part of the national capital, and must be looked after, and sickness causes a loss of national income, in addition to being liable to spread. But at the same time the State applies pressure to its citizens in their own interests, which it feels able, in some respects, to interpret and translate into action better than they can themselves. Though we may boggle at Rousseau's idea that citizens in a democracy 'will be forced to be free', we can accept more easily the view that they may be induced to be healthy.

The important thing to note here is the difference between these rights to education and health, as conceived in the twentieth century, and the rights of the citizen as envisaged in the eighteenth and nineteenth, of which the right to property was the prototype. Locke and others maintained that they were 'natural rights', inherent in the individual and not created for him by the society of which he was a member. Even when this extreme view was not accepted, the rights to property and personal freedom were seen as the basis of the individual's power to assert and protect himself against his fellowmen and the State - the power, in the last resort, to isolate himself by converting his home into his castle. The modern rights to education and health are, on the contrary, not merely recognised by all as being social in origin, but are part of the mechanism by which the individual is absorbed into society (not isolated from it), and simultaneously draws upon and contributes to its collective welfare.

The case of the welfare services, in the technical administrative sense, is different.   It cannot be said that society needs happy old people in the same way that it needs a healthy and educated population.   Nor would it suffer any grave loss if the mentally handi-capped were not assisted (at considerable cost in time and money) to make the most of their limited capaci-ties.   The motive that inspires the services rendered to these people is compassion rather than interest. And though compassion (or 'the impulses of common humanity') may create a right, having almost the force of law, to minimal subsistence, it cannot establish the same kind of right to the benefit of services which are continuously striving to extend the limits of the possible, and to replace the minimum by the optimum.   So this particular right to welfare is bound to be more dependent than the others for its driving and sustaining force on the fact that it is a moral right.   And that is why its champions have had, and are still having, so hard a struggle to win for it full recognition on the only terms they can accept. Furthermore, those in need of these welfare services are minority groups, set apart from the general body of normal citizens by their disabilities.   The principle of universality which is a characteristic feature of the modern rights of citizenship does not apply, and the right cannot be reinforced, as in the case of education and health, by a corresponding duty to exercise it.   The most one can say is that the handicapped have a moral duty to try to overcome their misfortunes as far as in them lies.

Every right to receive implies an obligation to give.   It is, perhaps, not too fanciful to suggest that, whereas in the relief of the poor (in its early days) the obligation was that of one human being to another, and in the case of social security and the health and education services it is the obligation of the State to its citizens, or of the society to itself, the obligation to promote the welfare of the old, the ill-treated and the handicapped rests on one's duty towards one's neighbour.   It is natural, therefore, that welfare services of this last kind should be generally regarded as involving a local, or neighbour-hood, responsibility.

In conclusion there are two points that need to be stressed.   First, a right to receive certain benefits or services does not necessarily imply the right to receive them free of charge.   It means only that the rendering of the service should not be conditional on

the ability to pay.   The cost of the service may be
met by pre-payment out of taxes, rates or insurance
contributions, or may be recovered, in part at least,
by levying *ad hoc* charges in proportion to the ability
to pay, ranging from the full cost of the particular
service received down to nothing at all.   The choice
of financial arrangement is a matter of importance,
and the decision will vary according to the nature of
the service concerned.   But these are questions secondary to the existence of the right itself.

Secondly, welfare is only to a very limited extent
the product of social services or of social policy.
Its roots lie deep in the social and economic system
as a whole.   Its realisation and enjoyment depend,
therefore, on a number of other rights, which I have
barely mentioned, including those to property and personal freedom, to work and to justice.   The national
wealth is produced and distributed by men exercising
these rights within the framework of national institutions, and national wealth is the material source of
national welfare.   Sometimes in the course of history
it has seemed that the crucial point was production
and that, if production throve, distribution could be
left to take care of itself.   At other times it has
been the inequalities of distribution that have
impressed men's minds and caused some people to urge
that these must be corrected even if production
suffered in the process.   Very broadly speaking the
former view prevailed in the early nineteenth century
and the latter was prominent in the early twentieth.
Today the emphasis is once again on production.
This is not because distribution is considered to be
unimportant or able to look after itself, but rather
because the machinery for correcting the major
inequalities has been established and been functioning
for a long time.   This machinery is far from perfect
and nobody is entirely satisfied with it.   But it is
there, and with it general acceptance of the ends
which it is designed to achieve.   So today efforts to
increase the supply of homes, hospitals, doctors,
schools and teachers are seen to be getting nearer to
the root of the problem than attempts to improve the
apparatus through which access to these sources of
welfare is distributed, while great stress is laid on
the need to raise the output of goods and services of
all kinds.   For success in this will not only increase
the sum total of welfare, but also greatly ease the
problem of rectifying defects in its distribution, and
the work on the welfare apparatus is quite certain to

go on. If new resources are created, the pressure to spread the benefits is likely, in the long run, to be irresistible.

It follows that the claim to, and the clamour for, welfare are one aspect of the now general expectation that social and economic progress will be continuous and that the standard of living will keep on rising. And nothing is clearer than that this expectation can be realised only if the people who entertain it are ready to work for it.   Their right to welfare is the right to their fair share of the individual enjoyment of the fruits of their collective labour.

NOTES

Based on a lecture delivered at the University of Keele on 12 February 1965.

1 Edith Abbott, 'Public Assistance', vol. I, p. 5.
2 Ibid., p. 74.
3 W.I. Jennings, 'The Poor Law Code' (1930), p. lxxvi.
4 George R. Nelson (ed.), 'Freedom and Welfare', pp. 448-55.
5 Abbott, op. cit., pp. 20-2.
6 Elizabeth Wickenden, 'The Legal Needs of the Poor' (paper given at a Conference in Washington in November 1964).
7 Abbott, op. cit., p. 9.
8 W.H. Beveridge, 'Insurance for All and Everything', pp. 6-7.
9 R.C. Davison, 'British Unemployment Policy since 1930', pp. 22 and 69.
10 'Beveridge Report', para. 369.
11 Wickenden, loc. cit.

2   The concept of welfare

Richard B. Brandt

One area in which the moral philosopher might say something useful for the thinking of economists is that of
welfare economics - not by improving formalizations or
criticizing proofs as to conditions necessary or sufficient for an optimum situation, much less by suggesting what particular state of society would be optimal.
Rather, he can do this by pointing out some distinctions
(e.g., explaining why assigning 'social welfare' a
certain meaning obscures important points), by suggesting how some terms used by economists can profitably be
defined, and by questioning some assumptions which seem
to lie behind the thinking of some economists.

The following discussion is aimed along these lines.
The main goal of the argument will be to produce helpful
definitions of 'increase the welfare of an individual'
and 'increase social welfare.' But the logical points
and distinctions introduced in the course of the discourse may be of more interest to the economist and
can be accepted on their merits irrespective of one's
appraisal of the main definitions. My discussion will
draw upon recent work in 'philosophical psychology' and
moral philosophy, but it would be misleading, in view
of controversies among philosophers, to suggest that it
represents any 'agreed results' of philosophical
inquiries.

THE WELFARE OF INDIVIDUALS

The term 'welfare' seems to carry a meaning, in ordinary talk about the welfare of individuals, different
from what it carries in many recent discussions in
which it appears in the expression 'social welfare.'
Hence, it will be useful to begin by examining the

meaning of 'welfare' in our more familiar discourse
about the welfare of individuals.   Since I shall argue
later that a useful concept of social welfare *involves*
the concept of individual welfare, it behooves us to be
clear about the latter notion before we try to define
the former.

The 'Shorter Oxford Dictionary,' among others,
equates the meaning of 'welfare' with that of 'good
fortune, happiness, or well-being; prosperity.'   This
proposal is hardly helpful for our purposes.   For if
clarification of 'welfare' is needed, it is equally
needed for the terms 'well-being' and 'good fortune.'
The other two terms are at least somewhat more explicit,
although for 'prosperity' one may wonder whether money
income, real income, or something else is meant.   But
in the case of these two terms it is mistaken to assert
an equivalence of meaning with 'welfare.'   It is un-
true that a person's welfare increases if and only if
his prosperity increases, for, to cite an example, we
should say that a person's welfare was enhanced by a
happy marriage, although such a marriage need not contribute to one's prosperity.   'Happiness' is rather
closer; but we should not want to say that a person's
welfare is increased *only* if, and *to the extent that,*
his happiness is increased.   There is room for reasonable doubt about this last point, partly because
'welfare' is a somewhat vague term; the reader will
be in a better position to judge at a later stage.

A different reason for objecting to the Oxford proposal is that it undiscriminatingly mixes terms of
entirely different kinds.   'Well-being' and 'good
fortune' appear to be value-words and probably do not
designate anything observable (probably are not parts
of an 'empiricist language'); whereas 'happiness' and
'prosperity' are not value-words and, with reservations
about vagueness, are parts of an 'empiricist language.'
Since it is helpful to place these distinctions in
clear focus, in view of their importance for the con-
firmation of judgments containing these terms, let us
pause to formulate the concepts of 'empirical language' and 'value-judgment' (or 'value-word').

Let us consider the notion of an 'empiricist language.' (1)   Such a language may be explained or
defined in terms of its vocabulary.   First, it includes words for the concepts of logic - those essential for discourse and argument about any subject
matter - and in particular words like 'all,' 'some,'
'the,' 'if ... then ...' (and including 'if it *were*
the case that ... then it *would be* the case that ...'),

'not,' and 'or.'   Second, it includes terms for *observable* properties and relations, such as 'red,' 'between,' 'painful,' and 'joy.'   There are debates about which terms should be classified as observation terms, but for the present this rather technical epistemological point may be ignored.   Third, it includes all terms synonymous with any complex of terms formed from the vocabulary already admitted.   Fourth - and here we get into deeper water - it includes other terms (like 'electron') which are tied to terms of the second and third classes by virtue of appearing in laws or rules in which terms of the other classes also appear.   Such laws or rules are often said to accomplish a 'partial definition' of terms of this fourth type.   Rudolf Carnap has argued that this fourth class is very large indeed, in science, but we need not pursue this question.

Whether a statement belongs to an empiricist language in this sense is an important matter.   For any statement in an empiricist language is open to assessment by the methods of empirical science, whereas this is not possible for any statement which does not belong to an empiricist language.

If we overlook some points of vagueness, it is clear that 'happiness' and 'prosperity' belong to an empiricist language; the same is true for 'welfare' *if* its meaning were equated with that of these terms. (I.D.M. Little has doubted this claim about 'happiness' in contexts of talk of 'increasing the happiness of the community'; explanations are needed if we are to use the term in such a context.)

Let us turn now to the concepts of 'value-judgment' and 'value-word.'   Some writers classify a judgment as a value-judgment if and only if it *cannot be formulated in an empiricist language*.   If this proposal were acceptable, we could drop 'value-judgment' as a *second* conceptual tool, and get along with the first one alone.   But the proposal is too broad.   Statements in books on theology, or on metaphysics, or even inductive logic (statements containing 'probable' or 'well-warranted') appear not to be formulable in an empiricist language, but it would be odd to say that they necessarily express value-judgments.   Moreover, some philosophers ('naturalists' in value theory) hold that value statements *do* belong to an empiricist language, and we do not wish to prejudge this issue by linguistic legislation.   (Even if we did, we should not succeed in settling any important issue, for the question could still arise whether judgments to the

effect that 'It is a good thing that ...' were value-
judgments in that sense.)   I believe, then, that we
should adopt a neutral definition of 'value-judgment'
which at least begs no important questions.   I propose
the following, while conceding that it needs to be
spelled out more elaborately than is possible here.
Let us say that a judgment is a value-judgment if, and
only if, it entails or contradicts some judgment which
could be formulated so as to involve any one of the
following terms, in its ordinary sense, in an essential
way: (i) 'is a good thing that' (or 'is a better thing
that'), (ii) 'is morally obligatory,' (iii) 'is repre-
hensible' and (iv) 'is morally praiseworth.'   If one
wishes to use 'value-judgment' more narrowly, so as to
distinguish it from specifically ethical or moral judgments, one could define it by reference to just the
first of the foregoing phrases.   Now a 'value-word' or
'value-phrase' is one the occurrence of which in a
statement marks the statement as a value-statement
expressing a value-judgment.   'Is a good thing that'
is a clear case of a value-phrase.

If we ask whether, by this criterion, judgments
about the welfare of individuals are value-judgments,
the correct answer appears to be affirmative.   For
take the phrase, which is the important one for the
economist, 'is on a *higher level of welfare.'*   The
statement, 'X is on a higher level of welfare if he is
in situation S rather than S´' appears to imply or even
mean the same as 'X is *better off* in S than in S´, if
we abstract from all questions of moral obligation and
the rights of others'; and the same for, 'If we
abstract from all questions of moral obligation and
the rights of others, it is a *better thing* for X to be
in S than in S´.'   If this is correct, then such
judgments are value-judgments in our sense, and 'welfare' appears to be a value-word.   The same is not,
however, true of 'happiness.'   From 'X is happier in
S than in S´' it does not appear to *follow* that he is
necessarily better off.   This is shown by the fact
that it is not inconsistent to think that knowledge is
better than ignorance, and therefore, that, whereas a
person might be happier in S than in S´, he is worse
off because he is more ignorant in S (perhaps he is
happily half-witted in situation S).   'Happiness,'
then, is not a value-word - which is an additional
reason for denying that it is synonymous with 'welfare.'

So far, then, our tentative conclusion about 'welfare' is (i) that it is a value-word and (ii) that it
does not mean the same as either 'prosperity' or 'happi-

ness.'   Since we have defined 'value-word' (and 'value-judgment') in a neutral way, so as not to commit us on the question whether value-words belong to an empiricist language, we are not yet committed to any conclusion about whether welfare-judgments can be confirmed by the methods of science.

It might seem that the next order of business, then, must be to state the outcome of the enormous philosophical literature on the meaning and function of value-words in general and then to attempt to map the place of 'welfare' among value-words (viz., map the logical relations to other value-words) as all of these are used in ordinary speech.

This undertaking would be all very well for the authors of a dictionary, but I do not believe it would be very profitable for economists or philosophers. (2) The fundamental reason for this is that value-words, in their ordinary use, are very vague, and the authors of value-statements do not have any definite meaning in mind when they make them.   Moreover, there is some reason to think that what meaning they have varies a good deal from one person to another, the extent depending largely upon the cultural history of the individual. What is called for, in contrast to laboring with ordinary usage, is that we *assign* some definite meaning to these terms, doubtless within the rough and vague limits prescribed by present usage, and that we do so for definite, statable, and relevant reasons.   This holds, I believe, for the term 'welfare.'

It may seem that the job of picking a useful and relevant meaning for 'welfare' is a wholly amorphous one, too indefinite to qualify as a job at which one could either succeed or fail.   But let us see.   In fact, it will be possible to be quite brief, although at the outset we must consider some facts which may seem extraneous to our concern about 'welfare.'

Let me begin by pointing out that there are a great many choices or decisions which an individual has to make when we think he is free to attend only to his own welfare - when no moral obligations to others are involved and no considerations of the rights of others arise.   An example of such a choice, in normal circumstances, is which profession to prepare for, whether law, or teaching philosophy, and so on.   Another and humbler example is whether to enter this drugstore for a breakfast egg or to seek the same in the cafeteria across the street.   Let us consider only choices of this sort.

Suppose there is such a choice to be made.   The

agent may be in doubt what to do.   Or, having made the
choice, he may be in doubt whether he did not 'make a
mistake.'   If there is this element of doubt or puzzle-
ment, the question arises whether one possible choice
may be defended, supported, or justified, as compared
with others.   It is obvious that people *do* engage in
some sort of reflection which they think sometimes
results in a justification of a choice, to their own
satisfaction.

About this process of reflection, we can sensibly
raise two questions: is there any particular kind of
consideration or reflection which in practice thoughtful
people in general find weighty or conclusive support or
justification of this sort?   And, if so, is it possible
to give an account, universally persuasive to thoughtful
people, of *why* attention should be given this kind of
consideration, in guiding one's conduct? (3)

I believe there is a particular kind of reflection
which thoughtful persons do find weighty, and for good
reasons.   Something close to it was indicated by John
Stuart Mill, when he said that the only way to find
whether something is desirable is, in the end, to find
whether people do desire it.   A more adequate account
is, roughly, to say that a choice is considered justified, and with good reason, if it is shown that it is
one which the agent, if he were 'rational,' would
prefer to any alternative open to him.   Or, to spell
out the term 'rational' just a bit, a choice is considered justified, and with good reason, if it is
shown that the agent would prefer it to any other
open to him at the time, if he were in a normal frame
of mind and believed correctly all the facts relevant
to the choice and had them vividly before his mind.
To say this is still so brief as to be cryptic: I
shall, therefore, proceed now to spell out what I mean
by 'prefer,' and by 'rational'; and I shall sketch
the reasons which may be given for saying that one
should pay attention to one's rational preferences in
making one's decisions.

But first let me acknowledge that other proposals
have been made about how to justify one's choices,
some of them highly implausible and unrealistic.   One
of these I shall discuss at some length in a moment:
it is the by no means implausible proposal that a
choice is justified, for the limited type of context
we are discussing, if and only if it would (or probably
would) maximize the net enjoyment or satisfaction of
the agent.

Let me now explain the concept or rational preference,

and then the alternative proposal.   After I have done
this, we shall be in a position to consider what
meaning may fruitfully be assigned to 'increases the
welfare of an individual.'

Preference

What is it to 'prefer'?   First, it is convenient to
say that what we prefer is always *that one situation be
the case* rather than that another be the case.   Thus,
we may prefer *that* Jones be elected mayor rather than
that Smith be elected.   We often *say* we prefer *things,*
say chocolate to vanilla.   But we can always rephrase
such remarks in our standard vocabulary; e.g., we can
say that we prefer *that* we be savoring chocolate than
that we be savoring vanilla.

Now, what I mean by '*X* would *prefer* that *p* to that
q' (e.g., that he do *A* rather than that he do *B*) is '*X*
would *want* that *p more* than that *q*' or else 'would
have less of an *aversion* to *p* than to *q*,' if the alternatives were before him as possibilities.   It is
perhaps obvious that it does not follow, from the fact
that *X chooses* that *p* rather than that *q*, that he
wants that *p* more than that *q*.   For a person may
select a cake from a plate of cakes offered him, when
he does not prefer (want more) that one to any other
cake on the plate, simply because he is busy talking
with someone.   Moreover, people often act impulsively
without attending carefully to what they most want.
Further, people can make mistakes about what they want:
a person can think he wants a good character, when in
reality he simply has an aversion to a bad reputation.
Since what a person does is more closely related to
what he thinks he wants than to what he does want,
there is a further reason why what one does may not be
an indicator of what one most wants or prefers.

But what then is it to *want* that *p*?   This is a
more elusive concept than might appear at first, as
anyone will know who when making a difficult decision
has tried to follow the advice 'Do what you most *want*
to do!'   It seems quite clear that wanting something
is not a simple introspectible datum like a tickle.
The exact logic of the concept of wanting is a difficult matter, (4) but I believe the central portion of
the concept of wanting is captured in the following
propositions, relating wanting to observable events:
(a) If, given that *X* had not been expecting *p* but now
suddenly judged that *p* would be the case, *X* would feel

joy, then X wants p.   (b) If, given that X had been
expecting p but then suddenly judged that p would not
be the case, X would feel disappointment, then X wants
p.   (c) If daydreaming about p is pleasant to X, then
X wants p.   (d) If X wants p, then, under favorable
conditions, if X judges that doing A will probably
lead to p and that not doing A will probably lead to
not-p, X will feel some impulse to do A.   (e) If X
wants p, then, under favorable conditions, if X thinks
some means M is a way of bringing p about, X will be
more likely to notice an M than he would otherwise
have been.   (f) If X wants p, then, under favorable
conditions, if p occurs to the knowledge of X, without
the simultaneous occurrence of events X does not want,
X will be pleased. (5)

It seems plausible to suppose that evidence for
wanting p more than q is provided by occurrence of the
events cited in a more intense form, in connection with
judgments about p, than with judgments about q.

If the foregoing conception is well taken, then what
a person wants is fixed by what he has to *think about*
in order for these effects to occur.

I have suggested that there is not a simple relation
between what a person wants and the choices he makes.
For very similar reasons there is not a simple relation
between what a person wants (or wants more or less)
and the bets he will lay.   It would, of course, be
unreasonable to deny that betting behavior is strong
evidence about the relative strength of wants.

Rational preference

I have suggested that preference may be called
'rational' when it meets certain conditions.   Let me
explain these more fully.

When we prefer one event p to another q, it is
always because we think (at least take for granted or
believe) that these events have different properties.
(These could be just the properties defining what it
is to be a 'p' or a 'q' occurrence.)   For instance,
we may prefer the profession of medicine because we
think the life of a physician, as compared with that
of a philosopher, is one of more contact with other
persons or one which produces more definite and tangible results.   This fact points to one possible way
of criticizing a preference: that of showing that the
beliefs on which it is based are incorrect, or even
unintelligible.   It also points to a second possible

way: that of showing that the beliefs on which it is based are incomplete, that there are further facts such that if the agent had thought about them, he would have preferred what he did either more or less. It seems, then, that one condition of a fully justified preference could be this: that it is based on all true beliefs about the object in question which would tend to move the agent one way or the other. I propose calling a preference 'rational' only if this condition is met.

There is a second and closely related condition. Sometimes in a sense we *know* all the pros and cons relevant to a preference, but we do not have them *all before our mind*. Sometimes when we think of one feature of an alternative, we feel drawn toward it; when we think of another feature, we feel repelled. This raises the question: what would we prefer if we could get *all* the relevant features before our mind with full vividness - as vividly as if we could actually perceive them all? I propose to call a preference fully 'rational' only when it is as it would be if this condition were met.

There is a third defect from which a preference may suffer. It may be formed, and be capable of being formed, only in a peculiar mood or frame of mind. Some features of something may appeal to us more in some frames of mind than others, for instance, under the smart of a wound to our pride. So, again, I propose to call a preference 'rational' only when this defect is absent - when the preference is one that would be framed in a state of mind undistorted by temporary mood or emotion or by some temporary craving.

I suggest that we call a preference for p over q a *rational* preference *if, and only if,* these three conditions are met.

We should notice that the question whether a person rationally, in this sense, prefers p to q is one that in principle can be answered by empirical means, by the person and also within limits by other people (assuming they can get information about his wants and aversions) - of course, in some cases by no means easily; for answering requires finding the actual properties of p and q, correct beliefs about which would tend to move a person if he had them.

When thoughtful people have an important decision to make and are in some doubt what to do, I believe that in fact they try to see whether their tentative preference is rational in this sense. If they are convinced it is, they are satisfied with a corresponding decision. The reader is invited to introspect, to determine whether or not this is the case.

But is there any reason, which will be universally persuasive to thoughtful people, why they should guide their conduct by this sort of reflection? (i) For one thing, there is not really a serious alternative, if one is going to be reflective about choices, to paying attention to what we *want* to do. This will be clearer after we have considered the major alternative. (ii) *If* we aim to make it a policy to do what we most want to do, presumably the policy will be to do the thing we most want of the *actual* alternatives open to us, as they really are, and not the thing we most want among mere caricatures of the alternatives. And to this end we need knowledge of the relevant facts before us. (iii) It is sensible to pay attention to 'normal' preferences since we have to live with our decisions. It would be imprudent to favor the fleeting preference of a moment in making a decision we may long dislike and regret. To this it may be replied that no reason has been given why we now should take an interest in whether we shall regret something; but at any rate we can say that it is arbitrary to favor only the preference of the present moment and also that in fact most persons do take an interest in whether they will regret a decision later, when they reflect that they are the very same person who will have to endure the later regrets.

I have already acknowledged that there are other possible systems for appraising choices of the limited kind under consideration. I shall discuss a closely related method in a moment. But there are some quite different ways. A person might think he should choose only what conforms with the 'purpose' of the universe, or with God's will. Conceivably reasons might be given for using such a method (although I suspect such reasons would reduce to the method already described). I do not see how we can rule out, in advance, all such possibilities as being absurd. But we also need not worry about them until they are formulated and we know what they are. What we can say now is that up to the present no comparably supported method (aside from the one to be discussed next) has been produced (6) and that a choice which meets the conditions described has met the known possible objections which might seriously be raised against it.

Pleasure, happiness, and satisfaction

There is one possible way of supporting or justifying
one's choices (in cases where no questions arise about
moral obligation or the rights of others), which is
different from the one just outlined, and which has
some plausibility.   This is the familiar view that an
agent's choice is justified if, and only if, it will
(or probably will) result in maximizing the agent's
pleasure, happiness, or satisfaction.   This conception
has appealed to many economists and philosophers
influenced by the utilitarian tradition.

We can simplify discussion without loss by con-
struing the proposal in terms of maximizing the
agent's net long-run *pleasure*, dropping out explicit
reference to happiness and satisfaction.   At least we
can do this if we construe 'pleasure' broadly enough
so as not to imply merely sensory pleasure but to
include such enjoyments as that of reading a book and
if we construe 'displeasure' broadly enough so as to
include such displeasures as those of anxiety and
embarrassment in addition to physical discomforts.

It might be objected to this simplification that it
distorts and reduces the plausibility of the proposal.
But this can hardly be correct, for it appears that we
can define 'happiness' in all its various senses in
terms of 'pleasant.'

For instance, 'I was happy all evening until he
said ...' means the same as 'I was enjoying myself
this evening until he said ...' or 'I was having a
perfectly pleasant evening until he said ...'   It is
often asserted, however, that 'happiness' is not a sum
of pleasures.   In this statement, 'happy' is being
used in a different and somewhat narrower sense.   To
be happy in this sense is to be pleased, or at least
not discontent, with one's achievements or prospects
with respect to one's major goals in life.   Indeed,
some recent work suggests that people call themselves
'happy' if they are pleased, or at least not discontent,
with achievement, or prospects, with respect to what
they consider their most important goals.   So we
might define 'is happy' in this sense as meaning 'does
not feel any unpleasant emotion at the thought of
where he is or is getting with respect to certain
major aims in life' and perhaps also 'goes about his
work with a pleasant cheer and zest.'   In other words,
when one is happy in this sense, one's life is not
marred with unpleasant emotions when one reflects on
certain matters and by and large one's activities are

pleasant.   If we conceive 'happiness' thus, then it is
true that a sequence of sensual pleasures does not
amount to happiness; but it is also true that happiness
is nothing other than the enjoyment (or absence of displeasure) resulting from being able to take an optimistic view about progress toward important goals.
There are doubtless other senses of 'happy' which we
should recognize; and we must remember that the term
is a rather vague one.   There is no reason to believe,
however, that such other senses cannot be explained in
terms of 'enjoys' and 'pleasant.'

Much the same is true of 'satisfaction.'   Suppose
a person says he gets much satisfaction out of the
progress of his former graduate students in the academic
world.   What he means is no more than that reflection
on the success of certain former students is pleasant.
Explanations of other uses of this term will readily
come to mind.

With these preliminaries out of the way, the
question is this: might we regard a choice as sensible
(in the limited context described above), if it will
(or probably will) maximize one's net long-run
pleasure, as contrasted with being in conformity with
one's rational preference?   It will help us adjudicate
this question if we consider briefly the nature of
pleasure or pleasantness, about which there has
recently developed a considerable literature. (7)

The first thing to be noted is that what is pleasant
is always some conscious state, or activity, of a
person.   Things that are pleasant are things like
dozing in the sun, listening to a symphony, reading a
novel, or hearing good news.

It follows that on this second theory the class of
'ultimate reasons' justifying a choice is narrower
than on the first theory.   The reason for this is
that people actually *want* other things besides their
own conscious states or activities.   Of course, people
do want enjoyment and do have an aversion to pain,
anxiety, and other unpleasant states.   But there are
other things they want: such as to get a manuscript
in better shape, to have a daughter happy in her
marriage and financially secure after her parents'
death.   Some writers have thought that what a person
desires is always some state (or, more particularly,
some pleasant state) of himself; but by any reasonable
criterion for identifying what a person desires (such
as the criteria sketched above), people desire some
things which cannot be described as states of themselves.   It is true that if one's manuscript gets in

better shape, one will feel 'happier' about it, and if
one's daughter is happily married and provided for, one
will feel less unpleasant anxiety about her.   But
these states of one's self are obviously not the
targets of one's desire.   For this reason it is quite
natural and unconfused for people to ask themselves
whether it is sensible to sacrifice personal enjoyments
in order to achieve something important;   this is a
real alternative and some people prefer one course,
some another.   Of course, it may be that one can
rationally want something only to the extent that
getting it will make one happier;   but the rational-
preference theory leaves open the possibility that this
is not the case.   And it is surely not obvious that a
'rational' want would be only for some pleasant state
of one's self.

A second feature of pleasure is important for our
purposes.   What precise kind of state or activity is
a 'pleasant' one?   On this the experts are much less
fully agreed.   Some suppose that 'pleasure' consists
in relaxation-feelings or bright pressure-feelings, but
others find it impossible to introspect such feelings
when they are enjoying themselves.   Others have held
that 'pleasure' is always a case of activity in which
one is absorbed or to which one attends without effort,
but this description hardly fits what is happening
when one is dozing in the sun, and one wonders how
such writers would describe how one feels when the
dentist is drilling.   I think myself that the property
which most clearly belongs to all pleasant states and
activities is simply that *at the time the person wants
them to continue for their own sakes* (which is consistent both with not *thinking* that one wants them to
continue, and also with *not wanting* to continue them,
everything considered, in view of consequences or of
other things one ought to be doing).   And, for one
experience to be *more* pleasant than another, is for
the person to want to continue it, more intensely, for
itself.   We should notice that things as diverse as
playing a game and having a certain kind of sensation
may be pleasant in this sense. (8)

If I am right in this, then pleasure is a *species* of
wanting: it is wanting some *present* state or activity
to *continue, for its own sake.*   Incidentally, one can
want a state or activity to continue at the time, but
afterward wish it had not.   Whether one wants something, and how much, seems to be partly a function of
the state of one's glands, so that there may be some
inconstancy in what one wants, perhaps even in what one

rationally wants.   (*If* there is, there may be a limit
to the consistent direction we can get for action from
appeal to our rational preferences.)

I can now explain why I believe that the traditional
hedonist view of how choices (for our limited context)
are to be appraised should not be substituted for the
'rational-preference' proposal.   The major reason is
simply that to adopt the hedonist view amounts to an
arbitrary decision in favor of conscious states or
activities which one wants at the time one has them.
It is true that we want these, both at the time and
often beforehand, but what is so sacrosanct about them
so that all other wants must be dismissed?   If a
person, after careful reflection, finds that he wants
some things (to make an important discovery or the
security of his children) more than states of personal
enjoyment, it is not clear that there is any persuasive
ground for abandoning these desires (as there is for
abandoning desires which we would not have except in
depressed moments).   Of course, the rational-preference
proposal leaves open the possibility that a rational
want is never directed at anything but a pleasant state
of consciousness or a pleasant activity.   The rational-
preference proposal, therefore, leaves open the possibility that the hedonist is right in his conclusion.
But to adopt it at the outset as a method of appraisal
is to opt arbitrarily for a special sort of want: for
wants directed at the continuance of some state or
activity of the self at the time.

There is a second difficulty in the proposal.   In
order to make rational decisions by the hedonist standard, one must compare enjoyments of certain duration
and intensity, for magnitude, with enjoyments of
different duration and intensity.   But this is impossible: we can compare the intensities of different
experiences (strength of wanting to continue at the
time), but we cannot compare intensities with dura-
tions.   We *can* make the comparisons necessary for
decision, however, if we take the notion of preference
as basic.   We can prefer to endure, say, a certain
stretch of pain of a given intensity for the sake of a
different stretch of enjoyment of a given intensity.
(It does not follow from this that there is *more
enjoyment* in the preferred experience.)   So it appears
that the hedonist can make judgments he needs to make,
only if he falls back on the preference standard after
all.   (He can refuse to do this if he admits that
there is no rational answer to questions about conduct
which could be answered only by comparisons of the
sort described.)

Levels of individual welfare

Thus far I have argued that one might support a choice
by showing that it conforms with one's 'rational
preference' in a sense explained.   I have suggested
that thoughtful people do appraise actual or possible
choices in this manner and that there are reasons which
would dispose a thoughtful person to pay attention to
his rational preference in deciding what to do.
Further, I have suggested that there is no other mode
of appraising choices which has a comparable claim on
conduct for those cases in which moral obligations and
the rights of others are not involved.

   We must now revert to the original question what
meaning can usefully be assigned to 'welfare' or 'on
a higher level of welfare.'

   It might be argued that we do not have to 'assign'
any meaning here, for it is clear that what we *already*
mean, in English, by these terms is such that 'X is on
a higher level of welfare if p rather than if q' just
means 'X rationally prefers that p to that q' in the
above-defined sense of 'rationally prefers.'   (And
the same for, 'X is better off if p than if q.')   At
one time I inclined to this view myself, but I believe
that 'better off' and 'welfare' are too vague for this
suggestion to be correct.   Therefore, if 'welfare' is
to have a meaning of the kind indicated, it must be an
assigned one.

   What purpose should guide our assignment of
meanings?   We need not aim to preserve the vagueness
of ordinary language.   We need, rather, to have meanings so assigned that things which are important to
say can be said clearly and unambiguously.   Further,
we need terminology related to choice and conduct which
enables us to raise and distinguish all the questions
it is important to raise, in view of our total understanding of the human scene.   And, if I am right in
thinking that there is a preferred method for resolving
doubts about choices and for appraising choices, we
shall need some terms indicative of the status of a
choice with respect to the application of this method.

   What meaning, then, all these points considered,
should we assign to 'is on a higher level of welfare'?
One possibility is simply to use it as a synonym for
'prefers.'   However, we already have a perfectly good
term for this concept.   Further, in ordinary speech
we often contrast preference with welfare (a person
may prefer what is bad for him).   I suggest, then,
that we are keeping reasonably close to the ordinary

associations of 'welfare,' and are at the same time
assigning a useful meaning to the term, if we decide
to use 'X is on a higher level of welfare if p than
if q' to mean 'X rationally prefers p to q.'

If we adopt this definition, it follows that one
person might be put on a higher level of welfare by
the very same kind of occurrence that will put another
person on a lower level.   It also follows that a
person's own rational desires are decisive for his
own welfare and that the desires of others are not -
however much another's wish for him may be more reliable
as an indicator of his rational desires than his own
actual wishes are.   If X conforms to what others want
him to do, when their wants are rational, he is adding
to *their* welfare, not necessarily to his own.   Also,
if X wants his son's happiness (rationally), then his
son's happiness really does raise $X's$ level of welfare,
the extent depending upon how much X wanted it.

Some propositions appear to be true about the
rational wants of all persons; but whether they are
logically or only empirically true, I shall not discuss.
Among them are the following: (i) If a person
rationally wants both p and q, and is indifferent
between them, he will rationally prefer a given probability of getting p to a smaller probability of getting
q.   (ii) A person will not rationally prefer p to q
on account of temporal position *alone*.   (iii) Knowledge that an event will be pleasant for a person will
always arouse, so far, a favorable rational interest
in the event; and knowledge that it will be unpleasant
will always arouse, so far, a rational aversion toward
the event.   (iv) The rational preferences of a person
will be transitive.

Given the above definition, we shall want to specify
that a good or service has *utility* for a person if he
would rationally prefer to have it rather than not have
it.   To say that two goods have equal utility for a
person will be to say that the person would be rationally indifferent between them.

If the foregoing definition is accepted, 'welfare'
and 'utility' both belong to an empiricist language
and at the same time are 'value-words' which can
function essentially in the expression of a value-
judgment.

SOCIAL WELFARE

The foregoing definitions do not commit us to any particular definitions of 'social welfare' or 'increases social welfare,' terms which appear frequently in the literature of welfare economics. Let us now consider what would be a useful way to construe these terms. Our results will enable us to appraise the status of the proposition 'The social welfare is increased by the change from S to S' if this increases the welfare of at least one person and the welfare of no one is diminished by the change,' a proposition which is viewed by some economists as an ultimate value-judgment. My conclusion will be that this proposition is true by definition.

Space limitations forbid considering various possible meanings that could be assigned to the above expressions. So let us go at once to the heart of the matter: the question what an economist might do, with good reason, to *support* advice he might offer to a public official as to some proposed rule or law. We could follow lines of thought similar to those pursued in the preceding section to justify saying that what one must do, in order to support a recommendation of a rule or law, is show that the rule or law is one *he (or others) would want adopted, if he (they) were rational (in the above-defined sense) and also were a person (persons) whose concern for others were equal to his (their) concern for self or family.*

I shall have to pass by the question what complications are raised by the possibility that two rational and sympathetic persons might disagree in their recommendations. I incline to think that in fact they *would* disagree to some extent, but I also believe there are some principles on which they (9) will necessarily agree - parallel to what was suggested for the case of individual welfare.

Now we could, with some sense, propose to assign to 'Rule A will *increase the social welfare* more than Rule B' the meaning 'If I [alternatively: anyone] were rational and sympathetic I [he] would prefer to have Rule A adopted rather than Rule B.' But in fact this would be inconvenient and misleading, for there are different fundamental reasons on account of which thoughtful people have wanted rules adopted - not only considerations of welfare, but also considerations of justice or equality. (Witness how people have favored equality of income when they have not argued that this would increase the total real income; or they have

argued that it should be illegal to purchase ration
tickets or to buy a substitute for military service,
although they have not denied that such exchanges might
increase total welfare.) Indeed, the difference
between utilitarians and their critics has been that
the utilitarians have said that in the end only increasing welfare is a relevant and forcible reason for
adopting an institution, whereas their critics have
denied this. In order to preserve at least the
possibility of debating these controversial points, it
is necessary to assign a meaning to 'increases social
welfare' so that it is not *self-contradictory* to say
'If I [one] were rational and sympathetic I [one]
would prefer to have Rule *A* adopted rather than Rule *B*,
for reasons of justice, and despite the fact that Rule
B would enhance social welfare more.'

How might we assign meaning to 'increases social
welfare' so as to meet this condition in a helpful way?
I see no alternative to a formulation equating
'increases social welfare' with 'increases the *sum* of
individual welfare' where 'individual welfare' is
explained as in the preceding section. It remains to
be shown, of course, that the welfares of individuals,
in that sense of 'welfare,' *can* be summed. But it is
clear, at least, that if 'social welfare' is defined
in this way, it follows that the social welfare is
increased if the welfare of at least one person is
increased and that of no one else decreased. It is
for this reason that I suggested above that it is an
analytic proposition, as we must construe 'increased
social welfare,' that social welfare will be increased
under these conditions. Thus, if this definition is
adopted, part of welfare economics rests on the sound
foundation of an analytic proposition.

It is well-known, however, that if we are to speak
of the 'sum' of individual welfares and also in principle to be able to determine which of two laws
increases the sum of individual welfares the more,
certain other propositions must be true. Most important, we must be able to compare for size the prospec-
tive utility of one person or persons with the pros-
pective disutility of some other person or persons,
if a certain law is adopted. And, if we explain
'utility' as above suggested, this means that at
least sometimes we must be able to affirm reasonably
the following proposition: that *X* wants *A* more than
Y wants *B*. (We are ultimately concerned with a comparison between the *rational* wants of *X* and *Y*, but
that problem can be ignored for the present.)

Since the possibility of reasonably affirming propositions of this sort is so central to application of this (traditional) concept of 'social welfare' that I am suggesting, and since I happen to think that some economists take an unreasonably purist view about this matter, I shall conclude my remarks with some queries about the epistemology of these economists.

Since according to suggestions made above, the intensity of a person's wanting is measured by various things such as the disappointment he would feel if he did not get it, we may as well simplify our problem by asking simply whether we can know that one person has some conscious state (e.g., disappointment, pain) more intensely than does some other person.

One difficulty a noneconomist has in discussing this problem is that he does not know exactly what is behind the economist's conclusions. If the economist thinks we cannot have sufficient reasons for thinking other persons conscious at all, that is one thing. If, however, he thinks we have sufficient reasons for thinking other persons are conscious, and perhaps for asserting *some* things about their states of consciousness, that is another.

Let us begin with the second possibility. Presumably in this case the purist economist thinks that certain pieces of evidence are good and sufficient for making some assertions about the consciousness of others. Then our question must be: why draw the line here? Are the reasons you think adequate for these assertions not essentially of the same kind as those available for other affirmations? Suppose the purist economist thinks another person has at least three different colors in his visual field (he may say we cannot know what these colors are like). If this is asserted because it is necessary to explain the other's color discriminations, then one might go on to suggest that the other person's ability to predict that a proctoscopic examination will hurt *me* more than a mosquito bite is good reason for saying that the former hurts *him* more than the latter sort of thing. It is, perhaps, obvious how we might go on. Exactly what we should do is necessarily unclear, of course, until we have information about exactly what the purist is prepared to concede.

The purist economist may be much more radical, however. He may say we have no good reason for making any assertions about the conscious states of other persons, even for asserting that other persons are conscious at all. We should notice, incidentally,

that it would not be to the point for him to say merely
that we do not have *certain* knowledge about the experiences of others, for this would not disparage our
grounds for statements about experiences of others in
comparison with grounds for other assertions.   If we
grant that such knowledge is not certain, it may still
be more nearly certain that the man having the proctoscopic examination is in pain than that there will not
be a business recession next year.   So let us suppose
the purist is saying we have *no good and coercive*
reasons for beliefs of this sort *at all*.

    This position is an extreme one.   What are the
purist's reasons for adopting it?   (One is inclined
to say that these reasons are very likely to be more
dubious than the reasons for regarding the man having
the proctoscopic examination as being in pain.)   Presumably the economist thinks that some *type of inference* is required for assertions about the experiences
of other persons which is not required in the rest of
science and is dubious.   (He might go further: he
might say we have no good reason for believing, unless
it can be shown to *follow logically* from observations,
that another person's experience is so and so.   But
to say this is to condemn all of science, for no law
or theory in science anywhere follows logically from
a description of the observations.)   What kind of
inference might this be?   Perhaps the purist will
reply: 'inference *by analogy*.'   If he does, we
must then ask him (a) what he *means* by 'analogical
inference' (this term is used in many different
senses) and (b) why he thinks that analogical inference
in that sense is required for the present context. (10)

    It is not unfair to demand that the purist produce
his epistemology, for he is the one who is departing
radically from common sense.   The purist obviously
does not believe his creed in practice: if his child
were about to have an operation, he would not question
the advisability of using an anesthetic or of giving
morphine after the operation!   Nevertheless, it is
worthwhile to produce two positive reasons on the
other side.

1 In physics it is thought proper to extrapolate laws
confirmed for observable entities, to the unobserved
(e.g., Newton's laws are extrapolated to the realm of
microscopic entities).   It is supposed that if
postulates about the unobservables, plus these extrapolated laws, lead to correct predictions, the postulates and the extrapolation are justified.   But the
logic is the same for inferences about other minds.

We know in our own case (a) that we feel pain when
having a proctoscopic examination, (b) that we seldom
succeed in making witty sallies when in severe pain,
(c) that we feel grief when we learn of the death of
our mother, (d) that we find it hard to take an
interest in things, or to act in a vivacious manner,
when we feel severe grief, and (e) that the passage of
time reduces the poignancy of grief.   On the basis
of this, we predict that a man having a proctoscopic
examination will seldom come out with witty remarks
and that the person whom we have just apprised of his
mother's death will not behave vivaciously this evening
although he probably will do so in a month's time.
These predictions work out magnificently.   Why, then,
as compared with the physicist, are the extrapolations
and assumptions wholly dubious?   We use mentalistic
assumptions in making a good many predictions about the
behavior of others, and it is not clear how we would
make them without mentalistic assumptions.   The
correctness of the predictions would seem to reflect
glory on the assumptions, in principle just as in
physics (although, of course, the predictions are non-
quantitative and much more humble).

2   Other people succeed in making a good many correct
assertions about *our* mental states.   One's mother,
when dropping iodine on the wound or in stripping back
one's injured fingernail, says 'That must hurt badly!'
How was she able to guess if she has never experienced
pain herself?   The books on psychology are very successful in predicting all sorts of visual illusions
and various facts about the emotional life.   How are
the psychologists able to predict how things will look,
or feel, if they are unconscious?   Indeed, the very
availability of a rich language for description of our
mental life must be explained by the purist - and also
how it was possible to teach us the use of this language.   The minimal explanatory assumption appears
to be that other persons are built very much along our
lines and so there has been a point in the existence
of such a language, and they have been able to teach
it to us because, on the basis of their own experience,
they have been able to know when we have experiences to
which these terms properly apply.

Whether the purist in economics will want to deny
the force of these lines of reasoning, I do not know.
Perhaps he will wish to fall back on the less extreme
position, described earlier, that it is only some
kinds of information about others which we cannot
claim with strong supporting grounds.

We need not deny that it is difficult to know whether an increase in the tariff on bicycles would do more harm than good. But I venture to suggest that some economists are locating the source of the difficulty in the wrong place; they are giving way to a penchant to attribute all our predictive ills to one disease - the philosophical problem about knowledge of other minds - instead of attributing them to the various difficulties of knowing exactly what will happen to various individuals, or classes of individuals, if the tariff were raised. If we knew exactly what difference to the *total conditions of living insofar as these are publicly observable* an increase in tariff would bring about, it seems doubtful to me that the impossibility of observing others' mental states would be much of a further problem. Indeed, if we even knew such a simple fact as that the total effect of a tariff increase would be that one hundred not very sturdy newsboys could not afford bicycles and must, therefore, spend one more hour each day delivering their papers on foot and also (on the credit side) that one man would be able to buy a third air-conditioned Cadillac, it is hard to believe that the purist would doubt that more harm than good was done. Unfortunately the effects of a change of tariff are so hard to predict in detail that we cannot well say just what people are doing, eating (etc.) given the change which they would not have been doing without it. But such effects are essentially knowable, if we wish to spend the time and money.

NOTES

1 For a discussion of the concept of an empiricist language, and some of its difficulties, see C.G. Hempel, Problems and Changes in the Empiricist Criterion of Meaning, reprinted, with afterthoughts, in A.J. Ayer, ed., 'Logical Positivism,' New York, Free Press, 1959. This paper includes a useful bibliography.
2 I have argued this at some length in 'Moral Philosophy and the Analysis of Language,' The Lindley Lecture for 1963, published by the Department of Philosophy, University of Kansas, 1963. I have discussed the varieties, and difficulties, of various theories about the meaning of value-words in ordinary language in 'Ethical Theory,' Englewood Cliffs, N.J., Prentice-Hall, 1959, chs 7 to 9.

3 It may be interesting to reflect on whether the
   accepted standards for inductive inference in science can be given support fundamentally different
   from that which can be given for choices.
4 See the discussion by R.B. Brandt and Jaegwon Kim,
   Wants as Explanations of Actions, 'Journal of Philosophy,' 60 (1963), pp. 425-35. For some differences between wants and aversions see Stephen Pepper,
   'The Sources of Value,' Berkeley, University of
   California Press, 1958, ch. 10; and E.C. Tolman,
   'Purposive Behaviour in Animals and Men,' New York,
   Appleton, 1932. See also Fritz Heider, 'Psychology
   of Interpersonal Relations,' New York, Wiley, 1958,
   chs 4 and 5.
5 These propositions are drawn from Brandt and Kim,
   'Journal of Philosophy.' Some of them require
   refinement. I do not believe that at present we
   can give any satisfactory general explanation of
   'under favourable conditions.' We shall wish to
   include as 'unfavourable' conditions such things as
   extreme fatigue, emotional excitement, and temporal
   remoteness of the event judged about.
6 I have discussed the merits of the theological proposal in 'Ethical Theory,' pp. 63-82 and 252-3.
7 See G. Ryle, 'The Concept of Mind,' London, Hutch-
   inson's University Library, 1949, ch. 4; also his
   'Dilemmas,' Cambridge University Press, 1954, ch. 4;
   and G. Ryle and W.B. Gallie, Pleasure, symposium,
   Aristotelian Society, supplementary vol. 28 (1954),
   pp. 135-64. T. Penelhum, The Logic of Pleasure,
   'Philosophy and Phenomenological Research,' 17
   (1957), pp. 488-503; and T. Penelhum, W.E. Kennick,
   and A.I. Isenberg, symposium, Pleasure and Falsity,
   'American Philosophical Quarterly,' 1 (1964), pp.
   81-100. C.W.W. Taylor, Pleasure, 'Analysis,'
   Supplement, 23 (1963), pp. 1-19. R.M. McNaughton,
   A Metrical Concept of Happiness, 'Philosophy and
   Phenomenological Research,' 14 (1953), pp. 172-83.
   A.R. Manser, Pleasure, 'Proceedings,' Aristotelian
   Society (1960-1961), pp. 223-38. B. Williams and
   E. Bedford, 'Pleasure and Belief,' symposium, Aris-
   totelian Society supplementary vol. 33 (1959), pp.
   57-92. R.B. Brandt, 'Ethical Theory,' pp. 304-07.
   P. Nowell-Smith, 'Ethics,' Harmondsworth, Penguin,
   1954, ch. 10.
       For interesting psychologists' discussions, see
   Fritz Heider, 'The Psychology of Interpersonal
   Relations,' New York, Wiley, 1959, ch. 5; J.G.
   Beebe-Center, 'The Psychology of Pleasantness and

Unpleasantness,' New York, Van Nostrand, 1932,
pp. 394-413; and his Feeling and Emotion in H.
Helson, ed., 'Theoretical Foundations of Psychology,'
New York, Van Nostrand, 1951; P.T. Young, 'Emotion
in Man and Animal,' New York, Wiley, 1943, ch. 7;
Magda Arnold, 'Emotion and Personality' vol. I, New
York, Columbia, 1960. Perhaps most interesting of
all is K. Duncker, On Pleasure, Emotion, and
Striving, 'Philosophy and Phenomenological Research,'
1 (1941), pp. 391-430.

8 An objection sometimes raised to this proposal is
that we can tell directly, by inspection, whether
we are enjoying something, whereas we would (it is
supposed) have to stop and reflect in order to know
that we want to continue some experience or activity
for itself (assuming the correctness of the above
account of 'wanting'). Various points may be made
in reply to this. One is that we know, without
elaborate reflection, that we would like to have a
lot of things: an increase in salary, a trip to
Europe, a drink of water, to find misplaced glasses.
Another, is that it is not impossible to become
conditioned to respond with 'Yes,' when stimulated
by the question, 'Are you enjoying yourself?', when
and only when we want some present state or activity
to continue. Many analogous phenomena have been
found in experiments on concept formation.

9 See my 'Ethical Theory,' chs 5, 6, and 11; also
'Value and Obligation,' New York, Harcourt, 1961,
pp. 433-40; and 'Hopi Ethics: A Theoretical
Analysis,' University of Chicago Press, 1954, ch.
16 and following.

10 It is possible some economists are influenced by the
logical positivism or operationalism which was
influential in the 1930s. They may then be saying
that statements about the experiences of others are
meaningless because in principle we cannot observe
them. (We can, of course, observe our *own* mental
events, and presumably other persons can observe
their mental events.) But if he does, is he not
condemning most of modern physics? Most of the
assertions in the area of quantum mechanics, for
instance, are about occurrences which in principle
we cannot observe in the required sense.

3   The good of man

G. H. Von Wright

1

The notion of the good of man, which will be discussed
in this chapter, is the central notion of our whole
inquiry. The problems connected with it are of the
utmost difficulty. Many things which I say about them
may well be wrong. Perhaps the best I can hope for is
that what I say will be interesting enough to be worth
a refutation.

We have previously (Ch. III, sect. 6) discussed the
question, what kind of being has a good. We decided
that it should make sense to talk of the good of everything, of the *life* of which it is meaningful to speak.
On this ruling there can be no doubt that man *has* a
good.

Granted that man has a good - what *is* it? The
question can be understood in a multitude of senses.
It can, for example, be understood as a question of a
name, a verbal equivalent of that which we *also* call
'the good of man'.

We have already (Ch. I, sect. 5) had occasion to
point out that the German equivalent of the English
substantive 'good', when this means the good of man or
some other being, is *das Wohl*. There is no substantive 'well' with *this* meaning in English. But there
are two related substantives, 'well-being' and
'welfare'.

A being who, so to speak, 'has' or 'enjoys' its
good, is also said to *be well* and, sometimes, to *do well*.

The notion of being well is related to the notion of
health. Often 'to be well' means exactly the same as
'to be in good, bodily and mental, health'. A man is
said to be well when he is all right, fit, in good shape
generally. These various expressions may be said to
refer to minimum requirements of enjoying one's good.

Of the being who does well, we also say that it
flourishes, thrives, or prospers. And we call it
happy. If health and well-being primarily connote
something privative, absence of illness and suffering;
happiness and well-doing again primarily refer to
something positive, to an overflow or surplus of
agreeable states and things.

From these observations on language three candidates
for a name of the good of man may be said to emerge.
These are 'happiness', 'well-being', and 'welfare'.

The suggestion might be made that 'welfare' is a
comprehensive term which covers the whole of that which
we also call 'the good of man' and of which happiness
and well-being are 'aspects' or 'components' or 'parts'.
It could further be suggested that there is a broad
sense of 'happiness', and of 'well-being', to mean the
same or roughly the same as 'welfare'. So that, on
one way of understanding them, the three terms could be
regarded as rough synonyms and alternative names of the
good of man.

The suggestion that 'the good of man' and 'the welfare of man' are synonymous phrases I accept without
discussion. That is: I shall use and treat them as
synonyms. (Cf. Ch. I, sect. 5; also Ch. III, sect. 1.)

It is hardly to be doubted that 'happiness' is
sometimes used as a rough synonym of 'welfare'. More
commonly, however, the two words are not used as synonyms. Happiness and welfare may, in fact, become distinguished as two concepts of different logical category
or type. We shall here mention three features which
may be used for differentiating the two concepts
logically.

First of all, the two concepts have a primary connexion with two different forms of the good. One could
say, though with caution, that happiness is a 'hedonic',
welfare again a 'utilitarian' notion. Happiness is
allied to pleasure, and therewith to such notions as
those of enjoyment, gladness, and liking. Happiness
has no immediate logical connexion with the beneficial.
Welfare again is primarily a matter of things beneficial and harmful, i.e. good and bad, for the being
concerned. As happiness, through pleasure, is related
to that which a man enjoys and likes, in a similar
manner welfare, through the beneficial, is connected
with that which a man wants and needs. (Cf. Ch. I,
sect. 5.)

Further, happiness is more like a 'state' (state of
affairs) than welfare is. A man can become happy, be
happy, and cease to be happy. He can be happy, and

unhappy, more than once in his life.   Happiness, like
an end, can be achieved and attained.   Welfare has not
these same relationships to events, processes, and
states *in time*.

Finally, a major logical difference between happiness
and welfare is their relation to *causality*.   Considerations of welfare are essentially considerations of how
the doing and happening of various things will causally
affect a being.   One cannot pronounce on the question
whether something is good or bad for a man, without
considering the causal connexions in which this thing
is or may become embedded.   But one can pronounce on
the question whether a man is happy or not, without
necessarily considering what were the causal antece-
dents and what will be the consequences of his present
situation.

The facts that happiness is primarily a hedonic and
welfare primarily a utilitarian notion, and that they
have logically different relationships to time and to
causality, mark the two concepts as being of that which
I have here called 'different logical category or
type'.   It does not follow, however, that the two concepts are logically entirely unconnected.   They are,
on the contrary, closely allied.   What then is their
mutual relation?   This is a question on which I have
not been able to form a clear view.   Welfare (the
good of a being) is, somehow, the broader and more
basic notion.   (Cf. Ch. III, sect. 12.)   It is also
the notion which is of greater importance to ethics and
to a general study of the varieties of goodness.
Calling happiness an 'aspect' or 'component' or 'part'
of the good of man is a non-committal mode of speech
which is not meant to say more than this.   Of happiness I could also say that it is the consummation or
crown or flower of welfare.   But these are metaphori-
cal terms and do not illuminate the logical relationship between the two concepts.

2

By an end of action we shall understand anything, *for
the sake of which* an action is undertaken.   If something, which we want to do, is not wanted for the sake
of anything else, the act or activity can be called an
end in itself.

Ends can be intermediate or ultimate.   Sometimes a
man wants to attain an end for the sake of some further
end.   Then the first end is 'intermediate'.   An end,

which is not pursued for the sake of any further end,
is 'ultimate'. We shall call a human act 'end-
directed', if it is undertaken either as an end in
itself or for the sake of some end.

What is an ultimate end of action is settled by the
last answer, which the agent himself can give to the
question, *why* he does or intends to do this or that.
It is then understood that the question 'Why?' asks
for a reason and not for a causal explanation of his
behaviour. (Cf. Ch. IV, sect. 8.)

In the terms which have here been introduced, we
could redefine Psychological Hedonism as the doctrine
that every end-directed human act is undertaken, ultimately, for the sake either of attaining some pleasure
or avoiding something unpleasant. The doctrine again
that every end-directed human act is undertaken, ultimately, for the sake of the acting agent's happiness
we shall call Psychological Eudaimonism. A doctrine
to the effect that every end-directed act is ultimately
undertaken for the sake of the acting agent's welfare
(good) has, to the best of my knowledge, never been
defended. We need not here invent a name for it.

Aristotle sometimes talks (1) as though he had sub-
scribed to the doctrine of psychological eudaimonism.
If this was his view, he was certainly mistaken and,
moreover, contradicting himself. It would be sheer
nonsense to maintain that every chain of (non-causal)
questions 'Why did you do this?' and answers to them
must terminate in a reference to happiness. The view
that man, in everything he does, is aiming at happiness (and the avoidance of misery) is even more absurd
than the doctrine that he, in everything he does, is
aiming at pleasure (and the avoidance of pain).

I said that, if Aristotle maintained psychological
eudaimonism, he was contradicting himself. (And for
this reason I doubt that Aristotle wanted to maintain
it, though some of his formulations would indicate
that he did.) For Aristotle also admits that there
are ends, other than happiness, which we pursue for
their own sake. He mentions pleasure and honour
among them. (2) Even 'if nothing resulted from them,
we should still choose each of them', he says. (3)
On the other hand, those other final ends are sometimes
desired, *not* for their own sake, but for the sake of
something else. Whereas happiness, Aristotle thinks,
is *never* desired for the sake of anything else. (4)
Pleasure, e.g. pleasant amusement, can be desired for
relaxation, and relaxation for the sake of continued
activity. (5) *Then* pleasure is not a final end.

I would understand Aristotle's so-called eudaimonism in the following light: among possible ends of human action, 'eudaimonia' holds a unique position. This unique position is *not* that 'eudaimonia' is the final end of all action. It is that 'eudaimonia' is the only end that is never anything except final. It is of the nature of 'eudaimonia' that it cannot be desired for the sake of anything else. *This* is, so Aristotle seems to think, why 'eudaimonia' is the highest good for man. (6)

It is plausible to think that a man can pursue, i.e. do things for the sake of promoting or safeguarding, his own happiness only as an ultimate end of his action. A man can also do things for the sake of promoting or safeguarding the happiness of some other being. It may be thought that he can do this only as an intermediate end of his action. The idea has an apparent plausibility, but is nevertheless a mistake. The truth seems to be that a man can pursue the happiness of others either as intermediate *or* as ultimate end.

The delight of a king can be the happiness of his subjects. He gives all his energies and work to the promotion of this end. Maybe he sacrifices his so-called 'personal happiness' for the good of those over whom he is set to rule. Yet, if this is what he likes to do, it is also that in which his happiness consists. To say this is not to distort facts logically. But to say that the king sacrifices himself for the sake of becoming happy and not for the sake of making others happy, would be a distortion. It would be a distortion similar to that of which psychological hedonism is guilty, when it maintains that everything is done for the sake of pleasure, on the ground that all satisfaction of desire may be thought intrinsically pleasant.

Can a man's *welfare* be an end of his own action? The question is equivalent to asking, whether a man can ever be truly said to do things for the sake of promoting or protecting his own good. It is not quite clear which is the correct answer.

On the view which is here taken of the good of a being, to do something for the sake of promoting one's own good, means to do something *because* one considers doing it *good for* oneself. And to do something for the sake of protecting one's own good means to do something *because* one considers neglecting it bad for oneself.

For all I can see, men sometimes do things for the reasons just mentioned. This would show that a man's welfare *can be* an end of his own action.

Yet the good of a being as an end of action is a very
peculiar sort of 'end'. Normally, an end of action is
a state of affairs, something which 'is there', when the
end has been attained. But welfare is not a state of
affairs. (Cf. the discussion in section 1.) For
this reason I shall say that welfare, the good of a
being, can only in an *oblique* sense be called an end of
action.

Obviously, the reason why a man does something, which
he considers good for himself, is not always and necessarily *that* he considers doing it good for himself.
Similarly, the reason why a man does something, which
he considers bad for him to neglect, is not always and
necessarily *that* he considers neglecting it bad for himself. This shows that a man's own welfare is not
always an ultimate end of his action. It also shows
that a man's own welfare is not always an end of his
action at all. It does not show, however, that a man's
own welfare is sometimes an intermediate end of his
action. Whether it *can* be an intermediate end, I shall
not attempt to decide. If the answer is negative, it
would follow that, when a man's own welfare is an end
of his action, it is necessarily an ultimate end.

Sometimes a man does something because he considers
doing it good for another being, and neglects something
because he considers doing it bad for another being.
It is obvious that another man's good can be the *intermediate* end of a man's action. The reason why the
master takes heed to promote and protect the welfare
of his servants, can be that he expects them to serve
him more efficiently if they thrive and are happy.
Then his servants' welfare is an intermediate end of
the master's. It may be suggested that, when the end
of a man's action is another being's welfare, then it
is necessarily an intermediate end. This suggestion,
I think, is false. We shall return to the topic
later (Chapter IX), when discussing egoism and altruism.

Beings can be handled or treated as means to somebody's ends. This is the case, e.g. with domestic
animals and slaves. Philosophers have sometimes
entertained the idea that beings could also be treated
as 'ends' or 'ends in themselves'. It is not clear
what it means to say that a being, e.g. a man, is an
'end in itself'. But treating a man as an end in
itself *could mean*, I suggest, that we do certain things
because we consider them good for that man. In other
words: whenever a being's good is an ultimate end of
action, that being is treated as an end in itself. A
man can treat other men thus, but also himself. That

men *should be* thus treated is an interesting view of
the nature of moral duty.   We shall briefly talk of
this in Chapter X.

In the next five sections of the present chapter we
shall be dealing with various aspects of the concept
of happiness and in the last five sections with questions relating to the concept of welfare.

3

Happiness, we said, is a hedonic notion.   It is, of
course, not *the same* as pleasure.   Nor can it be
defined, as has been suggested, as 'pleasure and the
absence of pain'.

Moralists who have written about happiness have
sometimes associated the notion more intimately with
one, sometimes with another, of the three principal
'forms' of pleasure, which we have in this book distinguished.   One could, accordingly, speak of three
types of 'ideals of happiness' or of the happy life.

The first I shall call 'Epicurean ideals'.   According to them, 'true happiness' derives above all from
having things which please.   'Pleasure' need not here
be understood in the 'grosser' sense of sensuous
pleasure.   It includes the enjoyment of agreeable
recollections and thoughts, of good company, and of
beautiful things.   Moore's position in 'Principia
Ethica' can, I think, be called an Epicureanism in
this broad sense.

Can a man find happiness entirely in passive
pleasure? i.e. can following an Epicurean recipe of
living make a man completely happy?   I can see no
logical impossibility in the idea.   If a man's
supreme desire happened to be to secure for himself a
favourable balance of passive pleasure over passive
'unpleasure', i.e. of states he enjoys over states he
dislikes, and if he were successful in this pursuit of
his, then the Epicurean recipe of living would, by
definition, make him happy.   It may be argued - from
considerations pertaining to the contingencies of
life - that the chances are strongly against his suc-
ceeding.   It may also be argued - this time from
considerations pertaining to the psychology of human
nature - that very few men are such pleasure-lovers that
the supreme thing they want for themselves in life is
a maximum of passive pleasure.   But the facts - if
they be facts - that Epicurean ideals are risky and not
very commonly pursued throughout a whole life, must not

induce us to deny that a man - if there be such a man -
who successfully pursued such ideals was genuinely
happy and flourishing.   To deny this would be to mis-
understand the notions of happiness and the good of
man and would be symptomatic, I think, of some 'moral-
istic perversion'.

The second type of ideals of the happy life probably
comes nearer than the Epicurean ideals to something
which the classical writers of utilitarianism had in
mind.   It seems to me true to say that the utilitarians
thought of happiness, not so much in terms of passive
pleasure, as in terms of satisfaction of desire.
Happiness, on such a view, is essentially contentedness
- an equilibrium between needs and wants on the one
hand and satisfaction on the other.

Yet one of the great utilitarians - protesting
against unwanted consequences of a view which he was
himself, though not wholeheartedly, defending - made
the famous dictum, 'It is better to be a human being
dissatisfied than a pig satisfied'.   I am not a utilitarian myself.   But I would like to protest, in a
sense, against Mill's remark.   The ultimate reason why
it is not good for man to live like a pig, is that the
life of a pig *does not satisfy* man.   The dissatisfied
Socrates, to whom Mill refers, we may regard as a symbol of man in search of a better and therewith more
satisfying form of life.   If his cravings were all
doomed to be nothing but 'vanity and the vexation of
spirit', then to idealize the dissatisfied Socrates
would be to cherish a perverted view of the good life.

If one adopts the view that happiness is essentially
an equilibrium between desire and satisfaction, one may
reach the further conclusion that the safest road to
happiness is to have as few and modest wants as possible,
thus minimizing the chances of frustration and maximizing those of satisfaction.   This recipe of happiness I
shall call 'the ascetic ideal' of life. (7)   When
carried to the extreme, this ideal envisages complete
happiness in the total abnegation of all desire what-
soever.

Ascetism, in this sense, can be termed a *crippled*
view of happiness.   In order to see in which respect
it is crippled, it is helpful to consider the contrary
of happiness, i.e. unhappiness or misery.   It would
seem that there is a more direct connexion between unhappiness and dissatisfaction of desire than there is
between happiness and satisfaction.   Frustration of
desire is a main source of unhappiness.   Never or
seldom to get that for which one is craving, never or

seldom to have a chance of doing that which one likes
to do, *this* is above all what makes a man miserable.

To call extreme asceticism a crippled ideal is to
accuse it of a logical mistake.   This is the mistake
of regarding happiness as the *contradictory*, and not
as the *contrary*, of unhappiness.   By escaping frustration a man escapes unhappiness - provided, of
course, that it does not befall him in the form of
such affliction, which accident or illness or the acts
of evil neighbours may cause him.   The man of *no*
wants, if there existed such a creature, would not be
unhappy.   But it does not follow that he would be
happy.

The third type of ideals of the happy life which I
wanted to mention here, seeks happiness neither in
passive pleasure nor in the satisfaction of desire,
but in that which we have called active pleasure, i.e.
the pleasure of doing that on which we are keen, which
for its own sake we like *doing*.   In the activities
which we are keen on doing, we aim at technical goodness or perfection.   (See Ch. II, sect. 12.)   The
better we are in the art, the more do we enjoy prac-
tising it, the happier does it make us.   Therefore,
the more talented we are by nature for an art, the
more can the development of our skill in it contribute
to our happiness.

It may be argued - chiefly against Epicureanism I
should think - that the pleasures of the active life
are those which are best suited to secure the attainment of lasting happiness.   It is more risky to be,
for one's well-being, dependent upon things we *have* or
get than upon things we *do* (or *are*).   That is: it is
more risky to seek happiness in passive than in active
pleasure.   There is probably a great deal of truth in
the argument.   But it would certainly be wrong to
think that the road to happiness through an active
life were completely risk-free.

4

The factors which determine whether a man will become
happy, we shall call 'conditions' of happiness.   Of
such conditions one may distinguish three main groups.
Happiness, we shall say, is conditioned partly by
'chance' or luck, partly by innate 'disposition', and
partly by 'action'.   'Action' here means action on
the part of the individual concerned himself.   That
which is *done to* a man may, for present purposes, be
counted as chance-factors conditioning his happiness.

Illness can befall a man or he can become bodily or mentally injured without any fault of his own.   If such misfortune assumes a certain permanence, it may affect a man's happiness adversely.   It may do so either as a cause of pain or as a cause of frustration of desire or because it prevents the victim from engaging in activity which, for its own sake, he enjoys.   However, luck may also favour a man's good.   The benefit a person draws from good friends or good teachers or financial benefactors has, partly if not wholly, the character of luck.   It is something which life has in store for some men but not for others to make them happier, independently of their own doings and precautions.

It is an aspect of that which we called the ascetic ideal of life, that man is well advised to *make* himself as independent as possible of chance and luck as conditions of his happiness.   This he can try to do in various ways: by hardening himself to sustain pain, by withdrawing from political and social engagements, or by not aspiring too high even in those activities, which he enjoys for their own sake.   The belief that a man could make himself altogether independent of external affectations of his good, is a conceit peculiar to certain 'ascetic' and 'stoic' attitudes to life. It overrates man's possibilities of conditioning his happiness and peace of mind by assuming a certain attitude to contingencies.

The innate dispositions of happiness have to do both with bodily health and with mental equipment and temper.   A man of weak health is more exposed to certain risks of becoming unhappy than a man of good health.   A man of many talents has more resources of happiness than a man of poor gifts.   A man of good temper and cheerful outlook will not let adversities frustrate his efforts as easily as the impatient and gloomy man.   To the extent that such temperamental dispositions can be developed or suppressed in a man, they fall under those conditions of happiness which a man controls through his action.

Human action, which is relevant to the happiness of the agent himself, is of two types.   Action of the first type are things which the agent does, measures which he takes for the sake of promoting or protecting his happiness.   Such action is 'causally' relevant to his happiness.   Action of the second type are things which the agent does or practises for their own sake, as ends in themselves, i.e. simply because he wants to do or likes to do them and for no other reason.

Action in which a man delights one could call 'constitutive' of his happiness, 'parts' of his happiness.

Now it may happen that action, which is thus constitutive of a man's happiness, *also* affects his happiness causally.   It may affect his happiness promotingly, but also affect it adversely.   For example: a man is immensely fond of playing various games.   He plays and enjoys playing them all day long.   In so doing he neglects his education and his social duties and maybe his health too.   Thus the very same thing, which is constitutive of his happiness, may, by virtue of its consequences, accumulate clouds of unhappiness over the agent's head, while he is rejoicing in this thing.   This possibility is responsible for the major complications, which are connected with a man's own action as a conditioning factor of his happiness and welfare generally.

5

When is a man happy?   It is obvious that a man can be truly praised happy, even though many painful and unpleasant things have happened to him in the course of his life.   But not if he never had any pleasures. What must the preponderance of the pleasant over the unpleasant be, if he is still to be called happy?

Here it is helpful to consider the states which we call gladness and sadness.   They occupy a kind of intermediate position between happiness and unhappiness on the one hand, and pleasure and its contrary on the other hand.   It may be suggested that pleasant and unpleasant experiences and activities are constitutive of gladness and sadness in a manner similar to that in which states of joy and depression are constitutive of happiness and unhappiness.   A man can be glad although he has toothache, and he can be a happy man even though he chances to be very sad for a time.   But he could not be glad if he had no pleasures to compensate such pains as he may have at the time of his gladness;   and he cannot be happy if he is not *on the whole* more glad than sad.   But we cannot tell exactly what must be the balance.

Pleasure, joy, and happiness are things of increasing degrees of permanence and resistance to changes. Something can please a man without cheering him up, and cheer him up without making him happy.   Something can be a terrible blow to a man and make him sad, but whether it makes him unhappy is another matter.

Consider, for example, a man whom we praise happy and
who is hit by a sudden blow of bad luck, say, the loss
of a child in an accident.   He will experience painful
agonies and extreme sadness.   'News of the disaster
made him dreadfully unhappy', we might say, thinking of
these emotional effects on him.   If, however, we were
to say that the news made him *an unhappy man,* we should
be thinking not only, or maybe even not at all, on those
emotional effects, but on effects of a less immediate
showing and of a longer lasting.   If we can say of him
some such things as, 'For years after he was as para-
lysed; none of the things, which used to delight him,
gave him pleasure any longer', or 'Life seemed to have
lost meaning for him, - for a time he even contemplated
suicide', then the accident made him *unhappy* as distinct
from merely *sad.*   But whether things, bearing on the
distinction, can be truly said of the man, is not to be
seen in an inkling.

Analogous things can be said about changes in the
reverse direction.   A piece of news, say of an unexpected inheritance, can make a man jump with joy.   But
whether it makes him *happy* as distinct from merely *glad*
can only be seen from effects of a longer lasting and
less obvious showing on his subsequent life.

Should we say 'the *whole* of his subsequent life'?
I think not.   Happiness is neither a momentary state
nor is it a sum total to be found out when we close our
life's account.   A man can *become* happy, *be* happy, and
change from happy to unhappy.   Thus, in the course of
his life, a man can be both happy and unhappy.   And
he can be happy and unhappy more than once.   (See
section 1.)

We could make a distinction between a happy *man* and
a happy *life* and regard the second as a thing of wider
scope.   This would make it possible to say of somebody that he had a happy life although, for some time,
he was a most unhappy man.

6

A judgment to the effect that some being is happy or is
not happy or is unhappy we shall can an 'eudaimonic'
judgment.

I think it is illuminating to compare the logic of
the eudaimonic judgment to the logic of the statement
'This is pleasant'.   Of the sentence 'This is pleasant'
we said that it conceals a logical form.   (See Ch. IV,
sect. 6.)   It suggests that pleasantness is a property

which we attribute to some object or state, whereas in
fact to judge something pleasant is to verbalize a relationship in which the judging subject stands to this
thing.   To judge something hedonically good is to
manifest an *attitude*, one could also say, to certain
things (activities, sensations, the causes of sensations).   The logically most adequate form of the
verbalization is therefore, it seems, the relational
form 'I like this' or some similar relational form.

In an analogous sense the sentence 'He is happy' may
be said, I think, to conceal a logical form.   It
suggests a view of happiness as a property which the
happy individual exhibits - which shines forth from him.
Whereas, in fact, to be happy is to be in a certain
relationship.   A relationship to what? it may be asked.
A relationship to one's circumstances of life, I would
answer.   To say 'He is happy' is similar to saying 'He
likes it', the 'it' not meaning this or that particular
thing or activity but, so to speak, 'the whole thing'.
One could also say, 'He likes his life as it is.'

On this view, if a man says of himself 'I am happy',
he manifests in words an attitude which he takes, or a
relationship in which he stands, to his circumstances
of life.   Happiness *is* not in the circumstances - as
it were awaiting the judgment - but springs into being
with the relationship.   (Just as hedonic goodness does
not reside in the taste of an apple, but in somebody's
liking the taste of an apple.)   To judge oneself happy
is to pass judgment on or value one's circumstances of
life.

To say 'He is happy' can mean two different things.
It can mean that the man, of whom we are talking, is
in the relationship to his circumstances which, if *he*
were to verbalize his attitude, he could express in
the words 'I am happy'.   Then 'He is happy' is not a
value-judgment.   It is a true or false statement to
the effect that a certain subject values certain
things, i.e. his circumstances of life, in a certain
way.   We could also call it a statement to the effect
that a certain valuation *exists* (occurs, takes place).

Quite often, however, 'He is happy' is not a judgment
about that which *he is* at all, but about that which *we
should be,* if we happened to be in his circumstances.
'He is happy' then means roughly, 'He *must be* happy,
viz. considering the circumstances he is in.'   Such
judgments are often an expression of envy.   To say with
conviction, 'Happy is he, who ...' is usually to pronounce on that which we think would make ourselves
happy.

We shall henceforth disregard the case, when the
third person judgment 'He is happy' is only a disguise
for our own valuations and thus really is a first
person judgment.

7

On the view which I am defending here, judgments of
happiness are thus very much like hedonic judgments.
The third person judgments are true or false.   In them
is judged that so-and-so is or is not pleased with his
circumstances of life.   They are judgments *about*
valuations - and therefore are no value-judgments.
The first person judgments are not true or false.   They
express a subject's valuations of his own circumstances.
They are genuine value-judgments, and yet in an important sense of 'judgment' they are no judgments.
  Ultimately, a man is himself judge of his own happiness.   By this I mean that any third person judgment
which may be passed on his happiness, depends for its
truth-value on how *he himself* values his circumstances
of life.   This is so independently of whether he
verbalizes his attitude in a first person judgment or
not.
  In a sense, therefore, a man's own verdict 'I am
happy' or 'I am unhappy', should he happen to pass it,
will be final - whatever we may think we should say,
if we were in his circumstances.   We must never make
the presence or absence of circumstances, which would
determine our own first person judgments of happiness,
the *criteria* of truth of third person judgments.
  What may make it difficult to see clearly this
'subjectivity' of the notion which we are discussing,
is the fact that not every man is the best and most
competent judge of his *prospects* of happiness.   A man
may strongly want to do something, think his life
worthless if he is not allowed this thing.   But
another, more experienced man, may warn him that, if he
follows his immediate impulses, he will in the end
become a most miserable wretch.   The more experienced
man may be right.   But the criterion, which proves
him right, is *not* the mere fact that certain things -
illness, destitution, and what not - befall this other
man as a predicted consequence of his folly and wicked-
ness.   The criterion is that these consequences make
that other man unhappy.   If our fool accepts the consequences with a cheerful heart, the wise man cannot
insist that he must be right.   He cannot do so on the

ground, say, that those same consequences would have made him, or most people, miserable.   Nor can he pretend that the lightsome fellow is 'really' unhappy, though unaware of his own misery.

But cannot a man be mistaken in thinking that he *is* happy?   In a sense he can *not*, but in another he *can*. 'He says he is happy, but in fact he is not' can express a true proposition.   But does not the truth of this proposition entail that the person who professes to be happy is lying?   And is this not uninteresting? The answer is that, beside uninteresting lies, there exist profoundly interesting lies in the matters, which we are now discussing.   First person judgments of happiness can be insincere, and insincerity may be regarded as a species of lying.

The same, incidentally, holds good for first person hedonic judgments too.   A youngster may profess to like the taste of tobacco, which in fact he detests, just for the sake of showing off.   He may even make himself believe this, in some involved and twisted sense of 'believe'.   A polite man may say he likes the taste of a wine merely to please his host.   The insincerity of such first person judgments may be relatively easy to unmask.

In the case of first person judgments of happiness and misery, the problem of sincerity is most difficult - both psychologically and conceptually.   I shall not here try to penetrate its logical aspects, which I find very bewildering.   (I am not aware of any satisfactory discussion of the topic in the literature.)   I shall make a shortcut through the difficulties and only say this much in conclusion:

However thoroughly a man may cheat himself with regard to his own happiness, the criterion of cheat or insincerity must be that *he* admits the fraud.   A judgment is insincere when the subject 'in his innermost self' admits that it is not as he says it is. If his lips say 'I am happy' and he is not, then in his heart he must already be saying to himself 'I am not happy'.   He, as it were, does not hear the voice of his heart.   These are similes, and I am aware of the temptation to misuse them.   (They are the same sort of similes that are used and misused in psychoanalysis - the similes of the subconscious, the superego, etc.)   What I mean by them could perhaps be said most plainly as follows: the fact that first person judgments of happiness can be insincere must not be allowed to conflict logically with the fact that, whether a person is happy or not depends upon *his own*

attitude to his circumstances of life.   The supreme
judge of the case *must be* the subject himself.   To
think that it could be otherwise is false objectivism.

8

Judgments of the beneficial and the harmful, i.e. of
that which is good or bad for a man, involve two components.   We have called them the 'causal' and the
'axiological' component.   (See Ch. III, sect. 5.)
We must now say some words about each of them.

  When something happens, i.e. the world changes in a
certain respect, there will usually also be a number of
subsequent changes, which are bound (by so-called
'natural necessity') to come about, once the first
change took place.   These subsequent changes we here
call the 'consequences' of the first change.   If the
first change is of that peculiar kind which we call a
human act, then the subsequent changes are 'consequences
of action'.   The change or changes upon which a certain
further change is consequen (i.e. the consequence of
which this further change is) we shall call the
'cause(s)' of this further change.

  Most things which happen, perhaps all, would not
have happened, *unless* certain antecedent changes had
taken place in the world.   These antecedent changes
we shall call the 'causal prerequisites' or 'requirements' of the subsequent change.   They are sometimes
also called 'necessary causes'.   The necessary causes
may be, but need not be, 'causes' in the sense defined
above.

  These explanations are very summary.   Not least of
all considering the importance to ethics of the notion
of consequences of action, it is an urgent *desideratum*
that the logic of causal relationships be better
elaborated than it is.   We shall not, however, attempt
this here.   Only a few observations will be added to
the above.

  The notions both of consequences and of prerequisites
and of causes of a change are relative to the further
notion of a *state of the world*.   Thus, e.g., a change
which is required in order to effect a certain change
in the world as it is to-day, may not be required in
order to effect this same change in the world as it is
tomorrow.

  It is sometimes said that every event (change)
'strictly speaking' has an infinite number of consequences throughout the whole of subsequent time, and

that for this reason we can never know for certain
which all the consequences of a given event are.
These statements, if true at all, hold good for some
different notion of consequence, but not for the
notion with which we are here dealing.   Exactly what
could be meant by them is not clear.   Yet we need not
dismiss them as nonsense.   When, for example, something which happens to-day is said to be a consequence
of something which took place hundreds of years ago,
what is meant is perhaps that, if we traced the
'causal history' of this event of to-day we should
find among its 'causal ancestry' that event of hundreds
of years ago.   Here the notions of causal ancestry
and causal history could be defined in terms of *our*
notions of cause, consequence, and prerequisite and
yet it need not follow that, if an event belongs to
the causal ancestry of another event, the first must be
a cause or prerequisite of the second or the second a
consequence of the first.   For example: let event *b*
be a consequence (in our sense) of event *a* and a causal
prerequisite (in our sense) of event *c*.   It would then
be reasonable to say that event *a* is a 'causal ancestor'
of event *c*, or that tracing the 'causal history' of *c*
takes us to *a*.   In some loose sense of the words, *a*
may be said to be a 'cause' of *c* and *c* a 'consequence'
of *a*.   But in the more precise sense, in which we are
here employing the terms, *a* is not (necessarily) a
cause of *c*, nor *c* (necessarily) a consequence of *a*.

The causes and consequences of things which happen,
are often insufficiently known and therefore largely a
matter of belief and conjecture.   Sometimes, however,
they *are* known to us.   The statement, should it be
made, that they *cannot* ('in principle') be known
either is false or applies to some different notions
of cause and consequence from ours.

By knowledge of the causes and consequences of
things which happen, I here mean knowledge relating to
particulars.   An example would be knowledge that the
death of N.N. was due to a dose of arsenic, which had
been mixed into his food.   Such knowledge of particulars is usually grounded on knowledge of general propositions - as for example that a dose of arsenic of
a certain strength will (unless certain counteracting
causes intervene) 'inevitably' kill a man.   Whether
all such knowledge of particulars is grounded on
general knowledge, we shall not discuss.

When in the sequel we speak of *knowledge* of the
causes and consequences of things, or of known causes
and consequences, 'knowledge' is short for 'knowledge

or belief' and 'known' for 'known or believed'.   The
consequences which are known (i.e. known or believed)
at the time when the thing happens, we shall also call
foreseen consequences.

So much for the causal component involved in judgments of the beneficial and the harmful.   We now turn
to the axiological component.   A preliminary task
will here be to clarify the notions of a *wanted* and an
unwanted thing.

9

The notion of a wanted thing, which I shall now try to
explain, is not the same as that of an end of action.
I shall call it the notion of being *wanted in itself*.
How things which are wanted in themselves, are related
to things which are wanted as ends of action, will be
discussed presently.   Correlative with the notion of
being wanted in itself is the notion of being *unwanted*
in itself.   'Between' the two falls a notion, which
we shall call the notion of being *indifferent in itself*.

The notion of being wanted in itself is the nearest
equivalent in my treatment here to the notion of
intrinsic value in Moore and some other writers.
Moore, when discussing the notion of intrinsic worth,
often resorts to a logical fiction which, *mutatis*
mutandis, may be resorted to also for explaining the
meaning of a thing being wanted, unwanted, or indifferent 'in itself'.

This fiction is that of a preferential choice
between two alternatives.   A major difficulty is to
formulate the terms of the choice correctly for the
purpose of defining the axiological notions under discussion.   (Moore's explanation of intrinsic value in
terms of betterness of alternatives cannot be regarded
as *logically* satisfactory - apart from questions of
the meaningfulness of the very notion. (8))   Our proposal here of a solution to the problem is tentative
only.

Assume you were offered a thing *X* which you did not
already possess.   Would you then rather take it than
leave it, rather have it than (continue to) be without
it?   The offer must be considered apart from questions
of causal requirements and of consequences.   That is:
considerations of things which you will have to do in
order to get *X*, and of things which will happen to you
as a consequence of your having got the thing *X* must
not influence your choice.   If then you would rather

take *X* than leave it, *X* is *wanted in itself*.   If you have the opposite preference, *X* is *unwanted in itself*. If you have no preference, X is *indifferent in itself*.

As readily noted, the ideas of the in itself wanted and unwanted, which we have thus tried to explain in terms of a fictitious preferential choice, are necessarily relative to a *subject*.   Nothing is wanted or unwanted 'in itself', if the words 'in itself' are supposed to mean 'apart from any rating or valuing subject'.   The words 'in itself' mean 'causal prerequisites and consequences apart'.   A thing, which for one subject is a wanted thing, may be regarded as unwanted by another subject.   A thing, furthermore, which is wanted *now,* may be unwanted at another time - the subject being the same.   The notion of being wanted or unwanted in itself is thus relative, not only to a subject, but also to a particular time in the life of this subject.

Moore did not think that intrinsic value was relative to subject and time.   In this respect his 'objectivist' notion of the intrinsically good and bad differs from our 'subjectivist' notion of the in itself wanted and unwanted.

It is important to note that from our definition of the in itself wanted, unwanted, and indifferent it does not follow that, if *X* is wanted in itself, then not-*X* (the absence of *X*) is unwanted in itself.   That not-*X* is wanted, unwanted, and indifferent in itself corresponds on our definitions, to the following set of preferences:

Consider a thing *X*, which you have.   Would you rather get rid of it than retain it, rather be without it than (continue to) possess it?   The proposal must be considered apart from things which you will have to do in order to get rid of *X* and from things which will happen to you as a consequence of your having got rid of *X*.   Then not-*X* is wanted in itself, if you prefer to get rid of *X*, unwanted in itself, if you prefer to retain *X*, and indifferent in itself, if you have no preference.

10

Anything which is an - intermediate or ultimate - end of action, can be called a *good* (for the subject in pursuit of the end).   (Cf. above Ch. I, sect. 5 and Ch. III, sect. 1.)   Anything which is an end of action, can also be said to be a *wanted thing*.

Also every thing, which is wanted in itself, can be called a good (for the subject to whom it is wanted). And every thing, which is unwanted in itself, can be called a bad (for the subject who shuns it).

Ends of action and things wanted in themselves thus both fall under the category 'goods'. Ends of action also fall under the category 'things wanted'.

The question may be raised, how ends of action and things wanted in themselves are mutually related. The question is complicated and I shall not discuss it in detail. It is reasonable to think that only things, which are attainable through action, *can be* ends of action. 'Craving for the moon' is not aiming at an end. But things other than those which are attainable through action, can be wanted in themselves - sunshine on a chilly day, for example. The only simple relationship between ends of action and things wanted in themselves, which I can suggest, is that ultimate ends of action are also things wanted in themselves.

Intermediate ends of action are either things wanted in themselves or things indifferent in themselves or, not infrequently, things unwanted in themselves. To get the in itself unwanted can never be an ultimate end of action, since the assumption that it is involves a contradiction. But to escape the in itself unwanted sometimes is an ultimate end of action. The unwanted is that which we shun, except when occasionally we pursue it as intermediate end for the sake of something else or suffer it as a necessary prerequisite of something coveted.

When a man gets something which is, to him, wanted in itself, without having pursued it as an end, we shall say that this wanted thing *befalls* him. Similarly, when a man gets something which is, to him, unwanted in itself and which he has not pursued as an intermediate end, we shall say that this thing befalls him.

The question may be raised whether a thing which befalls or happens to a man can appropriately be said to be 'wanted'. 'Wanted' in English has many meanings and must therefore be used with caution. Sometimes it means 'desired', sometimes 'needed', sometimes 'wished for'. When the wanted thing is an end of action, the nearest equivalent to 'wanted' is 'desired'. Perhaps things which happen to a man and which satisfy our explanation of the in itself wanted, should better be called 'welcome'. They are things we 'gladly accept' or are 'happy to get'. Often we just call them 'good'. When I here call them 'wanted', it is

by contrast to 'unwanted', which word is certainly
correctly used for shunned things that befall or
happen to a man.

11

Consider something, which an agent pursues as an ultimate end.   Assume that he gets it.   Attaining the
end is usually connected with a number of things as
its causal prerequisites and a number of other things
as its consequences.   Of the things which are thus
causally connected with his end, some are perhaps
known and others not known to the agent.   Some, moreover, may be known to him already at the time when he
pursues the end, others become known to him after he
has attained it.   That is: their causal relationship
to the end is (becomes) known to him.
     The thing which the agent pursues as an ultimate
end, is to him a good and something he wants in itself.
Of those things again which are causally connected -
either as prerequisites or as consequences - with his
attainment of the end, some are wanted in themselves
(by him), others are unwanted in themselves (by him),
others indifferent in themselves (to him).   The sum
total of those things, which are unwanted in themselves, we shall call the *price*, which the agent has
to pay for the attainment of his ultimate end.
     This notion of 'price', be it observed, includes
consequences as well as causal prerequisites.   On
this definition of the notion, not only those things
which the agent has to endure, in order to get his
wanted thing, but also those which he has to suffer as
a consequence of having got it, count as part of that
which he has to *pay* for the good.   One can define the
notion of a price in different ways - for other purposes.   This is how we define the notion for present
purposes.
     For anything which is wanted in itself, the question
may be raised: is this good worth its price?   The
question can be raised *prospectively*, with a view to
things which have to be gone through as a consequence
of starting to pursue this good as an end, or it can
be raised *retrospectively*, with a view to things
already suffered.
     To answer the question whether a certain good is
(was) worth its price, is to pass a value-judgment.
It is to say of something, a good, that it is better or
worse, more or less worth, than something else, its

price. How shall this value-judgment be properly
articulated?

I think we must resort here, for a second time, to
the logical fiction of a preferential choice. We
said (in section 9) that things which we do not have,
are wanted in themselves when, ignoring their causes
and consequences, we would rather get them than continue to be without them, and unwanted in themselves
when we would rather continue to be without them than
get them. This question of taking or leaving, having
or being without, we can also raise for things, *considering their causes and consequences*. A correct
way of presenting the choice which we should then be
facing, is, I think, as follows:

Assume that X is something, which is not already in
our world (life), i.e. is something which we do not
already possess or which has not already happened or
which we have not already done. Would we then want X
to become introduced into our world (life), considering
also the causal prerequisites of getting (doing) X and
the consequences of having got (done) X? Or would we
prefer to continue to be without X? In making up our
mind we should also have to consider the causal prerequisites and the consequences of *not* having this
change in our world (life). It may, for example, be
necessary for us to take some in itself unwanted
action to prevent X from coming into existence, if we
wish to avoid having X, and it may be necessary for us
to foresake some other in itself wanted thing Y as a
consequence of *not* having had X.

We introduce the symbol '$X+C$' for the complex whole,
consisting of X and those other things, which are
causally connected with it either as prerequisites or
as consequences of its coming into being, i.e. of the
change from not-X to X. The symbol 'not-$X+C'$'' shall
stand for the complex whole, consisting of the absence
of X and the presence of those things which are
causally connected, either as prerequisites or as consequences, with the continued absence of X.

The question which is presented for consideration in
the fictitious preferential choice we are discussing, is
whether we should prefer $X+C$ to not-$X+C'$ or whether we
should have the reverse preference or whether we should
be indifferent (have no preference).

Let the answer to the proposal be that we should
rather have than continue to be without X, i.e. prefer
$X+C$ to not-$X+C'$. Then we shall say that $X+C$ or the
complex whole, consisting of X and the causal prerequisites and consequences of the coming into being of X,

is a *positive constituent* of our good (welfare). Of
the thing X itself we say that it is *good for us* or
beneficial. This we say of X independently of whether
X is wanted or unwanted or indifferent in itself.

Let the answer to the proposal be that we should
rather continue to forego than have X, i.e. prefer
not-X+C' to X+C. Then we shall say that X+C is a
negative constituent of our good. Of the thing X
itself we say that it is *bad for us* or *harmful*. This
we say independently of whether X is wanted or unwanted
or indifferent in itself.

The answer can, of course, also be that we should be
indifferent to the alternatives. Then X+C is neither
a positive nor a negative constituent of our good, and
X is neither beneficial nor harmful.

Let us call X the *nucleus* of that complex whole,
which consists of X and the causal prerequisites and
consequences of the coming into existence of X. We
could then say that the things which are beneficial or
harmful, good or bad for a man, are nuclei of those
complex causal wholes, which are positive or negative
constituents of his good (welfare).

We can now state the conditions for answering the
question whether a certain good is worth its 'price'.
When a certain causal whole is a positive constituent
of our good *and* its nucleus is a thing, which is wanted
in itself, then we say that this thing or good *is* worth
its price. When, however, the whole is a negative
constituent of our good, *although* its nucleus is a
thing, which is wanted in itself, then we say that this
thing or good is *not* worth its price.

From our definitions of the beneficial and the harmful it does *not* follow that, if not-X is harmful, then
X is beneficial, and *vice versa*. If, however, not-X
is harmful, then X will be called *needed*. The needed
is that, the lack or loss of which is a bad thing, an
evil. The needed and the harmful are opposed as con-
tradictories, *in the sense* that the contradictory of
the needed is harmful, and *vice versa*. The beneficial and the harmful are opposed as contraries.

To provide a being with that which is beneficial for
it is to *promote* its welfare. To provide it with that
which it needs and to take care that it does not lose
the needed is to *protect* its welfare. Things (acts,
events) which are protective of a being's welfare are
good for the being in the sense of 'good for' which
can also be rendered by 'useful', but not in that sense
of 'good for' which we call 'beneficial'. (Cf. Ch.
III, sect. 1.)

12

The preferential choice, in the terms of which we have
defined the notions of the beneficial and the harmful,
we have called a 'logical fiction'.   That it is a
fiction implies two things.   First, it implies that
we are talking of how a man *would choose*, if he were
presented with the choice, and not of what he actually
chooses.   Secondly, it implies that we assume the
causal component involved in the value-judgment to be
completely known to the subject at the time of the
choice.   This second assumption entails that there are
no imperfections in the subject's knowledge which are
such that, if they were detected and corrected, the
subject would revise his preferences.

Thus, on our definitions, the answer to the question
whether a certain thing is good or bad for a man, is
independent of the following two factors: first, it is
independent of whether he (or anybody else) *judges* or
does not judge of the value of this thing for him.
Secondly, it is independent of what he (and everybody
else) happens to *know* or not to know about the causal
connexions of this thing.   Yet, in spite of this
independence of judgment and knowledge, the notions
of the beneficial and the harmful are in an important
sense *subjective*.   Their subjectivity consists in
their dependence upon the *preferences* (*wants*) of the
subject concerned.

Considering what has just been said, it is clear
that we must distinguish between that which *is* good or
bad for a man and that which *appears,* i.e. is judged
or considered or thought (by himself or by others), to
be good or bad for him.

Any judgment to the effect that something is good or
bad for a man is based on such knowledge of the relevant causal connexions which the judging subject happens
to possess.   Since this knowledge may be imperfect,
the judgment which he actually passes may be different
from the judgment which he would pass, if he had perfect knowledge of the causal connexions.   When there
is this discrepancy between the actual and the potential
judgment, we shall say that a man's *apparent* good is
being mistaken for his *real* good.

Of certain things it is easier to judge correctly
whether they are good or bad for us, than of certain
other things.   This means: the risks of mistaking our
apparent good for our real good are sometimes greater,
sometimes less.   It is, on the whole, easier to judge
correctly in matters relating to a person's health than

in matters relating to his future career.   For example:
the judgment that it will do a man good to take regular
exercise is, on the whole, safer than the judgment that
it will be better for him to go into business than
study medicine.   Sometimes the difficulties to judge
correctly are so great that it will be altogether idle
and useless to try to form a judgment.

Sometimes we know for certain that a choice, which
we are facing, is of great *importance* to us in the
sense that it will make considerable *difference* to our
future life, whether we choose the one or the other of
two alternatives.   An example could be a choice
between getting married or remaining single or between
accepting employment in a foreign country or continuing
life at home.   But certainty that the choice will make
a great difference is fully compatible with uncertainty
as to whether the difference will be for good or for
bad.   The feeling that our welfare *may* become radically
affected by the choice, can make the choice very agon-
izing for us.

Also of many things in our past, which we did not
deliberately choose, we may know for certain that they
have been of great importance to us in the sense that
our lives would have been very different, had these
things not existed.   This could be manifestly true,
for example, of the influence which some powerful personality has had on our education or on the formation
of our opinions.   We may wonder whether it was not
bad for us that we should have been so strongly under
this influence.   Yet, if we know only that our life
would have been very different but cannot at all
imagine *how* it would have been different, we may also
be quite incompetent to form a judgment of the beneficial and harmful nature of this factor in our past
history.

It is a deeply impressive fact about the condition
of man that it should be difficult, or even humanly
impossible, to judge confidently of many things which
are known to affect our lives importantly, whether
they are good or bad for us.   I think that becoming
overwhelmed by this fact is one of the things which can
incline a man towards taking a religious view of life.
'Only God knows what is good or bad for us.'   One
could say thus - and yet accept that a man's welfare
is a subjective notion in the sense that it is determined by what *he* wants and shuns.

13

Are judgments of the beneficial or harmful nature of
things objectively true or false? When we try to
answer this question, we must again observe the distinction between a first person judgment and a third
person judgment. (Cf. Ch. IV, sect. 5 and this
chapter, sections 6 and 7.)

When somebody judges of something that it is (was,
will be) good or bad for somebody else, the judgment is
a third person judgment. It depends for its truth-
value on two things. The one is whether certain causal
connexions are as the judging subject thinks that they
are. The other is whether certain valuations (preferences, wants) of another subject are as the judging
subject thinks that they are. Both to judge of causal
connexions and to judge of the valuations of other subjects is to judge of empirical matters of fact. The
judgment is 'objectively' true or false. It is,
properly speaking, not a value-judgment, since the
'axiological' component involved in it is not a valuation but a judgment *about* (the existence or occurrence
of) valuations.

The case of the first person judgment is more complicated. Its causal component is a judgment of matters
of fact. In this respect the first person judgment is
on a level with the third person judgment. Its axiological component, however, is a valuation and not a
judgment about valuations. With regard to this component the judgment cannot be true or false. There is
no 'room' for mistake concerning its truth-value. In
this respect the first person judgment of the beneficial
and the harmful is like the first person hedonic or
eudaimonic judgment.

Although the first person judgment cannot be false
in its axiological component, it can be *insincere*.
The problem of sincerity of judgments concerning that
which is good or bad for a man is most complicated.
It is intimately connected with the problems relating
to the notions of *regret* and of *weakness of will*. A
few words will be said about them later.

A subject can also make a statement about his own
valuations in the past or a conjecture about his valuations in the future. Such a statement or conjecture
is, logically, a third person judgment. It is true or
false both in its causal and in its axiological
component.

Whether a judgment is, *logically*, a first person
judgment, cannot be seen from the person and tense of

its grammatical form alone.   A man says 'This will do
me good'.   In saying this he could be anticipating
certain consequences and *expressing* his valuation of
them.   But he could also be anticipating certain consequences and *anticipating* his valuation of them.   In
the first case, the judgment he makes is of the kind
which I here call a first person judgment of the beneficial or harmful nature of things.   In the second
case, the judgment is (logically) a third person judgment.   The subject is speaking *about* himself, i.e.
about his future valuations.

Sometimes a judgment of the beneficial or the harmful is clearly anticipative both of consequences and of
valuations.   Sometimes it is clearly anticipative with
regard to consequences and expressive with regard to
valuations.   But very often, it seems, the status of
the judgment is not clear even to the judging subject
himself.   The judgment may contain *both* anticipations
and expressions of valuations.   Perhaps it is true to
say that men's judgments of what is good or bad for
themselves tend on the whole to be anticipative rather
than expressive with regard to valuations.

The distinction between the *apparent* and the *real*
good, it should be observed, can be upheld both for
third person and for first person judgments of the
beneficial and the harmful.   In this respect judgments
of the beneficial and the harmful differ from hedonic
and eudaimonic judgments.   (For the two last kinds of
judgment the distinction vanishes in the first person
case, i.e. in the genuine value-judgments.)   Because
of the presence of the causal component in the judgment,
a subject can always be mistaken concerning the beneficial or the harmful nature of a thing - even when
there is no 'room' for mistake with regard to
valuation.

14

A man's answer to the question whether a certain good is
worth its price or whether a thing is beneficial or
harmful, may undergo alterations in the course of time.
Such alterations in his judgments can be due either to
changes in his knowledge of the relevant causal connexions or to changes in his valuations.   For example:
a man attains an end, which he considers worth while to
have pursued, until years afterwards he comes to
realize that he had to pay for it with the ruin of his
health.   Then he revises his judgment and *regrets*.

There are two types of regret-situation relating to
choices of ends and goods in general.   Sometimes the
choice can, in principle if not in practice, be repeated.   To profess regret is then to say that one would
not choose the same thing again next time, when there
is an opportunity.   But sometimes the choice is not
repeatable.   The reason for this could be that the
consequences, of which one is aware and which are the
ground for one's regret, continue to operate throughout one's whole life.   There is no opportunity of
making good one's folly in the past by acting more
wisely in the future.   Then to express regret is to
pass judgment on one's *life*.   It is like saying: if
I were to live my life over again, I would, when
arrived at the fatal station, act differently.

The value-judgments of regret and no-regret, like
hedonic judgments and judgments of happiness, are
neither true nor false.   But they may be sincere or
insincere.   A person can say that he regrets, when in
fact he does not, and he can stubbornly refuse to admit
regret which he 'feels'.   How is such insincerity
unmasked?   For example in this way: if a man, after
having suffered the consequences, says he regrets his
action, but on a new occasion repeats his previous
choice, then we may doubt whether his remorse was not
pretence only.   He was perhaps annoyed at having had
to pay so much for the coveted thing and therefore
said it was not worth it, but at the bottom of his
heart he was pleased at having got it.   These are
familiar phenomena.

Yet to think that a repetition of the professed
folly were a sure sign of insincere regret, would be
to ignore the complications of the practical problems
relating to the good of man.   A good, if strongly
desired in itself and near at hand, may be a temptation
to which a man succumbs, when the evil consequences are
far ahead and the recollection of having suffered them
in the past is perhaps already fading.   There is no
logical absurdity in the idea that a man sincerely
regrets something as having been a mistake, a bad
choice with a view to his welfare, i.e. with a view to
what he 'really' wants for himself, and yet wilfully
commits the same mistake over again, whenever there is
an opportunity.

When a man succumbs to temptation and chooses a
lesser immediate good, i.e. thing wanted in itself,
rather than escapes a greater future bad, i.e. thing
unwanted in itself, then he is acting wilfully against
the interests of his own good.   It is in such situations

that those features of character which we call *virtues*,
are needed to safeguard a man's welfare.   We shall
talk about them later (in Chapter VII).

That a man can do evil to himself through ignorance
of the consequences of his acts or through negligence
is obvious.   That he can also harm himself through
akrasia or weakness of will has a certain appearance
of paradox.   He then, as it were, both wants and does
not want, welcomes and shuns, one and the same thing.
When viewed in the short perspective, 'prerequisites
and consequences apart', he wants it;   when viewed in
the prolonged perspective of the appropriate causal
setting, he shuns it.   One could say that, if he lets
himself be carried away by the short perspective, then
he was not capable of viewing *clearly* his situation in
the long perspective.   Or one could say that, if a
man has an *articulated grasp* of what he wants, he can
never harm himself through weakness of will.   But
saying this must not encourage an undue optimism about
man's possibilities of acting in accordance with cool
reasoning.

NOTES

1 See, e.g., 'Ethica Nicomachea' (EN), 1094a 18-21,
   1095a 14-20, and 1176b 30-1.
2 EN, 1097b 1-2.   See also 1172b 20-3.
3 EN, 1097b 2-3.
4 EN, 1097b 1 and again 1097b 5-6.
5 Cf. EN, 1176b 34-5.
6 There is no phrase in Aristotle's ethics which corresponds to our phrase 'the good of man'.   'Eudaimonia' (happiness, well-being) Aristotle also calls
   the best or the highest good.   The notion of a
   'summum bonum', however, is not identical with the
   notion of the good of man as we use it here.   But
   the two notions may be related.
7 Ascetism as an abnegation of worldly desire for the
   sake of the good of the soul must be distinguished
   from that which I here call ascetism as an ideal of
   life.   To the first, ascetism is no 'end' or
   'value' in itself, but an exercise and preparation
   for the good life.
8 See 'Ethics', Oxford University Press, 1966, pp.
   42-4 and, in particular, Moore's reply to his
   critics in 'The Philosophy of G.E. Moore', pp. 554-7.

4   Alienation and self-realization

Kai Nielsen

1.

Self-realizationist theories are among the classical
attempts to develop a comprehensive normative ethical
theory. Plato and Aristotle, in giving classical
statements of such theories, argue that a man's distinctive happiness, a man's distinctive flourishing,
will only be realized when he realizes himself, i.e.
when he achieves to the fullest possible degree his
distinctive function. And to achieve one's function
is to develop to the full those capacities which are
distinctive of the human animal. In doing this we
are being most truly ourselves and in doing this we
are doing what it is our own nature to do. Men who
cultivate to the fullest that which men and only men
have will be the happiest men and in so acting they
will realize themselves most fully; they will achieve
their maximum potential or their fullest distinctively
human growth. To so realize oneself is the final end
of all moral activity. It defines what is to constitute 'the good life' and what is to count as 'a
good man'.

A self-realizationist would argue that to find a
good x is (i) to discover the function of x and (ii)
to find which x's will fulfil this function effectively.
And to find the best x is to find the sort of x that
most effectively (efficiently) fulfils this function.
We will find the end or rationale of all human activity
when we clearly apprehend the function of man. The
man who realizes himself most fully is the man who
develops to the full his distinctive capacities as a
man. This is self-realization, this is human growth,
and this is the end of all moral endeavour.

More generally, and apart from Plato's and Aristotle's

117

particular formulations, the ultimate moral ideal should be to attain the fullest degree of self-realization. That is to say, the end of moral activity is to enable us to be most truly ourselves.   This, a self-realizationist is contending, should be the underlying rationale and justification of morality.   Moral rules, actions, practices, attitudes and institutions are judged good or bad just to the extent that they contribute to self-realization.   Rule A or action A is better than rule B or action B if A is more conducive to self-realization than B.   The aim of all moral action is to further self-realization to the highest degree.   We should always aim to realize our potentialities or capacities - that is, ourselves - as fully as possible.

This comforting formula, as Rashdall calls it, has some very serious ambiguities and difficulties.   Taken together they raise a serious challenge to self-realizationist theories of ethics.   In fact many philosophers think such accounts are thoroughly discredited - that self-realization is not, and cannot be, the end of moral endeavour or the ultimate standard of moral appraisal. However, in rejecting what has been called - not without point - 'the murky doctrine of self-realization', philosophers have neglected to attend to what may be important insights embedded in the theory.   I shall try to show why it will not succeed as an ultimate moral criterion but I do not want to throw the baby out with the bath-water.   I think there are insights in such accounts that need to be brought out and that there are problems raised by such a moral theory which need to be faced.

First, we need to ask whether on such an account we are to realize or seek to realize *all* our potentialities as a man or only some.   If, in realizing our great Gyntian selves, we are to seek to realize all our potentialities, we are in reality seeking something that cannot be achieved, for we have an indefinitely large number of them, and furthermore, we frequently have conflicting capacities.   The plain fact is that they cannot all be realized.   We must choose which capacities we ought to realize.   But to do this, it would seem that we would need some other criterion than self-realization, for, on the above account, to realize ourselves is simply to realize our capacities to the fullest extent.

It might be replied that where we cannot realize both of two conflicting capacities we should realize that capacity which would tend on the whole to enable us to realize the greater number of our capacities to the fullest extent. Suppose Jones has a considerable potential for, and indeed a liking of, boxing and rapid driving, but he also has a potential for, and extensive liking of, intellectual work. If he develops the latter and inhibits the former he, in turn, is much more likely to develop more potentialities that are distinctive of the human animal. More generally, and in accordance with the above, a self-realizationist might argue that our self-realization standard should be: each man should realize as many of his capacities as possible and, where his capacities conflict, he should choose those capacities which will contribute as fully as possible to the actualization of his other potentialities.

To argue in this way is, in effect, to argue that we should become 'good, all round people'. But it seems to me that Rashdall is quite correct in claiming that such an ideal is, in effect, a defence of mediocrity or dilettantism. I can hardly develop my talents, such as they are, as a philosopher, bookie, long-distance runner, preacher, boxer, neuro-surgeon and pianist all at the same time, or without prejudice of one to the other. The analytical powers I develop as a philosopher hardly further my emotional outpourings as a preacher. The time I need to spend at the piano to play it really well, will hardly allow me to become much of a long-distance runner and the punishment to my hands in boxing will hardly serve me well in performing delicate operations or in playing Prokofiev's Second Piano Concerto. I could seek to be an 'all around' fellow and develop all of these capacities a little, but then I will most surely end up doing none of them well, so that in anything I set my hand to I will be a mediocrity. Is such a dilettantish life the best possible life? Would I not do better for myself and for others by developing my philosophic talents to the fullest? That way I indeed do not achieve the harmonious fulfilment of as many of my capacities as possible, but do I not, by doing something else instead - in this case developing my philosophic talents - do something which is more worthwhile and which also serves my own interests more adequately?

If this last question is answered in the affirmative, then self-realization appears at least *not* to be our ultimate moral standard. If answered in the negative, the question immediately springs to mind: what reason is there for claiming that each individual ought always to develop as many of his capacities as possible? Why not argue, alternatively, that each individual should develop those capacities that he *wants* most to develop? Or why not, instead, argue that he should develop those that will make for everyone involved the greatest amount of good all around?   It seems to me that in opting for the fullest development of all one's capacities and potentialities, such a self-realizationist theory is offering us an ultimate moral standard that will not survive critical scrutiny.

2

Suppose instead we mean by 'realizing yourself' essentially what Aristotle meant, namely that to realize yourself is to develop those capacities which are distinctive of *homo sapiens*.   That is to say, we should develop those capacities which are distinctive of, that is peculiar to, our species alone.   This is the quintessence of self-realization and morality.   Our injunction should be 'Develop those potentialities which will most fully realize your distinctive human function'.

   The rub is that man - if he can correctly be said to have any function at all - can be said to have many distinctive functions;   that is to say, there are many things which are peculiar to man - that men and only men do.   Even *if* being able to reason or more plausibly to carry on rational discourse and act in accordance with what is deliberated upon is distinctive of the human animal, so is having guilt feelings, the capacity for anguish and alienation, the capacity to laugh, to commit atrocities, to drive automobiles, to slaughter one's fellow human beings and other creatures with complicated weapons, etc., etc.   There are a multitude of things which are distinctive of man.   Why should we pick out reason over such other general distinctive traits or at least putatively distinctive traits as having an opposable thumb and walking upright, having a long period of infant dependency, having permanent sexual drives, having a sense of right and wrong, suffering anguish, or having the ability to laugh? Reason is indeed thought by Plato and Aristotle, and by others as well, to have a special excellence but that is not based on the fact that it is distinctive of human beings, for there are other things which are ignored in a specification of the function of man, which are also distinctive of human beings.   This makes it evident that no adequate reason has been given for taking reason - the capacity to reason or the activity of reasoning - as the function of man, as that which makes a man a man.

In defending Aristotle, people may reply to the above argument by saying that to find the function of a thing we not only need to find what is distinctive of it but we also need to find its *essential* characteristics. When this is recognized, it will become evident that having the capacity to laugh is not essential to man while having the ability to reason is.

With respect to this argument, it should be noted that 'essential' in 'essential characteristic' itself functions evaluatively.   Thus, in order to specify the function of man or self-realization, one must invoke some unspecified but still more fundamental *normative* criterion to establish what counts as an '*essential* characteristic'.   There are many activities which are distinctively and peculiarly human but some are more important than others and thus are more essential. But what is our criterion for importance here?   Surely if A is taken to be more important than B, A is something we take to be more valuable, i.e. desirable, as we take the ability to carefully deliberate and reason to be more valuable than the capacity to laugh.   But then we still have not decided how we ascertain what is more or less valuable.   Certainly we do not do it by appealing to a criterion of self-realization, for we have to know already what counts as a more essential and hence more valuable characteristic in order to know what would count as attaining or approximating self-realization.

It might be replied that we can easily tell that the capacity to reason is more essential to the human animal than the capacity to laugh, for the human animal could survive without laughter or even the ability to laugh but not without the ability to reason. And to the response that this argument presupposes, as a still more fundamental value, the value of survival, it could in turn be answered that it does not presuppose it as a higher value but only as a necessary condition for self-realization.   That is to say, trivially speaking, unless man survives, he cannot achieve self-realization or anything else.   But this does not mean that the end of life is mere survival without equal attention being given to questions concerning the quality or character of that survival.   Moreover, just as there could be some fundamental genetic shift in man such that men no longer laughed, so too there could be a radical change so that men no longer reasoned in the complicated way prized by Aristotle.   Both changes are

compatible with the continued existence of man as a
species, though, given such changes, if we (the present
group of people who might read such an essay), unlike
the rest of mankind, continued as we are, we would no
doubt say that such men 'were scarcely human'.   But
in saying this, we reveal the *normative* way we are
using 'scarcely human'.

We have many characteristics which are distinctive
of (peculiar to) mankind, but not all of them are regarded as essential characteristics, yet the standard by
which we decide which characteristics are essential and
which are not remains unspecified and whatever the
standard is, it is plainly not derived from a conception
of self-realization, but is actually *presupposed* in the
specification of self-realization and in the specification of the function of man.

We might argue alternatively that by realizing his
highest and *best* capacities man does what is most distinctive of him.   And thus in recognizing what these
highest and best capacities are, we find out what the
function of man is, and so come to see what constitutes
self-realization.   But here we even more obviously presuppose, as a still more fundamental moral standard
than self-realization, some alien and unexplained
criterion.   For how do we ascertain what are our
highest and best capacities?   If we knew what they
were, we could know what self-realization is but then
we wouldn't need self-realization as an ultimate standard.   But that aside, just how do we ascertain what
our highest and best capacities are?   We are not told.
We only have an unexplained and unexplicated reference
to 'highest and best capacities'.

3

There are further difficulties in any self-realizationist account which appeals to a conception of the function
of man.   For the very notion of man's having a function
to have even a tolerably clear meaning, it must be the
case that man is conceived on close analogy with an
artifact, a functional part of the body such as the
liver or heart, or with someone such as a policeman or
barber who has a social role.   But man *qua* man has no
social role and he is too unlike an artifact or a
functioning part of a body for that analogy to be helpful.   We can say quite unequivocally what it would be
like for a corkscrew to be a good one by specifying the
function of a corkscrew and by saying what constitutes

an efficient performance of that function.   The concept
of the function of a corkscrew is not at all problematic.
Similar things hold for our bodily organs even though
they are not artifacts made for a purpose.   We can
find out what it is to have a good heart or good liver
by finding out what hearts and livers are for, that is
by finding out what role they play in the bodily economy.
Similarly, people have different social roles to play
in society and we can find out what a good policeman or
barber is by finding out what roles policemen or
barbers play in society.   When we understand what
policemen and barbers are for, and what it is to perform that function efficiently, we know what it is for
someone to be a good policeman or barber.

The function of a policeman or teacher is not quite
as definite as that of many artifacts, but we are still
not at a loss for words here, and the notions are by
no means utterly indeterminate, though they have their
controversial aspects.   But the fact still remains
that to the extent that we understand what teachers,
policemen or barbers are for and what it is to efficiently perform that function, we understand what it is
for someone to be a good teacher, policeman or barber.
But a man may be a good policeman or barber and still
be a bad man; he may be good in several social roles
and still be a bad man; conversely he may be a good
man and a bad teacher or barber.   The fact is that
men are not unequivocally *for* anything in the way
barbers and policemen are.   Being a human being is not
the assuming of a social role, though human beings are
socialized animals.

Only if we assume some extremely questionable theological framework in which we say that man was made to
worship God and fulfil his commands, can we give much
sense to the claim that 'human beings are for anything'.   But even here we are reluctant to assert
quite literally that human beings are for something.
And furthermore such a theological claim, particularly
if we try to construe it literally, is quite arbitrary.
The claim that human beings have a function is quite
baseless.   There is no unproblematic answer or even
sense to the putative question: 'What are human beings
for?'

If, to escape these difficulties, we speak instead
of a man as realizing himself or fulfilling his own
natural tendencies, powers and wants, we should recall
our earlier point that man has many different powers,
tendencies and wants, and that sometimes they conflict.
He cannot do them all, so again it is not clear what he
is to do to realize his own nature.

4

However, let us assume that somehow I have been mistaken
in what I have asserted above and that man does have a
function and that it is what Aristotle says it is.
That is to say, let us now assume that man's essential
and distinguishing mark is his capacity to reason - this
is what distinguishes him from other animals. Now,
assuming for the sake of the argument that reason is
such an essential characteristic, we still face difficulties. First, we face difficulties concerning
exactly what it is that we are claiming. Surely on
some readings of 'being able to reason', it is not something unique to men. The way a cat stalks a bird would
certainly seem to involve reasoning, i.e. thinking, on
the cat's part. We need a characterization here of
the ways human beings alone or distinctively act in
accordance with or for the sake of reasons. We need
a specification of the distinctive ways 'the rational
element' is embedded in human nature.

In talking about the function of man, we are talking
about what constitutes being a man. As playing the
flute is that which constitutes being a flute player,
so, Aristotle claims, acting on reasons constitutes
being a man. This is presumably the demythologization
of Aristotle's remark that 'the function of man is an
activity of the soul in conjunction with the rational
element'.

What exactly is it on Aristotle's account to act on
reasons? One commentator understands it as 'organizing or co-ordinating our desires and emotions, and
controlling or checking the immediate impulses to
action so as to enable ourselves to secure what we
really want'. (1) Human beings presumably can act
intentionally in this way and only human beings can
so act. (We are assuming now that this is a distinctive and essential human characteristic.) Being able
so to act is what constitutes human rationality. This
is what makes us distinctively human.

If this is what acting on reasons most essentially
comes to, then it may well be the case that two men,
acting in quite different and conflicting ways, could
on such an account be acting equally rationally and
each could equally well be doing what on this account
is right. For if they had different and conflicting
wants - wants which conflicted, even where they took
the most efficient means to satisfy their desires - it
would still remain the case (given the above reading of
Aristotle) that they were both being equally rational

in so acting and were both equally justified in their
moral judgments.   But if this is so, then ethical
relativism, at an extremely important point, would
not have been overcome.   But it is one of the accounts
which claims to overcome relativism and to show how
it is that moral beliefs can have an objective basis.
This is one of its main attractions; without this
promise such an obscure and puzzling account replete
with its metaphors would have little attraction.
Moreover, what is reasonable to do and what constitutes
self-realization would be crucially dependent on such
a reading on what *we just happen to want*.   We would
have no fundamental moral criteria by means of which
we could make a critique of wants.   Rather what was
good and bad on such a theory would be very dependent
on what we just happened to want.   The kind of sub-
jectivism and relativism that Aristotle's theory was
intended to combat would hardly be overcome.

It might be replied, deliberately shifting the
grounds of the argument somewhat, that I am neglecting
the fact that Aristotle lays great stress on the worth
of contemplation.   To understand the function of man
as that of acting on reasons, we need to understand
that contemplation is really the highest form of
rationality.   In it, according to Aristotle, man's
rational nature has its full flourishing.   It is in
this that man realizes himself and achieves his full
humanity.

However, it should immediately be recognized that
while the capacity to act on reasons is common to all
human beings who are not mentally defective in some
way, contemplation is not such a common trait.   There
are many people who are highly intelligent and indeed
are reasonable human beings as well who are not con-
templative and do not particularly prize contemplation.
Moreover, there are many people who by ordinary criteria
at least are fully moral beings and thoroughly reasonable beings, who are not at all given to contemplation.
It would appear that in placing such a stress on contemplation, Aristotle is doing little more here than
expressing a rationalist prejudice.   Contemplation is
no doubt unique to man but so is making change.   No
reason has been given for taking contemplation to be
that which is most essential to his human nature or as
being that in virtue of which a man realizes himself.
It is arbitrary to claim that contemplation is the
human activity which is of the highest value. (2)

Suppose we drop the bit about contemplation and
continue, in spite of the above arguments, to claim that

the function of man is to act on reasons or to reason in his actions and that only by doing this can he attain happiness.

If this is the move, it should be straight away noted that with such an appeal to happiness a new criterion has been introduced.   Living in accordance with reason, i.e. acting on reasons or reasoning in one's actions, is not intrinsically good but good because it tends to be conducive to happiness or (more sceptically) if anything like happiness is attainable, it will only be attainable by human beings who generally act on reasons.   But then self-realization is not the ultimate standard, happiness is.

Someone might try to avoid this conclusion by arguing that when we consider what Aristotle meant by the concept of happiness, to wit, a virtuous activity of the soul, we will see that happiness and self-realization are not independent concepts independently specifiable.   The point being made here is that human happiness is distinctive and can only be understood in terms of understanding man's function, namely his acting on reasons or reasoning in his actions.   A man will be happy if and only if he does this well.

However, this surely does not seem to be true of our ordinary and indeed reflective concept of happiness.   One might, by acting on reasons intelligently and efficiently, achieve one's aims and attain happiness, but it is also the case that one might be miserable and alienated.   And a man who did not think too clearly might be happier than a non-evasive, clear-headed individual who understood his condition very well.   This might even be true of an individual who was deceived or even deceived himself.   We need Dostoevski as a supplement to Aristotle's rationalism. We need to recognize that self-knowledge is often bitter and disillusioning - one loses certain consolations and an illusory flattering image of oneself. Indeed a clear insight into 'what makes one tick' may be self-destructive rather than something that furthers self-realization.   From Plato to Freud we have assumed that self-knowledge, though difficult, is a good thing and ultimately a source of happiness.   Both of these rationalist assumptions need challenging.

One thing to be said in reply here is *not* that we will be happy *if and only if* we act on reasons or are reasoning in our actions, but that we will be happy *only* if we act on reasons or are reasoning in our actions.   A reasonable creature may be unhappy but he cannot be happy unless he is at least in some measure reasonable.

   This is surely far more plausible than claiming one
will be happy if one is reasonable.   But all the same,
it is not a claim that is obviously *universally* true.
Yet it seems reasonable at least to believe that it
generally holds and incorporates what appears, at
least, to be the true claim, indeed the truism, that
if a 'man has goals or aims in life it is unlikely
that he will achieve his aims if he does not act on
reasons'. (3)   There is a value to be reasonably
placed on rational activity.   We need to understand
what we are doing and we need to be able to reason in
order to get what we want.   But this does not entail
or even go very far toward establishing that the fullest
possible clarity about ourselves and the rationale of
our actions carries with it a greater happiness than a
life in which one remains confused about some, humanly
speaking, very central things.   A minimum kind of
rationality, where reason is clearly a servant to one's
desires and a watchdog concerning desires which are
likely to be destructive, is absolutely crucial to anything approximating a human life or a happy life.
But a fuller measure of rationality might be counter-
productive as far as happiness is concerned.
   Perhaps it is an illusion to think that life will
ever be substantially freer from human degradation and
exploitation than it is at present, but all the same,
believing that it could be might enable a man to give
sense to his life where otherwise it would be without
sense.   But a clear knowledge of what was involved
here might lead him to despair and suicide.   A man
with a clear grasp of his condition could be a man in
despair and a man with a confused conception of life
might be happy.   All Aristotle shows about human
happiness and rationality is that if a man cannot
reason at all well, he is likely to make mistakes which
will make him miserable.   But people can have an
acute rational understanding of their positions and
still not flourish and they could be confused and
happy and indeed not terribly intellectually acute and
still be thoroughly good human beings.
   Self-realization can be so construed that it is tied
to acting on reasons or for the sake of reasons, in
which case it need not be a way to enhance human happiness to the fullest extent.   By contrast self-
realization may be so construed that it is conceptually
tied to happiness, but then self-realization is no
longer something which conceptually requires the
greatest rationality possible no matter what the circumstances.   Rationality and happiness are related but

not so tightly that it is the case that human beings
must, when there are alternative ways of acting, be
happiest when they do that action which gives them the
clearest - the most rational - understanding of their
situation.

In sum it should be stressed here that if what constitutes being a man is acting on reasons, it needs to
be pointed out that by so acting it does not necessarily
follow that one is discharging a moral obligation or
even doing anything beneficial to oneself.   No justification has been given for saying that by so acting we
realize ourselves or achieve the highest good.   If it
is responded that, if we act on reasons and consistently
reason in our actions, by definition we realize ourselves or achieve the highest good, it should be
replied that this definition is arbitrary and stipulative.   There is no reason (*pace* Plato) why an unprin-
cipled and immoral man could not act on reasons.   An
immoralist need not be an irrationalist.

5

In a way that has been too little noticed, self-realizationist theories suffer the same central defect from
which so-called ethical egoism suffers.   Recall that
for 'ethical egoism' the ultimate guiding principle is
that each person is to seek what he, on careful regard,
takes to be in his own self-interest and he is to consider the interests of others only when doing so will
directly or indirectly further his own interests.
Similarly for the self-realizationist theories the
fundamental moral imperative is for each person to
seek to realize himself.   But we have moral rules and
principles and indeed the institution of morality
itself, primarily or at least importantly, to adjudicate in a fair manner conflicts of interest. (4)   If
that is not its *raison d'être*, it is at least a central
function of such discourse.   But just as 'ethical
egoism' is of no help in adjudicating such conflicts,
for on such an account each man is told to seek his own
self-interest, including someone asked to arbitrate such
disputes, so too the self-realizationist tells men to
seek self-realization and this tells everyone, including
the arbitrator of a dispute, to look within himself and
do that which will most realize him.   But this does
not tell us what to do when a course of action which
will lead to A's self-realization conflicts with a
course of action which will lead to B's self-realization

and both cannot be done.   It does not guide a judge,
adviser or arbitrator of such a case in deciding what
he is to advise except, unhelpfully, particularly where
his own self-realization is not affected, to tell him
to seek to realize himself in such situations.   But
that is not what is needed or wanted in such a situation, and in many cases it is not at all evident what
would contribute toward his self-realization.   But
the crucial thing is that what would contribute to *his*
self-realization is not what is at issue in such situations.   In fact it very much looks as if self-realizationist theories are in reality a *form* of 'ethical
egoism'.

If it is retorted that what a self-realizationist
theory should be understood as claiming is that we
should work for, advocate, or at least hope for, the
greatest amount of self-realization for as many people
as possible, this indeed gets the theory out of the
difficulties associated with 'ethical egoism' but only
by making it into a kind of utilitarianism.   We should
always seek as our overriding aim to achieve the
greatest good for the greatest number.   Only here the
individual good, which is to be maximized for as many
people as possible, is not, as in hedonistic forms of
utilitarianism, pleasure, but individual self-realization.   This may be a plausible theory, provided that
utilitarianism stands up to critical scrutiny and provided that our earlier objections to self-realizationist
theories can be overcome.   But that, of course, is a
big if and it is also the case that the theory in
question has been so modified that it is no longer a
pure self-realizationist theory, for now it has a
utilitarian structure.   It only differs from the more
standard forms of utilitarianism in that it makes the
claim that for each individual what is good for him,
when others are not counted in, is self-realization.

6

Given the extensive array of mistakes I have trotted
out and shown to be involved in self-realizationist
ethical theories, how can I possibly be justified in
claiming that in spite of all that, such a theory contains its moral lessons and insights as well?   I
will argue that, while it does not serve as an ultimate
moral standard or principle and indeed cannot be
coherently put in this role, it is an important, though
tantalizingly vague, element to be utilized in spelling

out personal ideals of moral excellence.   Furthermore, in any adequate systematic, normative ethic, consideration must be given to these ideals; yet it is just such conceptions which receive scant attention in non-self-realizationist theories.

In this connection, we should not forget that we do not only ask: what am I bound to do or what ought I to do, but what should I become?   What should I make of my life and how should I live to live in a non-alienated, non-self-estranged way?   What, that is, should my life be like if I am to overcome self-estrangement?   But in answering these questions self-realizationist idioms come in quite naturally and indeed perhaps unavoidably.   If A can be estranged from himself, he must be able to find himself or perhaps even realize himself.   If there can be an alienated self or estranged self, there must be some concept of a true self or an unalienated self.

Suppose that this is resisted and what is claimed instead is that to make sense of your life - to attain your full human flourishing - you should go in an intelligent and single-minded way after pleasure.

However, this in turn should be challenged, for first, one typically does not attain much pleasure by going after it, it is rather something of a concomitant of certain activities - activities that can often be brought off only if one does not think about getting pleasure from what one is doing. (5)   Moreover, and second, even if pleasure could be such an end of action, it is hardly the only end of action.   A satisfying life indeed has pleasure in it, but it is not constituted by a life in which the rationale of all of one's activities is to maximize pleasure and minimize pain.

When we ask: what sort of things are *worth* having for their own sakes, we will indeed say pleasure and we will also, if we reflect, very likely say, an ability and an opportunity to direct our own lives.   But we are also very likely to say a 'fullness of life' and resist the question: 'What do you want a full life for?' as somehow conceptually inappropriate.

Yet how are we to understand 'fullness of life'? What is the literal rendering of this?   In trying to get a grip on it we are very likely to invoke notions such as 'a life in which one develops and flourishes', 'a fully human life', 'a life in which there is a measure of self-improvement and growth'.   But are not all of these notions, notions which presuppose or imply a conception of self-realization?   To grow or develop is to grow or develop into or toward something and is not that something naturally called one's more 'authentic self' or 'true self' or indeed a self which has achieved something in the direction of self-realization?

Note also that we frequently speak of creeds, institutions, forms of life, or practices which compress, stunt, or dwarf us. Are not their opposites those which aid or do not stand in the way of our self-realization? There could be no conception of a dehumanized humanity if we did not at least have some conception of what a humanity that attained or retained its humanity would be like. But to talk of this again is another way of talking of self-realization. The same type of contrast is at work in talk of empty lives, really dead people, zombies and the like. And when we talk of a good life as involving self-expression we imply that there is a 'true self' to be realized.

When Marx spoke of the estrangement of one's self from one's self and from one's own humanity and the humanity of others that we experience under capitalism, he contrasted this with a truly human life and a truly human society wherein man could attain emancipation and where one's labour would not be alienated. But in these very notions we have operating, though expressed by other words, conceptions of self-realization and the non-attainment of self-realization. What exactly this family of notions comes to remains vague - the doctrine of self-realization is indeed a murky one - but it all the same signifies something, we know not clearly what, that we quite unequivocally take as precious. An account of morality and the moral life which ignores these features of morality is plainly thereby impoverished.

NOTES

1 G.C. Field, 'Moral Theory', London, Methuen, 1966, p. 75.
2 This stress on contemplation and this conception of rationality also fits badly, as Bernard Williams observes, with his stress on practical wisdom and the importance of citizenly activities. Bernard Williams, 'Morality: An Introduction to Ethics', New York, Harper & Row, 1972, p. 60.
3 Frederick Siegler, Reason, Happiness and Goodness, in James J. Walsh and Henry J. Shapiro, eds, 'Aristotle's Ethics: Issues and Interpretations', Belmont, California, Wadsworth, 1967, p. 36.

4   Kurt Baier, 'The Moral Point of View',Ithaca, New
    York, Cornell University Press, 1958 and Kai Nielsen,
    On Moral Truth, in Nicholas Rescher, ed., 'Studies
    in Moral Philosophy', Oxford, Basil Blackwell, 1968.
5   Alasdair MacIntyre has importantly criticized such
    conceptions in his 'Against the Self-Images of the
    Age', New York, Shocken, 1971, pp. 173-90.

5   Human rights, real and supposed

Maurice Cranston

It is said that when that remarkable American jurist
Wesley Newcomb Hohfield tried to make the students at
Yale Law School discriminate carefully between different
uses of the term 'right' in Anglo-American law, he
earned himself considerable unpopularity; his pupils
even got up a petition to have him removed from his
Chair. (1)   If the analysis of positive rights is thus
resisted by law students we should not be surprised if
the analysis of human rights is ill-regarded by many
politicians, publicists, and even political theorists.
Some politicians, indeed, have a vested interest in
keeping talk about human rights as meaningless as
possible.   For there are those who do not want to see
human rights become positive rights by genuine enactments; hence the more nebulous, unrealistic or absurd
the concept of human rights is made out to be, the
better such men are pleased.

I shall argue in this paper that a philosophically
respectable concept of human rights has been muddied,
obscured, and debilitated in recent years by an attempt
to incorporate into it specific rights of a different
logical category.   The traditional human rights are
political and civil rights such as the right to life,
liberty and a fair trial.   What are now being put
forward as universal human rights are social and economic rights, such as the right to unemployment insurance,
old-age pensions, medical services and holidays with
pay.   I have both a philosophical and a political
objection to this.   The philosophical objection is that
the new theory of human rights does not make sense.
The political objection is that the circulation of a
confused notion of human rights hinders the effective
protection of what are correctly seen as human rights.

One distinction which seems now well established in

people's minds is that between human rights or the Rights
of Man or natural rights (I take these expressions to
mean the same thing) and positive rights, a distinction
which corresponds to the distinction between natural law
(or justice or the moral law) and positive law.   The
distinction has been made better understood by the
critics of natural rights, by men like Edmund Burke who
could understand what was meant by the rights of Englishmen but not by the Rights of Man, and Jeremy Bentham who
said 'Right is the child of law; from real laws come
real rights, but from imaginary law, from "laws of
nature", come imaginary rights.... Natural rights is
simple nonsense, natural and imprescriptibel rights [an
American phrase] rhetorical nonsense, nonsense upon
stilts'. (2)

   I do not think Bentham's remark is true, but it was
worth saying, because it obliges those of us who think
natural rights is *not* nonsense to explain what sort of
sense it is.   For Bentham - and for Burke - the only
test of a right was 'Is it actually enjoyed?', 'Is it
really enforced?'   In other words, 'Is it a positive
right?'   On this analysis, any right which is not a
positive right is not granted the name of a right at
all.   For Burke the Rights of Man were mere abstrac-
tions: the rights of Englishmen were realities - a
'positive recorded hereditary title to all that can be
dear to the man and the citizen'. (3)   Real rights,
again, were positive rights.

   Both Burke and Bentham had a political as well as a
philosophical interest in this question.   Both regarded talk about the Rights of Man as mischievous as
well as meaningless.   Burke, the conservative, objected to such talk because it stimulated revolutionary
sentiments, it injected 'false ideas and vain expectations into men destined to travel the obscure walk
of laborious life'.   Bentham, the radical, objected
to talk about the Rights of Man because it produced
declarations and manifestos that had no real significance in positive law, declarations which took the
place of effective legislation for the public welfare.
Burke disliked the rhetoric that led to public unrest
and Bentham disliked the rhetoric that enabled politicians to fob off the public with words instead of
deeds.   Being thus attacked from Right and Left, it
is no wonder that the idea of the Rights of Man, and
of Natural Law, became unfashionable in the nineteenth
century.

   The present century has seen a marked revival of
consciousness of what is now generally know as human

rights - a term which has the advantage over the older
expression 'natural rights' of not committing one too
ostentatiously to any traditional doctrine of Natural
Law. The reason for this revival is perhaps to be
sought in history, first, in the great twentieth-
century evils, Nazism, fascism, total war and racialism,
which have all presented a fierce challenge to human
rights; and secondly, in an increased belief in, or
demand for, equality among men. When the United
Nations was set up by the victorious powers in the
Second World War, one of the first and most important
tasks assigned to it was what Winston Churchill called
'the enthronement of human rights'. The efforts that
have been made at the United Nations to fulfil this
promise have much to teach a political theorist.

At the inaugural meeting of the Economic and Social
Council of the UN in May 1946, a Commission on Human
Rights was appointed to submit to the General Assembly
recommendations and reports regarding an 'International
Bill of Rights'. English-speaking delegates on this
Commission promptly put forward a draft 'Bill of
Rights' in the form of a draft convention or treaty
which both named the specific rights to be recognized
and provided for the setting up of international institutions to deal with any alleged breach of those rights.
The English-speaking delegations not unnaturally interpreted the expression 'Bill of Rights' as meaning an
instrument of positive law, and therefore understood
the duty of the Commission to be that of finding a
formula for making human rights positive rights by
making them enforceable. The Russian representative
objected to these proposals. He said that it was
premature to discuss any measure of a binding or
judicial nature; the Soviet Union was willing to
support a 'Bill of Rights' only if it was understood
as a manifesto or declaration of rights. Some years
afterwards the United States followed the Russian
example, and announced that it, too, would not commit
itself to any legally binding convention for the international protection of human rights.

In the UN Commission on Human Rights a compromise
was settled on. The Commission agreed first to produce a manifesto or declaration of human rights, and
then afterwards begin to work out 'something more
legally binding' which it was decided to call a
Covenant. The manifesto did not take long to produce.
It was given the name of Universal Declaration of
Human Rights and proclaimed by the General Assembly of
the United Nations in December 1948 (see Appendix,

p. 143).   The 'more legally binding' Covenant of
Human Rights, however, is still, after many years, at
the stage of discussion.

One of the difficulties of translating the Universal
Declaration of Human Rights into any kind of positive
law is that the Declaration contains so much.   It has
no fewer than thirty articles.   The first twenty spell
out in detail the sort of rights that were named in the
various classical statements of the Rights of Man: the
rights to life, liberty, property, equality, justice
and the pursuit of happiness are articulated as, among
other things, the right to freedom of movement;   the
right to own property alone as well as in association
with others;   the right to marry;   the right to equality before the law and to a fair trial if accused of
any crime;   the right to privacy;   the right to religious freedom;   the right to free speech and peaceful
assembly;   the right to asylum.   Among the institutions
outlawed are slavery, torture and arbitrary detention.

The Universal Declaration of 1948 did not, however,
limit itself to this restatement of the familiar
Rights of Man;   it includes a further ten articles
which name rights of a new and different kind. (4)
Article 21 states that everyone has the right to take
part in the government of his country, and further
articles affirm the right to education;   the right to
work and to form trade unions;   the right to equal pay
for equal work;   the right of everyone to a standard
of living adequate to the health and well-being of
himself and his family;   the right to security in the
event of unemployment, sickness, disability, widow-
hood, old age or other lack of livelihood;   the right
to enjoy the arts and to share in scientific advancement and its benefits;   and, what is even more novel,
the right to rest, leisure and 'periodic holidays with
pay'.

The difference between these new rights and the
traditional natural rights was not unnoticed by those
responsible for drafting the Declaration.   In the
records of the Commission, the first twenty articles
are called 'political and civil rights' and the
further rights 'economic and social rights'.   These
later rights appear to have been included under
pressure from the Left;   but there are many humanitarian
people, apart from those on the Left, who (in my
belief, unwisely) agree with their inclusion. (5)

So far as the United Nations is concerned, the
Commission on Human Rights soon discovered, when it
came to draft the 'more legally binding' Covenant, that

the two kinds of rights did not mix together well; and
the Commission was therefore obliged to draft *two* cove-
nants, one concerning the political and civil rights,
the other the social and economic rights. Neither
draft has so far proved acceptable to the General
Assembly. In the meantime altogether more progress
has been made in the field of human rights by another
international organization, the Council of Europe. In
1950 a European Convention for the Protection of Human
Rights was signed by the member States of the Council
of Europe at Strasbourg. This time the so-called
'social and economic rights' were omitted; the rights
that were named were the traditional 'political and
civil rights'. Moreover, in this case, a European
Commission and a European Court of Human Rights were
set up with full judicial powers to investigate and
remedy any alleged breach of the rights named in the
Convention. Here, clearly, is a tangible attempt to
translate the human rights into positive rights on an
international scale. The only weakness of the European
Convention is that some leading European powers, France,
Italy, Greece, and Turkey, have refused to recognize
the jurisdiction of the European Court or to grant the
right to individual petition to the Commission or the
Court. Nevertheless a dozen other nations *do* recognize these institutions; so that changes in positive
law have helped in those places to make men's 'human
rights' positive rights. (6)
    One of the objections to regarding the 'social and
economic' rights as authentic human rights is that it
would be totally impossible to translate them in the
same way into positive rights by analogous political
and legal action. There are other objections: but
the time has now come to consider more carefully what
is meant by a right, and then what kind of right a
human right is. We have already noted the distinction
between human rights and positive rights; I propose
now to rearrange rights into two other categories; the
one I shall call legal rights, the other moral rights.

1 Legal rights may be distinguished as follows:
    (a) General positive rights: the rights that are
enjoyed and fully assured to everyone living under a
given jurisdiction or constitution.
    (b) Traditional rights and liberties: Burke said
that the English people had risen against James II
because he had taken away their traditional rights and
liberties as Englishmen. The Vichy government took

away many of the traditional rights and liberties of
Frenchmen.   This class of rights includes lost positive
rights as well as existing positive rights.

(c) Nominal 'legal' rights: Even the least liberal
nations tend to have 'façade' constitutions (7) which
'guarantee' freedom of speech, movement, assembly, and
other such rights to their inhabitants.   But where
these nominal rights are not enforced, they cannot, of
course, be classed as positive rights.   We nevertheless
see the demand in some such places for the nominal
'legal' rights being made positive rights.   One example
is the demand of certain Polish intellectuals for that
freedom of expression which their constitution assures
them.   An even more publicized example is the demand
of the Negroes in the United States for the nominal
legal right to vote, enter State schools and so forth,
to be translated into positive rights.

(d) Positive rights, liberties, privileges and
immunities of a limited class of persons: Under this
category we should have to include all rights which are
attached to membership of a given category, e.g., the
rights of clergymen, of peers, of doctors, of graduates
of the University of Oxford and of freemen of the City
of London.   The twentieth century has become impatient
of privileges, and rights which were once enjoyed by a
limited class of persons are often now claimed by all
the inhabitants of a country.   For example, the privileges of citizenship, the rights of ratepayers, as they
were known in nineteenth-century England, are now
enjoyed by all adult British subjects.   A demand for
the extension of rights within a political society is
often confused with the demand for human rights.   But
the two are quite distinct.

(e) The positive rights, liberties, privileges and
immunities of a single person: Here the examples are
few, because the cases are few: the rights of the
President of the United States, of the Chairman of the
Senate; the rights of the King, or the Lord Chancellor,
or of the Archbishop of Canterbury, are examples.
Since the decay of the doctrine of the Divine Right of
Kings, this class of rights does not present much of a
problem.

The foregoing classes cover the category of legal
rights.   Next in turn is the category of moral rights.
In this case it will be convenient to reverse the order
of generality.

2   Moral rights

(a) Moral rights of one person only: We remember Bradley's famous phrase 'my station and its duties': we can equally speak of 'my station and its rights'. I, and I alone, have a network of rights which arise from the fact that I have done certain deeds, paid certain monies, been elected to certain places, and so forth.   Some of these rights are legal rights as well as moral rights.   But in considering them as moral rights the question is not 'Does the law uphold them?' but 'Have I just claim to them?'   Not all my moral rights may in fact be enjoyed.   Often we become most conscious of our moral rights precisely when they are *not* upheld.   I am inclined to say 'I have a moral right to be told what is going on in my own house' when I realize I am not being told.   So just as the crucial question with legal rights is 'Are they secured and enjoyed?', the crucial question in a moral right is 'Is there a just title?'   Is there a sound moral claim?   *Justification* is the central question.

(b) The moral rights of anyone in a particular situation: This is the class of moral rights which belongs to everyone who comes into a certain specific category, e.g., that of a parent, or a tutor, or an *au pair* girl.   So we can say of a person, if he is a member of this class, he is entitled to so and so. Claims to have such moral rights are pressed by proving that one does belong to the appropriate category.

(c) The moral rights of all people in all situations: Because these rights are universal we should naturally expect them to be few in number;   and we should expect them to be highly generalized in their formulation.   It is easier to agree, for example, about the kind of deed which violates the right to life than it is to agree about any philosophical expression of the right to life.   Moreover, it is inevitable that such a right as that to liberty will be somewhat differently understood in different societies, where the boundary between liberty and licence will be differently drawn.   Again, our understanding of the right to property will differ according to the meaning we give to that richly ambiguous word.

The place which human rights occupy in my classification is readily understood.   Human rights are a form of moral right, and they differ from other moral rights in being the rights of all people at all times and in all situations.   This characteristic of human rights

is recognized in the first paragraph of the preamble to
the Universal Declaration of 1948, which says: 'Whereas
recognition of the inherent dignity and of the equal and
inalienable rights of all members of the human family is
the foundation of freedom, justice and peace in the
world....'

Part of the difficulty of justifying human rights is
their very universality.   Moral rights of classes 2 (a)
and 2 (b) above are justified by reference to the definite station or situation of the claimants.   I claim a
right to be told about the health of Nicholas Cranston
by showing that I am his father.   I do not think anyone else (except his mother) has the same right.   But
human rights do not depend in any way on the station
or the situation of the individual.   This is part of
what is meant by saying they are 'rights that pertain
to a human being merely because he is a human being'.
If the validity of a moral right is commonly established
by reference to the station or situation of the
claimant, it is not altogether easy to see by what
tests one could validate the rights which are *not* considered in relation to any definite situation.

Nevertheless there are some tests for the authenticity of a human right or universal moral right.
Rights bear a clear relationship to duties.   And the
first test of both is that of practicability.   It is
not my duty to do what it is physically impossible for
me to do.   You cannot reasonably say it was my duty
to have jumped into the Thames at Richmond to rescue
a drowning child if I was nowhere near Richmond at the
time the child was drowning.   What is true of duties
is equally true of rights.   If it is impossible for
a thing to be done, it is absurd to claim it as a
right.   At present it is utterly impossible, and will
be for a long time yet, to provide 'holidays with pay'
for everybody in the world.   For millions of people
who live in those parts of Asia, Africa, and South
America where industrialization has hardly begun,
such claims are vain and idle.

The traditional 'political and civil rights' can
(as I have said) be readily secured by legislation;
and generally they can be secured by fairly simple
legislation.   Since those rights are for the most
part rights against government interference with a
man's activities, a large part of the legislation
needed has to do no more than restrain the government's
own executive arm'.   This is no longer the case when
we turn to 'the right to work', 'the right to social
security' and so forth.   For a government to provide

social security it needs to do more than make laws; it has to have access to great capital wealth, and many governments in the world today are still poor.   The government of India, for example, simply cannot command the resources that would guarantee each one of the 480 million inhabitants of India 'a standard of living adequate for the health and well-being of himself and his family', let alone 'holidays with pay'.

Another test of a human right is that it shall be a genuinely universal moral right.   This the so-called human right to holidays with pay plainly cannot pass. For it is a right that is necessarily limited to those persons who are *paid* in any case, that is to say, to the *employé* class.   Since not everyone belongs to this class, the right cannot be a universal right, a right which, in the terminology of the Universal Declaration, 'everyone' has.   That the right to a holiday with pay is for many people a real moral right, I would not for one moment deny.   But it is a right which falls into section 2 (b) of the classification of rights which I have set out above; that is, a right which can be claimed by members of a specific class of persons *because* they are members of that class.

A further test of a human right, or universal moral right, is the test of *paramount importance*.   Here the distinction is less definite, but no less crucial. And here again there is a parallel between rights and duties.   It is a paramount duty to relieve great distress, as it is not a paramount duty to give pleasure. It would have been my duty to rescue the drowning child at Richmond if I had been there at the time; but it is not, in the same sense, my duty to give Christmas presents to the children of my neighbours.   This difference is obscured in the crude utilitarian philosophy which analyses moral goodness in terms of the greatest happiness of the greatest number: but common-sense does not ignore it.   Common-sense knows that fire engines and ambulances are essential services, whereas fun fairs and holiday camps are not.   Liberality and kindness are reckoned moral virtues; but they are not moral duties in the sense that the obligation to rescue a drowning child is a moral duty.

It is worth considering the circumstances in which ordinary people find themselves invoking the language of human rights.   I suggest they are situations like these:

A black student in South Africa is awarded a scholarship to Oxford, and then refused a passport by the South African government simply because he is black.   We feel this is clear invasion of the human right to freedom of movement.

Jews are annihilated by the Nazi government, simply because they are Jews.   We feel this is a manifest abuse (an atrocious abuse) of the human right to life.

In several countries men are held in prison indefinitely without trial.   We feel this is a gross invasion of the human right to liberty and to a fair trial on any criminal charge.

In considering cases of this kind, we are confronted by matters which belong to a totally different moral dimension from questions of social security and holidays with pay.   A human right is something of which no one may be deprived without a grave affront to justice. There are certain deeds which should never be done, certain freedoms which should never be invaded, some things which are supremely sacred.   If a Declaration of Human Rights is what it purports to be, a declaration of universal moral rights, it should be confined to this sphere of discourse.   If rights of another class are introduced, the effect may even be to bring the whole concept of human rights into disrepute.   'It would be a splendid thing', people might say, 'for everyone to have holidays with pay, a splendid thing for everyone to have social security, a splendid thing to have equality before the law, and freedom of speech, and the right to life.   One day, perhaps, this beautiful ideal may be realized....'

Thus the effect of a Universal Declaration which is overloaded with affirmations of so-called human rights which are not human rights at all is to push *all* talk of human rights out of the clear realm of the morally compelling into the twilight world of utopian aspiration.   In the Universal Declaration of 1948 there indeed occurs the phrase 'a common standard of achievement' which brands that Declaration as an attempt to translate rights into ideals.   And however else one might choose to define moral rights, they are plainly *not* ideals or aspirations.

Rights have been variously defined by jurists and philosophers.   Some have spoken of them in terms of 'justifiable claims' or 'moral titles';   others have analysed rights in terms of duty ('what we have an overwhelming duty to respect');   others again have preferred to speak of right conduct or obligation or of ought ('a man has a right whenever other men ought not to prevent his doing what he wants or refuse him some service he asks for or needs').   All these words - 'right', 'justice', 'duty', 'ought', 'obligation' - are the key terms of what Kant called the 'categorical imperative'.   What ought to be done, what is obligatory, what is right, what is duty, what is just, is not what it would be nice to see done one day; it is what is demanded by the basic norms of morality or justice.

An ideal is something one can aim at, but cannot by definition immediately realize.   A right, on the contrary, is something that can, and from the moral point of view *must*, be respected here and now.   If this were not so, we should have to agree with Bentham; if the Rights of Man were ideals, to talk of them as rights at all would indeed be rhetorical nonsense.   We can give sense to human rights only because we can reasonably claim that men have moral rights, and that among the moral rights which each man has are some that he shares with all other men.

To deny that the 'economic and social rights' are the universal moral rights of all men is not to deny that they may be the moral rights of some men.   In the moral criticism of legal rights, it is certainly arguable that the privileges of some members of a certain community ought to be extended to other members (and perhaps all members) of that community.   But this matter is correctly seen as a problem of *socialization* or *democratization* – that is, the extension of privileges and immunities – rather than as a problem about the universal rights of all men; and the case for any such specific claims to an extension of legal rights must be argued on other grounds.

NOTES

1 Arthur L. Corbin in his introduction to Hohfield's 'Fundamental Legal Conceptions', Yale University Press, New Haven, 1964.
2 'Anarchical Fallacies'.
3 'The Philosophy of Edmund Burke', ed. Bredvold and Ross, Michigan University Press, Ann Arbor, 1960, p. 205.
4 C.J. Friedrich, in Rights, Liberties, Freedoms: A Reappraisal, 'American Political Science Review', LVII, 4 December 1963, shows that some 'social and economic rights' were known to the Age of Reason. He quotes the 'right to work' being named by Turgot and Robespierre, and gives references to eighteenth-century claims to the right to education.
5 E.g., Professor C.J. Friedrich (cf. previous note). Another champion of the view that social and

economic rights should be interpreted as human rights is the late Pope, John XXIII.   I have discussed his views in an article, Pope John XXIII on Peace and the Rights of Man, 'Political Quarterly', October 1963.

6 See A.H. Robertson, 'Human Rights in Europe', Manchester University Press, 1964.

7 See G. Sartori, Constitutionalism, 'American Political Science Review', Vol. LVI December 1962, pp. 853-65.

6   Welfare state and welfare society

R. M. Titmuss

INTRODUCTION

I did not choose this title.   It was chosen for me.
Despite this assistance, I must say that I am no more
enamoured today of the indefinable abstraction 'The
Welfare State' than I was some twenty years ago when,
with the advent of the National Health, National
Insurance and other legislative promissories, the term
acquired an international as well as a national
popularity.

The consequences have not all been intellectually
stimulating.   Generalized slogans rarely induce concentration of thought; more often they prevent us from
asking significant questions about reality.   Morally
satisfied and intellectually dulled, we sink back into
our presumptive cosy British world of welfare.   Meanwhile, outside these islands (as well as inside) there
are critics - economic and political critics - who are
misled into confusing ends and means, and who are discouraged from undertaking the painful exercise of
distinguishing between philosophical tomorrows and
the current truths of reality in a complex British
power structure of rationed resources, and great
inequalities in incomes and wealth, opportunities and
freedom of choice.

From what little is known about the reading habits
of international bankers and economists, I think it is
reasonable to say that they do not include much in the
way of studies on welfare and the condition of the poor.
How then are their views shaped about the British 'Welfare State'?   This we do not know, but at least we can
say that if we mislead ourselves, we shall mislead them.
But the matter does not end there.   Models of public
welfare can assume different forms and contain different

assumptions about means and ends.   Concepts of welfare
can imply very different things to different people -
as we can see from the Study Group Reports to this
Conference.

One particular model is the 'Public Burden Model of
Welfare'.   In general terms, this sees public welfare
expenditure - and particularly expenditure which is
redistributive in intent - as a burden;   an impediment
to growth and economic development.   Given this model
of the British patient, the diagnosis seems simple.
We are spending too much on 'The Welfare State'.   Such
explanations are, moreover, encouraged by the concept
of private economic man embedded in the techniques of
national income accounting.   An increase in public
retirement pensions is seen (as it was seen inter-
nationally during the balance of payments crisis in
1964) as an economic burden. (1)   A similar increase
in spending power among occupational (publicly subsidized
private) pensioners is not so seen.   Yet both involve
additions to consumption demand.

Or take another example: medical care, public and
private.   It is being argued today that by encouraging
the growth of private medical care through a voucher
system and by allowing people to contract-out of
taxation, the 'burden' of the Health Service would be
reduced.   The objective it seems is to reduce the
assumed 'burden';   thus, those who contract-out
diminish the burden.   Logically, we should extend to
them our gratitude and moral respect for contracting-
out of public commitments.   But, if Mr Enoch Powell
may be accepted as an authority (and I quote from his
recent book 'Medicine and Politics', (2) this 'voucher
scheme resolves itself merely into a method of increasing state expenditure upon medical care'.   In other
words, it is a proposal for redistributing more
medical resources in favour of private patients.   The
case for contracting-out must, therefore, be justified
on grounds other than the 'welfare burden' argument.

INTERNATIONAL ASPECTS OF WELFARE

If we insist, come what may, on the continued use or
misuse and misapplication of the term 'The Welfare
State' then we must accept the consequences of international misunderstanding.   We cannot assume that
observers abroad share, or will share, the social or
moral criteria we may apply to welfare; to many of
our creditors and currency colleagues in Western Germany,

France and the United States, the 'Welfare State' is
equated with national irresponsibility and decadence;
an easy way of living off foreign loans.   To the
political scientist as well as the economist these
opinions are relevant facts in the same way as (according to some sociologists) social class is what men
think it is.   These opinions do not, moreover, differ
markedly from those expressed in the published statements on welfare during the past fifteen years by
bankers, insurance directors, financiers and others in
the City of London. (3)

Many of these monetary experts abroad appear to place
a different valuation on countries which depend heavily
on 'borrowing' human capital as distinct from those
which borrow financial capital.   For such transactions,
no payment is made to the lending country;   there are
no interest charges, and there is no intention of
repaying the loan.

Since 1949 the United States has absorbed (and to
some extent deliberately recruited) the import of
100,000 doctors, scientists and engineers from developed
and developing countries.   In about eighteen years the
United States will have saved some $4,000 million by
not having to educate and train, or train fully, this
vast quantity of human capital. (4)   It has spent
more on consumption goods;   less on public services.
It has taxed itself more lightly while imposing
heavier taxation on poorer countries.   Estimates have
been made that this foreign aid to America is as great
or greater than the total of American aid to countries
abroad since 1949.   Moreover, such estimates leave
out of account the social and economic effects in
Britain (and much more significantly in the poor
countries of the world) of having to train more doctors, scientists and engineers, and of having to pay
heavily inflated rewards to prevent American recruitment with all their harmful repercussions on incomes,
prices and levels of taxation.

In medicine alone, foreign doctors now account for
nearly 20 per cent of the annual additions to the
American medical profession. (5)   The world now provides as much or more medical aid to the United States
in terms of dollars as the total cost of all American
medical aid, private and public, to foreign
countries. (6)   A study I have made recently of the
columns of the 'British Medical Journal' and the
'Lancet' from 1951 to 1966 shows that advertisements
for British doctors (often accompanied by recruiting
campaigns and sometimes actively encouraged by senior

British doctors (7)) rose from a yearly average of 134
in 1951 to over 4,000 in 1966. (8)   The total number
of newly qualified doctors in Britain in 1966 was around
1,700;   each of them cost about £10,000 to train,
excluding expenditure on student maintenance. (9)

The United States is not alone in attempting to
develop its welfare systems (and Medicare) at the
expense of poorer countries through the discovery that,
today, it is much cheaper and less of a public burden
to import doctors, scientists and other qualified
workers than to educate and train them.   Britain is
also relying heavily on the skills of doctors from
poorer countries - due in part to the belief less than
five to ten years ago among Ministers and leaders of
the medical profession that we were in danger of
training too many doctors. (10)   And, we may add, the
belief among liberal economists and sections of the
medical profession that Britain was spending too much
on the Health Service which was in danger of bankrupting
the nation.   Even as late as 1962, there were influential voices in the British Medical Association who
were speaking of the profession's recent experience of
a 'glut of doctors' and the need to avoid medical
unemployment in the late 1960s. (11)   Guilty as we
have been in our treatment of doctors from overseas,
and in our failure in the past to train enough health
workers for our own national needs, at least it cannot
be said that we are deliberately organizing recruitment
campaigns in economically poorer countries.

These introductory reflections on some of the international aspects of welfare point, I believe, to three
general conclusions.   First, they underline the
dangers in the use of the term 'The Welfare State'.
Second, they remind us that we can no longer consider
welfare systems solely within the limited framework of
the nation-state;   what we do or fail to do in changing
systems of welfare affects other countries besides
ourselves.   Third, to suggest one criterion for the
definition of a 'Welfare Society';   namely, a society
which openly accepts a policy responsibility for
educating and training its own nationals to meet its
own needs for doctors, nurses, social workers, scientists, engineers and others.   Just as we have recognized the injustices and the waste in the unrestricted
free international movement of goods, material and
capital, so we must now recognize the need for the
richer countries of the world to take action to protect
the poorer countries from being denuded of skilled
manpower.

To this end, a number of measures could be taken,
some unilaterally, some by international agreement.
Among the most important would be for the rich
countries to decide to spend less on personal consumption goods and more on training young people for
the social service professions; to decide to devote
more of their resources for genuine international aid
to the poorer countries; to decide to ban the deliberate recruitment overseas of skilled manpower; to
decide to revise and broaden their immigration
policies so that movement between countries is not
restricted to the highly educated and trained; and
to take other measures too complex to discuss in this
paper.

For the rich countries of the world to take action
in such ways would represent a few modest steps towards
the notion of 'a Welfare World'. Those countries
assuming leadership with policies of this nature might
then with some justification regard themselves as
'Welfare Societies'.

This principle of community responsibility for the
provision of adequate resources to implement the objectives of national legislation is particularly relevant
to the whole field of welfare. The quantity, territorial distribution and quality of any country's social
services - education, medical care, mental health,
welfare, children's and other personal community
services - depends enormously on the quantity and
quality of staff; professional, technical, auxiliary
and administrative. To enact legislation designed to
create or develop services yet not to invest adequately
in the training of doctors, nurses, social workers,
teachers, and many other categories of skilled manpower
and womanpower is a denial of this principle of
community responsibility. To rely on the private
market and autonomous professional bodies to fulfil
these training needs is nothing less than a ridiculous
illusion. The private national market has failed
lamentably in this country and in the United States
to produce enough doctors, teachers, social workers
and nurses. To resort to the international market to
remedy the deficiency of national social policies can
only have tragic consequences for the poorer countries
of the world.

In considering the international aspects of these
welfare manpower issues there is one further observation
I wish to make before turning to other Conference
themes. It seems to me the height of collective
immorality for the rich countries of the world to

preach to the poorer countries about the economic
benefits of family planning while, at the same time,
making it more difficult for these countries to
develop family planning programmes by drawing away
the skilled manpower they need for the infrastructure
of services required in which to provide birth control
as well as death control services.

Having delivered myself of these thoughts under the
conveniently broad umbrella-theme of this Conference,
I want now to consider certain other questions of
principle in systems of welfare.

UNIVERSALIST AND SELECTIVE SOCIAL SERVICES

In any discussion today of the future of (what is called)
'The Welfare State' much of the argument revolves round
the principles and objectives of universalist social
services and selective social services.   Prominence
was given to this issue in Chapters 2 and 4 of the
'Guide to Studies' prepared two years ago for this
Conference.   Time does not seem to have eroded the
importance of this issue.

I think it is unnecessary, therefore, to remind you
in detail of the many complex questions of principles,
goals, methods and assumptions involved in this debate.
In regard to some of them - and particularly the
question of freedom of choice - I have set out my views
in a recently published lecture 'Choice and The Welfare
State'.

Briefly, then, I will restate certain of the more
general points emphasized in this 'Guide'.   Consider,
first, the nature of the broad principles which helped
to shape substantial sections of British welfare
legislation in the past, and particularly the principle
of universalism embodied in such post-war enactments
as the National Health Service Act, the Education Act
of 1944, the National Insurance Act and the Family
Allowances Act.

One fundamental historical reason for the adoption
of this principle was the aim of making services available and accessible to the whole population in such
ways as would not involve users in any humiliating
loss of status, dignity or self-respect.   There should
be no sense of inferiority, pauperism, shame or stigma
in the use of a publicly provided service;   no attribu-
tion that one was being or becoming a 'public burden'.
Hence the emphasis on the social rights of all citizens
to use or not to use as responsible people the services

made available by the community in respect of certain
needs which the private market and the family were
unable or unwilling to provide universally. If these
services were not provided for everybody by everybody
they would either not be available at all, or only
for those who could afford them, and for others on
such terms as would involve the infliction of a sense
of inferiority and stigma.

Avoidance of stigma was not, of course, the only
reason for the development of the twin-concepts of
social rights and universalism. Many other forces,
social, political and psychological, during a century
and more of turmoil, revolution, war and change, contributed to the clarification and acceptance of these
notions. The novel idea of prevention - novel, at
least, to many in the nineteenth century - was, for
example, another powerful engine, driven by the Webbs
and many other advocates of change, which reinforced
the concepts of social rights and universalism. The
idea of prevention - the prevention and breaking of
the vicious descending spiral of poverty, disease,
neglect, illiteracy and destitution - spelt to the
protagonists (and still does so) the critical importance
of early and easy access to and use of preventive,
remedial and rehabilitative services. Slowly and
painfully the lesson was learnt that if such services
were to be utilized in time and were to be effective
in action in a highly differentiated, unequal and
class-saturated society, they had to be delivered
through socially approved channels; that is to say,
without loss of self-respect by the users and their
families.

Prevention was not simply a child of biological and
psychological theorists; at least one of the grand-
parents was a powerful economist with a strongly
developed streak of nationalism. As Professor
Bentley Gilbert has shown in his recent book, 'The
Evolution of National Insurance: The Origins of the
Welfare State', national efficiency and welfare were
seen as complementary. (12)   The sin unforgivable was
the waste of human resources; thus, welfare was
summoned to prevent waste.   Hence the beginnings of
four of our present-day universalist social services:
retirement pensions, the Health Service, unemployment
insurance and the school meals service.

The insistent drumming of the national efficiency
movement in those far-off days before the First World
War is now largely forgotten.   Let me then remind you
that the whole welfare debate was a curious mixture of

humanitarianism, egalitarianism, productivity (as we
would call it today) and old-fashioned imperialism.
The strident note of the latter is now, we may thank
our stars, silenced.   The Goddess of Growth has replaced the God of National Fitness.   But can we say
that the quest for the other objectives is no longer
necessary?

   Before discussing such a rhetorical question, we
need to examine further the principle of universalism.
The principle itself may sound simple but the practice
- and by that I mean the present operational pattern
of welfare in Britain today - is immensely complex.
We can see something of this complexity if we analyse
welfare (defined here as all publicly provided and subsidized services, statutory, occupational and fiscal)
from a number of different standpoints.

AN ANALYTICAL FRAMEWORK

Whatever the nature of the service, activity or function,
and whether it be a service in kind, a collective
amenity, or a transfer payment in cash or by accoun-
tancy, we need to consider (and here I itemize in
question-form for the sake of brevity) three central
issues:
(a)   What is the nature of entitlement to use?   Is
it legal, contractual or contributory, financial, discretionary or professionally determined entitlement?
(b)   Who is entitled and on what conditions?   Is
account taken of individual characteristics, family
characteristics, group characteristics, territorial
characteristics or social-biological characteristics?
What, in fact, are the rules of entitlement?   Are
they specific and contractual - like a right based on
age - or are they variable, arbitrary or discretionary?
(c)   What methods, financial and administrative, are
employed in the determination of access, utilization,
allocation and payment?
   Next we have to reflect on the nature of the service
or benefit.
   What functions do benefits, in cash, amenity or in
kind, aim to fulfil?   They may, for example, fulfil
any of the following sets of functions, singly or in
combination:
1 As partial compensation for identified disservices
caused by society (for example, unemployment, some
categories of industrial injuries benefits, war pensions, etc.).   And, we may add, the disservices

caused by international society as exemplified recently
by the oil pollution resulting from the Torrey Canyon
disaster costing at least £2 million. (13)
2 As partial compensation for unidentifiable disservices caused by society (for example, 'benefits'
related to programmes of slum clearance, urban blight,
smoke pollution control, hospital cross-infection and
many other socially created disservices).
3 As partial compensation for unmerited handicap (for
example, language classes for immigrant children,
services for the deprived child, children handicapped
from birth, etc.).
4 As a form of protection for society (for example,
the probation service, some parts of the mental health
services, services for the control of infectious
diseases, and so on).
5 As an investment for a future personal or collective
gain (education - professional, technical and industrial - is an obvious example here; so also are certain
categories of tax deductibles for self-improvement and
certain types of subsidized occupational benefits).
6 As an immediate and/or deferred increment to personal welfare or, in other words, benefits (utilities)
which add to personal command-over-resources either
immediately and/or in the future (for example, subsidies to owner-occupiers and council tenants, tax
deductibles for interest charges, pensions, supplementary benefits, curative medical care, and so on).
7 As an element in an integrative objective which is
an essential characteristic distinguishing social
policy from economic policy. As Kenneth Boulding has
said, '... social policy is that which is centred in
those institutions that create integration and discourage alienation.' (14) It is thus profoundly
concerned with questions of personal identity whereas
economic policy centres round exchange or bilateral
transfer.

This represents little more than an elementary and
partial structural map which can assist in the understanding of the welfare complex today. Needless to
say, a more sophisticated (inch to the mile) guide is
essential for anything approaching a thorough analysis
of the actual functioning of welfare benefit systems.
I do not, however, propose to refine further this
frame of study now, nor can I analyse by these classifications the several hundred distinctive and functionally separate services and benefits actually in operation in Britain today.

Further study would also have to take account of

the pattern and operation of means-tested services.   It
has been estimated by Mr M.J. Reddin, my research assistant, that in England and Wales today local authorities
are responsible for administering at least 3,000 means-
tests, of which about 1,500 are different from each
other. (15)   This estimate applies only to services
falling within the responsibilities of education, child
care, health, housing and welfare departments.   It
follows that in these fields alone there exist some
1,500 different definitions of poverty or financial
hardship, ability to pay and rules for charges, which
affect the individual and the family.   There must be
substantial numbers of poor families with multiple
needs and multiple handicaps whose perception today of
the realities of welfare is to see only a means-testing
world.   Who helps them, I wonder, to fill up all those
forms?

I mention these social facts, by way of illustration,
because they do form part of the operational complex of
welfare in 1967.   My main purpose, however, in presenting this analytical framework was twofold.   First, to
underline the difficulties of conceptualizing and
categorizing needs, causes, entitlement or gatekeeper
functions, utilization patterns, benefits and compensations.   Second, to suggest that those students of
welfare who are seeing the main problem today in terms
of universalism versus selective services are present-
a naïve and oversimplified picture of policy choices.

Some of the reasons for this simple and superficial
view are, I think, due to the fact that the approach is
dominated by the concept or model of welfare as a
'burden'; as a waste of resources in the provision of
benefits for those who, it is said, do not need them.
The general solution is thus deceptively simple and
romantically appealing; abolish all this welfare complexity and concentrate help on those whose needs are
greatest.

Quite apart from the theoretical and practical im-
maturity of this solution, which would restrict the
public services to a minority in the population leaving
the majority to buy their own education, social
security, medical care and other services in a
supposedly free market, certain other important questions need to be considered.

As all selective services for this minority would
have to apply some test of need - eligibility, on what
bases would tests be applied and, even more crucial,
where would the lines be drawn for benefits which
function as compensation for identified disservices,

compensation for unidentifiable disservices, compensation for unmerited handicap, as a form of social protection, as an investment, or as an increment to personal welfare?   Can rules of entitlement and access be drawn on purely 'ability to pay' criteria without distinction of cause?   And if the causal agents of need cannot be identified or are so diffuse as to defy the wit of law - as they so often are today - then is not the answer 'no compensation and no redress'?   In other words, the case for concentrated selective services resolves itself into an argument for allowing the social costs or diswelfares of the economic system to lie where they fall.

The emphasis today on 'welfare' and the 'benefits of welfare' often tends to obscure the fundamental fact that for many consumers the services used are not essentially benefits or increments to welfare at all;   they represent partial compensations for disservices, for social costs and social insecurities which are the product of a rapidly changing industrial-urban society.   They are part of the price we pay to some people for bearing part of the costs of other people's progress;   the obsolescence of skills, redundancies, premature retirements, accidents, many categories of disease and handicap, urban blight and slum clearance, smoke pollution, and a hundred-and-one other socially generated disservices.   They are the socially caused diswelfares;   the losses involved in aggregate welfare gains.

What is also of major importance today is that modern society is finding it increasingly difficult to identify the causal agent or agencies, and thus to allocate the costs of disservices and charge those who are responsible.   It is not just a question of benefit allocation - of whose 'Welfare State' - but also of loss allocation - whose 'Diswelfare State'.

If identification of the agents of diswelfare were possible - if we could legally name and blame the culprits - then, in theory at least, redress could be obtained through the courts by the method of monetary compensation for damages.   But multiple causality and the diffusion of disservices - the modern choleras of change - make this solution impossible.   We have, therefore, as societies to make other choices;   either to provide social services, or to allow the social costs of the system to lie where they fall.   The nineteenth century chose the latter - the *laissez faire* solution - because it had neither a germ theory of disease nor a social theory of causality;   an answer which can hardly be entertained today by a richer society equipped with more knowledge about the dynamics of change.   But knowledge in this context must not, of course, be equated with wisdom.

If this argument can be sustained, we are thus compelled to return to our analytical framework of the functional concepts of benefit and, within this context, to consider the role of universalist and selective social services.   Non-discriminating universalist services are in part the consequence of unidentifiable causality.   If disservices are wasteful (to use the economists' concept of 'waste') so welfare has to be 'wasteful'.

The next question that presents itself is this: can we and should we, in providing benefits and compensation (which in practice can rarely be differentially provided), distinguish between 'faults' in the individual (moral, psychological or social) and the 'faults of society'?   If all services are provided - irrespective of whether they represent benefits, amenity, social protection or compensation - on a discriminatory, means-test basis, do we not foster both the sense of personal failure and the stigma of a public burden? The fundamental objective of all such tests of eligibility is to keep people out; not to let them in. They must, therefore, be treated as applicants or supplicants; not beneficiaries or consumers.

It is a regrettable but human fact that money (and the lack of it) is linked to personal and family self-respect.   This is one element in what has been called the 'stigma of the means test'.   Another element is the historical evidence we have that separate discriminatory services for poor people have always tended to be poor quality services; read the history of the panel system under National Health Insurance; read Beveridge on workmen's compensation; Newsom on secondary modern schools; Plowden on standards of primary schools in slum areas; Townsend on Part III accommodations in 'The Last Refuge', (16) and so on. (17)

In the past, poor quality selective services for poor people were the product of a society which saw 'welfare' as a residual; as a public burden.   The primary purpose of the system and the method of discrimination was, therefore, deterrence (it was also an effective rationing device).   To this end, the most effective instrument was to induce among recipients (children as well as adults) a sense of personal fault, of personal failure, even if the benefit was

wholly or partially a compensation for disservices
inflicted by society.

THE REAL CHALLENGE IN WELFARE

Today, with this heritage, we face the positive challenge of providing selective, high quality services
for poor people over a large and complex range of welfare; of positively discriminating on a territorial,
group or 'rights' basis in favour of the poor, the
handicapped, the deprived, the coloured, the homeless,
and the social casualties of our society.   Universalism is not, by itself alone, enough: in medical care,
in wage-related social security, and in education.
This much we have learnt in the past two decades from
the facts about inequalities in the distribution of
incomes and wealth, and in our failure to close many
gaps in differential access to and effective utilization of particular branches of our social services. (18)
     If I am right, I think that Britain is beginning to
identify the dimensions of this challenge of positive,
selective discrimination - in income maintenance, in
education, in housing, in medical care and mental
health, in child welfare, and in the tolerant integration of immigrants and citizens from overseas; of
preventing especially the second generation from
becoming (and of seeing themselves as) second-class
citizens.   We are seeking ways and means, values,
methods and techniques, of positive discrimination
without the infliction, actual or imagined, of a sense
of personal failure and individual fault.
     At this point, considering the nature of the search
in all its ramifying complexities, I must now state my
general conclusion.   It is this.   The challenge that
faces us is not the choice between universalist and
selective social services.   The real challenge resides
in the question: what particular infrastructure of
universalist services is needed in order to provide a
framework of values and opportunity bases within and
around which can be developed socially acceptable
selective services aiming to discriminate positively,
with the minimum risk of stigma, in favour of those
whose needs are greatest.
     This, to me, is the fundamental challenge.   In
different ways and in particular areas it confronts
the Supplementary Benefits Commission, the Seebohm
Committee, the National Health Service, the Ministry of
Housing and Local Government, the National Committee

for Commonwealth Immigrants, the policy-making readers
of the Newsom Report and the Plowden Report on educational priority areas, the Scottish Report, 'Social
Work and the Community', and thousands of social
workers and administrators all over the country
wrestling with the problems of needs and priorities.
In all the main spheres of need, some structure of universalism is an essential pre-requisite to selective
positive discrimination; it provides a general system
of values and a sense of community; socially approved
agencies for clients, patients and consumers, and also
for the recruitment, training and deployment of staff
at all levels; it sees welfare, not as a burden, but
as complementary and as an instrument of change and,
finally, it allows positive discriminatory services to
be provided as rights for categories of people and for
classes of need in terms of priority social areas and
other impersonal classifications.

Without this infrastructure of welfare resources and
framework of values we should not, I conclude, be able
to identify and discuss the next steps in progress
towards a 'Welfare Society'.

NOTES

Lecture delivered at the British National Conference on
Social Welfare, London, April 1967, and published in
the 'Proceedings of the Conference'.

1 See for example, 'The Times', 28 July 1965, and 6
   August 1965; article by H. Heymann, Gnomes of
   Zurich with a London Address, in 'The Times', 8
   January 1966, and 'The Times', 4 April 1967
   (report by P. Jay, Economics Correspondent), and
   'The Economist', editorial Into the Wasteland, 23
   July 1966, and editorial note on 'Poverty', 22
   April 1967.
2 J. Enoch Powell, 'Medicine and Politics', London,
   Pitman, 1966, p. 72.
3 See R.M. Titmuss, 'Income Distribution and Social
   Change', London, Allen & Unwin, 1962.
4 G. Henderson, Institute for Training and Research,
   'New York Times', 6 November 1966, p. E 11.   See
   also J.A. Perkins, President of Cornell University
   and Chairman of the President's Advisory Committee
   on Foreign Assistance Programmes, 'Foreign Affairs',
   July 1966; Brinley Thomas, in The New Immigration,
   'The Annals of the American Academy of Political

and Social Science', September 1966; G. Sutherland,
'The Political Quarterly', vol. 38, no. 1, January-
March 1967; Lord Bowden, House of Lords, 'Hansard',
20 December 1966, cols 1971-80; and H.G. Grubel
and A.D. Scott, 'Journal of Political Economy',
University of Chicago, 1966, vol. 14, no. 4,
p. 231.

5 K.M. West, Foreign Interns and Residents in the
United States, 'Journal of Medical Education',
December 1965, vol. 40, pp. 1110-29.

6 'The dollar value per year of this "foreign aid" to
the United States approximately equals the total
cost of all of our medical aid, private and public,
to foreign nations'(K.M. West, ibid., p. 1127).
About three-fourths of all foreign medical trainees
in the USA are from developing countries.

7 T.C. Gibson, British Physicians on Medical School
Faculties in North America, 'Brit. Med. J.', 1967,
i, 692.

8 Israel, as well as many other countries, is affected
by the shortage of doctors in the USA. Of the 265
doctors graduating from Israeli medical schools in
1963-65, nearly 40 per cent left for the USA (statement by Minister of Health quoted in 'Haaretz',
21 March 1967).

9 K.R. Hill, Cost of Undergraduate Medical Education
in Britain, 'British Medical Journal', 1964, i,
300-2.

10 Ministry of Health and Department of Health for
Scotland, 'Report of the Committee to Consider the
Future Numbers of Medical Practitioners and the
Appropriate Intake of Medical Students', London,
HMSO, 1957.   Seven of this eleven-man Committee
were eminent members of the medical profession and
the Chairman was an ex-Minister of Health, Sir
Henry Willink.

11 In May 1962 a special committee set up by the
British Medical Association to consider recruitment
to the medical profession concluded in its report
that in spite of certain obvious indications of a
shortage of doctors it was not prepared to commit
itself on the need for more medical students ('The
Times', 11 May 1962).   Dr R.G. Gibson, chairman of
this committee (and now Chairman of the Council),
said two months later that the profession had
recently experienced a 'glut of doctors.   At
present there seemed to be a shortage, but care
must be taken not to create unemployment in the
profession a few years from now' ('Brit. Med. J.',
Supp., ii, 26, 27 July 1962).

12 B.B. Gilbert, London, Michael Joseph, 1966.
13 'The Torrey Canyon', Cmnd 3246, London, HMSO, 1967.
14 K.E. Boulding, The Boundaries of Social Policy,
    'Social Work', vol. 12, no. 1, January 1967, p. 7.
15 This study is to be published by Mr Reddin as an
    'Occasional Paper on Social Administration'.
16 P. Townsend, 'The Last Refuge', London, Routledge,
    1964.
17 See also R.M. Titmuss, 'Problems of Social Policy',
    London, HMSO, 1950.
18 See P. Townsend, 'Poverty, Socialism and Labour in
    Power', Fabian tract, 371, 1967, and R.J. Nicholson,
    The Distribution of Personal Income, 'Lloyds Bank
    Review', January 1967, p. 11.

7 Respect for persons and public morality

R. S. Downie and Elizabeth Telfer

1 PUBLIC MORALITY

In our first chapter we tried to elucidate in general
terms the view that respect for persons as ends
expresses what is fundamental to morality. In this
chapter we shall begin the more detailed defence of the
view by showing that respect for persons is the ultimate
principle presupposed in our ordinary judgments of
social morality.

The strategy of the chapter will be to begin by
suggesting the partial truth of utilitarianism as a
theory of public or social morality, and arguing that
this theory hardly makes sense at all unless we presuppose that persons are to be respected. We shall
then develop utilitarianism by showing how it can
accommodate the existence of moral rules and social
institutions. Ordinary moral judgments, however, lay
stress on the concept of equality - there is a minimum
equality of treatment which ought not to be overridden
by any degree of social utility. Hence, we need to
qualify our acceptance of the principle of utility by
making room for a second principle of equality. Equality, however, also presupposes respect for persons,
for the belief that a minimum equality of treatment is
morally required depends on the prior notion that each
person matters as an individual and so makes some
claims which cannot be overridden. Ordinary moral
judgments require us also to make room for a principle
of liberty, which is roughly to the effect that the
restrictions on a person's liberty which are morally
permissible ought to be the minimum necessary for the
maintenance of social utility and equality. The
reason why ordinary moral views lay stress on liberty,
we suggest, is that a person must have a certain elbow-

room if he is to develop in himself those attributes
which make him characteristically a person.

Our contention, then, is that an adequate theory
of social morality requires the three principles of
utility, equality and liberty, and these, we maintain,
all presuppose the principle of respect for persons as
their ultimate justification.   Alternatively, we may
say that they are all the expressions of the attitude
of *agape* in the face of the complexities of the organization of a social system.

2   UTILITARIANISM

It is one of the most generally agreed judgments of
ordinary morality that unselfishness is to be commended
and selfishness condemned.   We can therefore say that
ordinary moral judgments require us to make the ends
of others our own by helping them to get what they want.
This will include both a negative aspect - refraining
from *interfering* with their pursuit of their aims - and
a positive aspect of *co-operation*.   It also covers the
activity of helping them to avoid what they want to
avoid, which can be called by the blanket terms of
'pain', 'distress', 'frustration', 'embarrassment'.
Here again, helping people to avoid pain, distress or
the like has a positive and a negative aspect: the
negative aspect is not *causing* them pain or distress
and the positive aspect is the taking of steps to
relieve their pain or distress.   But this gives us no
clear guidance for action.   For an action may relieve
the sufferings of some while causing suffering to
others, or we may be faced with a choice between different possibilities of action each of which will bring
somebody something he wants.   We therefore need a
principle of action which would help us to decide what
to do in such situations;   and the principle which
suggests itself at once is some version of the utilitarian greatest happiness principle.   There are various
ways of stating the principle, but let us make use of
the most familiar, that of J.S. Mill: (1) 'Actions are
right in proportion as they tend to promote happiness,
wrong as they tend to promote the reverse of happiness.'

Now there is surely no point in organizing action
to maximize happiness unless we think that happiness
matters, and it is unintelligible to suppose that
happiness matters without supposing that the people
whose happiness is in question matter.   But to say
that they matter in this way is to say that they are

objects of respect.   Hence, the principle of utility
presupposes that of respect for persons.   Indeed, the
requirements of ordinary morality which (we have just
argued) give rise to the principle of utility are
precisely those for which the attitude of sympathy
provides a natural motivation (as we saw in Chapter I,
p. 24), and sympathy is an integral part of the attitude
of respect.

Instead of speaking of 'happiness' Mill could equally
well have used the language of wants and their satisfaction, and indeed would have avoided a good many
difficulties if he had done so.   We may therefore
reword Mill's formula to fit what we have said so far
about the fulfilment of others' wants, and suggest as
a guide to the requirements of the principle of respect
for persons the following rule: 'The right action is
that which fulfils the most desire' (including in
'desire' both desire to avoid things and desire to have
things, and calculating the amount of desire with
reference both to the numbers of people whose desire
is fulfilled and to the intensity with which they felt
it).

The criticisms which might be made of this formula
are almost endless, but we shall concentrate mainly on
those based on the nature of moral rules (which will
enable us to develop our theory of social morality by
bringing in the idea of institutional structure), and
on the claims of the principles of equality and liberty.

3   MORAL RULES

An objector to utilitarianism might say that although
it may be true in some contexts that we call those
actions right which make for the best consequences for
the majority, in other contexts we seem to call actions
right or wrong simply because they are or are not performed in conformity with moral rules.   Thus, when we
say, 'A promise is a promise', we have not thought
that keeping a promise will lead to the best consequences for the majority; we simply issue a reminder
that there is a moral rule that one ought to keep one's
promise.   Again, if a person has borrowed money it is
right and obligatory that he should return it simply
because there is a moral rule that debts ought to be
paid.   We do not say or think that a person ought to
pay back the money he has borrowed because this will
produce the best possible consequences for the
majority; we think he ought to pay it back because

there is a moral rule that debt-paying is obligatory.
Indeed, there may be cases where the consequences of
paying a debt will be worse for all than those of not
paying it; yet we should still say that debt-paying
is right. Suppose, for example, that a person has
borrowed £100 and that the lender intends to squander
the money in a selfish way when it is returned while
the borrower will use it in a worth-while way. The
best possible consequences for the majority would
seemingly result in this case if the money were not
returned, and yet we should still say that there is a
rule that debt-paying is obligatory and that therefore
the money ought to be returned. The objection, then,
is that our ordinary views are not precisely reflected
in the utilitarian thesis that actions are right or
wrong in so far as they produce the best possible consequences for the majority; some actions may be right
for this reason, but we regard others as right simply
because they are instances of moral rules.

It is necessary in a reply to the objection to distinguish between two possible ways of interpreting it.
The first interpretation takes the objection to be one
of fact: that, as a matter of fact, we do not always
in everyday life refer to consequences when we are
wondering whether acts are right or wrong. The second
interpretation takes the objection to be a conceptual
one: that there is a conceptual gap between the rightness of (some) actions and consequences, and a conceptual link between the rightness of (some) actions and
moral rules. The second interpretation is the one
which characterizes the deontologist's position. Let
us consider the interpretations in more detail.

The first interpretation is reminding us that we
often regard an action as right simply because it is
governed by a rule - of truth-telling, promise-keeping,
or the like - but it leaves open the question of the
connexion between rightness and consequences. Now if
the utilitarian can provide a justification for the
existence of rules it might seem that he can consistently meet the objection so interpreted.

In his attempt to provide such a justification the
utilitarian can point out that we do not as individuals
have the necessary capacities to work out the consequences of all our actions. Our experience is
limited and our knowledge and understanding are
limited and we therefore cannot always work out the
calculus of consequences for ourselves, let alone for
society as a whole. Moreover, supposing we could
calculate the effects of our actions, we do not always

have time to do so before acting; we are often obliged
to make up our minds quickly on what is right or wrong,
whereas it would take time to go into the probable
consequences of our actions.   Hence, the argument runs,
moral rules have grown up which express the accumulated
wisdom of mankind on the consequences of action.
Mill compares this function of moral rules to that of
signposts or the 'Nautical Almanack': we have signposts to guide us across country which may be unknown
to us. (2)   Again, the sailor does not need to make
his calculations at sea but goes to sea with his calculations already made for him in the 'Nautical Almanack',
and similarly, we go across the sea of life with the
consequences of our actions already calculated for us
in moral rules.   Thus, the utilitarian sees moral
rules as being rules of thumb or ready reckoners which
compensate for the deficiencies in the experience, knowledge, understanding and time of the individual person.

A utilitarian can also stress another function performed by moral rules.   The nature of this function
emerges if it is pointed out that in addition to the
deficiencies for which 'lightning calculators' can
compensate, human beings are also deficient in altruism
and therefore require the threat of coercion to
encourage them to seek majority interests rather than
their own.   The advantage of rules is that not only
do they prescribe the types of action which are conducive to majority interest, their very existence
helps to secure the compliance of most people.   The
reasons for this are, first, that habits of obedience
and the desire to conform to established custom are
deeply engrained in most forms of society, so that
people will conform to a rule simply because it is a
rule.   Second, where the rules are basic to the continued stability of a society they may be incorpora-
ted in a legal system and supported by the threat of
legal sanction, and also by the sanction of social
approval and disapproval.   Here then is another main
function of moral rules - by their very existence, and
by the legal and social sanctions which can be attached
to them, they can reinforce behaviour patterns of
proven utility.   It may therefore seem that far from
being an objection to a utilitarian view of the criterion of right action, such an interpretation of moral
rules enriches the theory and makes it more accurately
reflect our ordinary views.

But moral rules can be assimilated by the utilitarian
theory only in so far as they are regarded merely as
guides, as administrative rules to ensure that in view

of human weakness the best possible consequences for
the majority are in fact brought about.   It is
possible to argue, however, (and this is the second,
the deontological, interpretation) that such a view
of moral rules does not adequately reflect our
ordinary views about them. (3)   According to the
utilitarian interpretation, moral rules are guides -
signposts or almanacks - to help us calculate the
consequences of our actions.   But if we are ourselves
lightning calculators it would seem on this interpretation of them that we are entitled to ignore rules,
whereas our ordinary view is that we are not entitled
to be cavalier about rules.   Again, if for some
reason of flood or landslide a signpost no longer
points to the right route, we are entitled to pick our
own route; and so it would seem that if for some
reason keeping to a moral rule will no longer bring
about the best possible consequences then we may, or
perhaps should, ignore a rule such as that debts ought
to be paid.   But this, it may be argued, is precisely
not our ordinary view, which is rather that debts
ought to be paid regardless of the consequences.   We
may sum up the points of difference by saying that on
the utilitarian interpretation the rightness of actions
is necessarily connected with the production of the
best possible consequences, and only contingently connected with moral rules, whereas on the rival deontological interpretation the rightness of some actions
at least is necessarily connected with rules and only
contingently, if at all, connected with good consequences.   The objection of the deontologist - and it
seems a valid one - is that, if the existence of moral
rules admits of no justification other than the utilitarian one so far provided, we ought to have no
hesitation at all about ignoring a rule if we think
we can thereby bring about the best possible consequences; but this is simply not our ordinary attitude
towards moral rules.

In reply, the utilitarian can point to the consequences of the conceptual gap between rightness and
the production of the best possible consequences.   If
the deontologist is correct, it is theoretically ·
possible that the performance of a duty could on a
given occasion make the world a worse place than it
would have been if the duty had not been performed.
It might be argued that the very fact that a duty has
been performed must mean that some good consequences
will be brought about.   But even if we grant that the
mere fact of duty-performance is itself good, it still

may be the case that the total state of the world after
the duty-performance is worse than it would have been
if the duty had not been performed. And if this is a
consequence of the deontologist's interpretation of
moral rules his interpretation must be rejected as a
bad case of rule-worship. There are other objections
to deontology, but this is the strongest, and the one
which arises most directly from the utilitarian position. But, even if we grant that this utilitarian
criticism of deontology is valid as far as it goes,
the question still arises as to whether the utilitarian
can answer the criticism made by the deontologist.

It may be said that he can, by distinguishing two
different kinds of rules. (4)   Some rules, he may con-
tend, are, when all is said and done, only empirical
generalizations about the results of types of action.
Actions are not made right or wrong because of the
existence of these empirical generalizations forbidding
or enjoining them; rather we have the empirical generalizations because we have learned by experience that
certain types of action are liable to have consequences
which are morally bad or good. For example, 'One
ought not to pass on malicious gossip' is a rule based
on the fact that the transmission of malicious gossip
can be misleading, hurtful or injurious to a person's
reputation. It is not that any one case of malicious
gossip is wrong *because of* the rule, for in judging
the action as wrong in a given case one need not refer
to the rule at all; it is simply that the rule provides safe moral guidance if one is in doubt. Again,
it is often tiresome, irritating or hurtful to make a
joke to someone about his appearance, and consequently
one may make it a rule to avoid this line of witticism.
But such a rule merely expresses what experience
teaches; the wrongness of hurting a person's feelings
in this way does not depend on the existence of the
rule. The utilitarian can therefore recognize the
existence of rules in the form of 'wise saws and modern
instances', but the rightness or wrongness of the
actions is established independently of the rules.
Moreover, since rules of this type are only generalizations, they readily admit of exceptions - cases
where an action of a kind which normally has bad consequences will have good consequences, and *vice versa*.
When exceptions do occur we may abandon the rule without a qualm, since the rightness or wrongness of the
action does not depend on it. The utilitarian may
however add that we should be very cautious about
assuming that any particular case is an exception, and
perhaps leave a margin for error, as it were.

Other rules, however, have a different logical status.   They are not empirical generalizations about the consequences of actions;   rather they lay down the obligations inherent in some institution which is artificial in the sense that it owes its existence to rules.   This is the case, for example, with rules that one should keep promises and with rules concerning property, such as 'Do not steal' and 'Pay your debts'; there would be no such things as promises, stealing or debts if there were not rules of conduct defining them. The rightness of promise-keeping or debt-paying and the wrongness of stealing can therefore be said to depend essentially on the existence of rules, and thus to be artificial, in that it owes its existence to the institution which defines the practice.   Because of this, one can say that 'Promise-keeping is right' or 'Debt-paying is right' or 'Stealing is wrong' can all be in a sense analytic propositions: one could not explain the notion of promising, for example, without reference to the rule laying down the obligation to keep promises.   But it should be noted that it is only *within* the institution (as it were) that 'Promise-keeping is right' etc. are analytic;   there is pre-supposed a logically prior *synthetic* moral judgment that it is right that the given institution should operate.   The utilitarian argument is that the operation of such institutions as a whole may be in the general interest even although individual instances of promise-keeping and debt-paying (say) may seem to be against it.   We undermine the institution if we raise the question of interest in every case;   the rules of the institution must be applied to preserve the institution.   In this way the rules of institutions differ from empirical generalizations about the consequences of individual actions.

Now to say that the rules of institutions must be applied because they are rules sounds like an appeal to a new moral value of impartiality - 'If you keep your promise to A, you must also keep it to B'.   But in fact it is only a reminder that since we all benefit from the operation of the institution as a whole we are not justified in making exceptions to its rules simply because some bad consequences may result from keeping to them in a given instance.   Rather, since the utility of the institution depends on continued trust in its operation, *any* departure from its rules is *prima facie* wrong and to be regretted.   Here there is a contrast with empirical generalizations about conse-quences, which can be ignored without a qualm if a

person can calculate the consequences more accurately
for himself.   To say that any departure from an institutional rule is *prima facie* wrong is not to say that
exceptions are never permissible; but it is to say
that an essential element in any calculation of the
consequences of the projected exception must be the
effect that making an exception will have on the status
of the institution itself.   In other words, where the
rule is that of an institution from which we all
benefit, the consideration 'What would happen if everyone did it?' is morally relevant when an exception is
mooted.   No new moral value of impartiality is introduced simply by this consideration.   And, in fact, as
far as *moral* substance goes, rules such as 'Keep
promises' actually incorporate a certain partiality or
inequality.   The promisee or the creditor is in a
privileged position, and his claim overrides that of
others concerned.   We may say here that a man's position as promisee or as creditor gives him special
rights which must be considered in preference to the
majority interest; but that this inequality is justified in the majority interest.

The institutions of property and promise-making,
with the rights and correlative duties bound up with
these, are institutions in a rather vague and weak
sense; the rules are not necessarily written down but
are agreed upon by a kind of tacit consent.   In any
society, however, there will be many other institutions,
some of a far more formal character.   Indeed, viewed
as a system, society consists not of an aggregate of
individual persons but of a complex of institutions,
such as businesses, factories, trade unions, schools,
churches, military organizations, political and legal
institutions, welfare organizations, banks and so on.
An institution, in this sense, is a cluster of rights
and duties with some social function, although, of
course, it does not operate on its own but is operated
by individual persons, who are vested with the rights
and duties of the institution in which they operate.
As before, the exercise of specific institutional
rights or the performance of specific institutional
duties will not be directly connected with the general
welfare but obliquely so, *via* the operation of the
institution as a whole.   Thus, while it is not always
apt to ask whether a specific institutional duty promotes the general welfare it is always apt to ask
whether an entire institution, or the current form of
it, does so.

These facts about institutions explain many judgments

we make which at first sight go against the principle of
utility.   For example, we do not feel that a man is
doing wrong in confining the area of his service to
others to a small circle such as his immediate family
and friends, although it might seem that the general
interest would be better served if he did not merely
consider a privileged group.   The reason why we do
not think it wrong is now clear; a man should consider
his family in preference to others because he has
special duties to his family and they have special
rights against him; a man is justified in 'taking on'
these special duties because the institution of the
family is (we may suppose) more conducive to the general
interest than any viable alternative.   A great many of
the ordinary person's duties are institutional duties
of this kind; the scope left to him for direct consideration of the general welfare (such as by charitable
contribution of money or service) will be small.   To
say this (it must be repeated) is not to say that
institutional duties *never* admit of exceptions; such a
position would not be utilitarian and would smack
rather of the rule-worship of which we accused the
deontologist.   It is to say that exceptions to institutional duties will be very infrequent indeed, since
the connexion between the rightness of such a duty and
the best possible consequences is oblique; the good
consequences stem from the continued operation of the
system as a whole.
   We can now sum up our discussion by saying that it
is possible to state utilitarianism in a way which
does justice to our ordinary views on moral rules, provided we distinguish between empirical generalizations
about the consequences of actions and institutional
rules.   Such a distinction enables us to incorporate
the valid insights of deontology without committing us
to the conceptual gap between rightness and good consequences which was the weak point of the theory.
No crucial objection to utilitarianism can therefore
be based on a consideration of the place of moral
rules in our moral outlook.   But a crucial objection
can be based on an analysis of the concept of equality.

4   EQUALITY

So far we have suggested that rights are claims of
privilege, asserting an inequality which, if justifiable
at all, is justifiable in terms of majority interest.
But is extreme inequality morally justified if it pro-

motes the general welfare?   If this were so, it would
justify building the happiness of the majority on the
sufferings of the minority.

An example of this would be a society where there
are a few slaves in proportion to the free community,
and it seems that the majority of society will be more
prosperous under this arrangement than if the slaves
are freed.   We would, however, be likely to criticize
this society, on the grounds that it is *unjust* or
inequitable; it therefore seems that we judge such
situations not only in terms of the amount of benefit
but also in terms of the way the benefit is distributed, and may prefer a situation where it is reasonably
equally distributed to one where the total of benefit
is higher but the disparities between the best off and
the worst off are great.

Utilitarians have often quite cheerfully admitted
the need for the principle of equality, but have not
seen that this means abandoning the claim that the
principle of utility on its own can account for our
views on the rightness of actions.   Mill, for example,
in his chapter on Justice in 'Utilitarianism' (5) says
that the dictum - 'everybody to count for one, nobody
for more than one' - expresses the principle of
equality, and that it might be written under the
principle of utility as an explanatory commentary.
In a footnote he goes on: 'This implication, in the
first principle of the utilitarian scheme, of perfect
impartiality between persons, is regarded by Mr
Herbert Spencer (in his 'Social Statics') as a dis-
proof of utility to be a sufficient guide to right;
since (he says) the principle of utility presupposes
the anterior principle, that everybody has an equal
right to happiness.'   Mill, however, denies that the
impartiality to which Spencer refers involves a
second principle alongside that of utility.   Impartiality, he says, 'is not a *pre*-supposition; not a
premise needful to support the principle of utility,
but the very principle itself....   If there is any
anterior principle implied, it can be no more than
this, that the truths of arithmetic are applicable
to the valuation of happiness, as of all other measurable quantities.'   In the passage quoted Mill
seems to have missed the point Spencer was making.
Thus he says that Spencer's account of the anterior
principle to the principle of utility, that everyone
has an equal right to happiness, 'may be more correctly
described as supposing that equal amounts of happiness
are equally desirable, whether felt by the same or

different persons.'   But this latter thesis, so far
from being a mere re-wording of Spencer's, is surely
incompatible with it.   Mill's version allows the
grossest inequalities in the way the happiness is
distributed, whereas Spencer's does not.   Bentham's
dictum in itself seems to be ambiguous as between the
two possibilities;   but his general account of the
felicific calculus is clearly compatible with inequality
in distribution, and thus we may assume that his
account does not incorporate equality any more than
does Mill's thesis.

We have raised the question of equal distribution of
benefit in connexion with an institution or system of
rights and duties, but the same question can arise in
connexion with the consequences of an individual
action;   it sometimes seems that the best consequences
overall can be secured only at the price of the
suffering of a few.   Again, it seems that in judging
such situations we take account not only of the total
of benefit but also of the way in which it is distributed.   In short, we judge consequences not only by
a principle of utility but also by a principle of
equality.

The principle of equality demands that any inequality in treatment must be justifiable in some way;
the presupposition is that equal treatment is appropriate, and the onus is on him who discriminates to
justify his procedure by pointing to some difference
between the parties which affords a reasonable ground
for discrimination.   The concept of 'relevant
differences' between people (differences which do in
fact justify the discrimination being made) is thus
an important one in connexion with equality.

It is in this context that the idea of universalizability can be introduced.   There are really two
distinct notions covered by the term 'universalizability', the logical and the moral, and these notions
are employed in two distinct principles of universalizability.   The logical principle concerns rules
and reasons, and states that if a rule of action or
reason for action applies to one case, it must apply
to all similar cases.   In other words, if one is
applying a rule or acting for a reason no distinction
of treatment may be made which is not based on some
criterion of difference.   This principle simply
follows from the fact that rules and reasons are (at
least by implication) *general* in scope.   But it is of
the greatest importance in connexion with the rule-
following nature of persons.   For human beings often

justify their conduct in terms of rules and reasons;
and in so doing they are logically bound to see those
rules and reasons as justifying similar conduct by
others in similar situations. (This indeed is part
of what Kant meant when he spoke of men as legislating
for others.) This is not, of course, to say that
rules apply without exceptions, but only that differences in application logically must be on *principle* -
that is to say, they must really constitute qualifications in the original rule, rather than arbitrary
departures from it.

As an example of the logical principle of universalizability, consider a rule like 'All young men must
serve in the Army for two years'. This rule as it
stands applies to all young men. I cannot logically
hold this rule and then say that it does not apply to
some particular young man - unless I am prepared to
explain what is different about him which exempts him
(for example, poor eyesight) and thus in effect add a
qualifying clause to the rule which could exempt others
also. In other words, the rule becomes: 'All young
men except those with poor eyesight must serve in the
Army for two years'. This example shows how reasons
are universalizable too; if I say 'This young man
ought not to serve because he has poor eyesight' I am
giving a reason which would apply to all other young
men in the same situation.

The *moral* principle of universalizability is really
a statement of the presupposition that equal treatment
is appropriate. It may be expressed as follows: 'No
distinction of treatment may be made which is not
based on some *morally relevant* criterion of difference'.
It thus requires that differences of treatment be not
merely explained (as the logical principle demands)
but morally justified. For example, I would satisfy
the logical principle of universalizability if I gave
as grounds for exempting certain people from the Army
the fact that they all had blue eyes. But this fact
is of no moral relevance. If on the other hand the
criterion is something like 'being married' we can
see why such a factor might be held to *justify* discrimination, not merely explain it.

Often the kinds of difference which are held to be
morally relevant derive from the gap between equal
treatment and equal satisfaction; if people differ
sufficiently in need or capacity or situation they
will not get equal satisfaction from equal treatment.
For example, the married soldier's difference in situation means that treating him similarly to the unmarried

soldier will not produce similar results in terms of happiness.   But morally relevant differences may stem also from demands separate from equality altogether. Thus utilitarian grounds may justify a difference in treatment between some people and others, and so may grounds drawn from the principle of liberty.   We shall shortly see how this happens when we discuss education as an example of the working of the principle of equality.

Difference in treatment is held by some to be justified also by difference in *desert*. (6)   The notion of desert is the notion that how a man should be treated depends on his merits and demerits.   These may be either moral or non-moral.   Thus Aristotle, assuming that just distribution must be according to merit, suggests as possible candidates for merit free birth, noble birth, or wealth. (7)

Now opinions differ as to how far desert really creates a moral demand separate from those of utility and equality. (8)   An extreme view would be that it is desert which is the primary value and that equality is not a separate value at all but is simply a corollary of a principle of desert.   For if we have a principle that each should be treated according to his deserts, this implies that those of equal desert should be treated equally and those of unequal desert should be treated unequally, but it does not set up equality as an independent value.   This seems indeed to be Aristotle's view.

But our current moral views seem rather to assign a comparatively small part in justifying inequalities to the notion of desert.   This is especially so in the case of merits or demerits for which the possessor is not responsible, where we are apt to think that equality demands the rectifying of the imbalance rather than 'giving to him that hath'.   Exceptions to this, such as 'He's a bright boy and deserves to succeed' are often to be seen as expressions of the principle of liberty rather than of desert. (9)

The principle of equality, then, is not absolute. We do not hold that all people must be treated equally in all respects, but rather that the claim of equality must be balanced against other claims.   But at the same time we hold that there is a minimum claim of equality which *is* absolute.   There are inequalities so extreme that they cannot be justified by appeal to the general utility or to any other value.   This can be put another way by saying that each individual has rights to certain basic benefits (or at least to

freedom from certain basic evils) which must not be
infringed however far others would benefit thereby.
The degree of inequality allowable will depend partly
on whether those who come out of it badly choose or
consent to it in some sense, and also partly on
whether they (as well as the more privileged party)
will be better off than they would have been under a
more egalitarian arrangement (as may be the case for
example with the paying of high wages as an incentive
to acquire skills).

We can now see that even the moral principle of
universalizability ('No distinction of treatment may
be made which is not based on some morally relevant
criterion of difference') expresses only one aspect of
the principle of equality.   To do justice to the
demands of equality we must add another principle to
that of moral universalizability, viz 'Extreme inequalities are not permissible on any grounds'.

We shall now discuss briefly some concrete examples
of the interplay of the principles of utility and
equality.   Take first participation in government,
which for most people is equivalent to voting.

We would normally say that everyone has an equal
right to vote, and that differences such as the colour
of a man's skin could not be relevant grounds for
excluding him.   The only criterion for relevance here
is whether any fact about a man disables him from
benefiting by the exercise of the right.   This sounds
at first sight as though we could exclude people from
voting if they were sufficiently ignorant or unintel-
ligent, on the grounds that such people cannot know
what is in their interest and so the vote is of no use
to them.   But this would be a mistake.   Voting is
valuable not only for the benefits which the voter can
win for himself by exercising his vote wisely.   To
be able to vote is a benefit in itself; the right to
a say (however misguided) in matters which concern a
man is demanded by respect for persons as self-deter-
mining creatures.   One can indeed speak of a right to
make one's own mistakes, and this is one instance of
it. (10)

Education is another commodity which is good both
in itself and in the further benefits which it brings.
Here again the basic presumption is that everyone has
an equal right to education.   But educational resources, such as money, equipment and manpower, are
in practice concentrated on two groups: those who are
especially handicapped mentally or physically (and, if
the Plowden recommendations are adopted, by their

environment), and those who are especially gifted.
These two types of 'positive discrimination' (to use
Lady Plowden's expression) (11) can both be justified
by the principle of respect for persons, but in
entirely different ways.   Thus discrimination in
favour of the underprivileged is in reality an equal-
izing measure to reduce their handicap.   Unequal
treatment is needed to produce *results* which are not
too unequal.   On the other hand, discrimination in
favour of the gifted is justified partly by the fact
that they are especially capable of benefiting by
extended education and partly by utilitarian considerations.   The utilitarian justification is obvious;
this is an example of a situation where everyone, not
merely the privileged group, benefits from inequality.
The justification in terms of difference of capacity
is a more complex one and depends on an understanding
of what kind of benefit education is.   It seems to
be valuable because it contributes to a particular kind
of self-development - some would say the most important
kind.   (For a discussion of self-development see
Chapter III.)   Now one cannot speak of a right to
equal self-development through education, since this
type of self-development is not something of which
everyone is equally capable.   What we can say however
is that everyone has a right to benefit as far as he
is able from education, that equal capacities should
be treated equally.

We can now see why the public school system is
thought by some to be unjust - it gives educational
privilege to those who differ neither in need nor in
ability to benefit.   But if we consider the chief
arguments against abolishing it, we shall see the
workings of another principle which is a very important
part of respect for persons, that of liberty, or the
right to do as one wishes unless it causes harm to
others.   This principle is important enough to need
separate discussion and we shall turn to it when we
have touched on the right to a minimum standard of
living as a final example of the principle of equality.

Equality demands, not an equal standard of living
for all, but a minimum redistribution of resources
which ensures that everyone reaches a minimum standard
of living.   Greater equalization than this is ruled
out partly by utility, partly by what appears to be an
appeal to desert.   Thus we think that giving everyone
much the same standard of living whatever he does
removes all incentives to work, and also constitutes
an injustice to the industrious who 'deserve to

succeed' while the lazy man 'deserves to fail'.   Now
in saying that the lazy man deserves to fail we are
not necessarily condemning him morally.   Rather we
think that the lazy man may be deemed to have *chosen* a
lower standard of living for the sake of a quiet life,
and that if this seems to him the greater benefit we
should not introduce what is in effect an *inequality*
by allowing him to have it both ways.   But not everyone would rather be poor than hard-working.   Of
course, people can also be poor through no 'fault' of
their own but simply because they possess no talent of
high market value;   many a dustman would be a doctor
or a dancer if he could.   We still think, however,
that it is justifiable that dancers and doctors should
get more than dustmen,   partly as an incentive to them
to develop their talents, for which industry is needed,
and partly because it seems right that by and large a
man should be allowed to make what profit he can out
of his talents.   The first of these considerations
appeals to utility, the second to the principle of
liberty (which we shall discuss in the next section).

Before we sum up our argument so far let us consider
two terms which often cause confusion in this context,
namely, 'equity' and 'justice'.   'Equity' means
roughly 'treating people equally when they should be
treated equally, and differently when they should be
treated differently'.   Thus, equity is not the same
as equality, and is quite consistent both with the
view that equality has no independent claim, and with
the view that there is a minimum independent claim of
equality.   Accordingly, it is not very informative to
say that something is equitable;   it does at least
suggest however that due regard has been paid to the
desert and the claim to equality of the *individual*,
and that the issue has not been settled exclusively by
an appeal to the expedient, which is of merely utilitarian value.

'Justice' can be used in two ways.   It may refer
to a man's rights under the specific institutions of
a society, his institutional rights as we have called
them.   Or it may refer to deeper and more important
principles in the light of which both instutional
rights and the dictates of utility may be judged.
These rights are those of equality and of liberty
(which we shall discuss later).   Justice, if it is
conceived of in this more basic sense, is that which
asserts the claims of the individual against the utilitarian claims of society.   Because of this it is
easy to think of justice as embodying respect for

persons and of utility as hostile to it.   But to think
thus is to forget that the majority is made up of individuals.   As Raphael says: 'By contrasting the claim
of justice, as looking to the interests of the individual, with the claim of utility as looking to the
interests of society at large, I do not imply that
society is anything other than its members.   In our
practical deliberations, however, we often find it convenient to think of "the interests of society" as an
abstracted entity, since we may know from experience
that a course of action is likely to benefit or harm a
number of members of our society, while not knowing
which particular members will be affected on this
occasion.   The dangers of the abstraction are countered
by the concept of justice, which emphasizes the claims
of the individual as such.' (12)

We are now in a position to recapitulate the argument so far.   Our burden has been that the principle
of utility, in terms of the maximization of the satisfaction of desires, is related to ordinary moral rules
in two distinct ways: rules can either be empirical
generalizations about the best way to implement the
principle, admitting of exceptions like other generalizations, or they can lay down men's duties and rights
under some institution which can be justified as a
whole in utilitarian terms.   We compared this second
type of rule to the duties and rights of various roles
in the social system, and saw how in both cases rights
were privileges giving their possessor a claim prior
to that of utility.   We then suggested another kind
of claim which competes with and perhaps takes prece-
dence over what one might call institutional claims,
and modifies the claim of utility - namely, the claim
of equality.   This too can be expressed in the language of rights; it asserts the right of every man
to some basic necessities, however much society at
large might benefit by depriving him of them, and it
further asserts the right of everyone to equal treatment in all respects unless the inequality can be
justified by relevant differences.   This demand for a
minimum degree of equality in a system of social organization embodies the idea that each individual matters
in himself as a person quite apart from any special
features which may distinguish him.   Hence, equality,
no less than utility, presupposes the principle of
respect for persons.

5 LIBERTY

We have so far suggested by argument and example that
the principle of utility must be modified by one of
equality if we are to have an account of public morality
which reflects our ordinary moral attitudes, and that
both these principles presuppose that of respect for
persons.   We shall now suggest that ordinary moral
attitudes require us to modify the requirements of
utility yet further by making room for another principle
- that of liberty.

The principle of liberty states that it is wrong to
curb people's desires unnecessarily, to interfere without justification in people's pursuit of objectives
which are of interest to them.   This principle seems
especially germane to the principle of respect for
persons, as the word 'respect' is often used in just
this sense of 'tolerate' or 'refrain from interfering
with'.   The force of 'respect' in this sense is
brought out by the example given by the Shorter Oxford
Dictionary - that Louis respected the interests of his
Protestant subjects.   Again, in a characteristic
passage, Hare tells us that what 'distinguishes the
liberal is that he *respects* the ideals of others as he
does his own.   This does not mean that he agrees with
them - that would be logically impossible, if they are
different from his own....   In saying that the liberal
respects the ideals of others we mean that he thinks
it wrong to interfere with other people's pursuit of
their ideals just because they are different from his
own;   and that he also thinks it wrong to interfere
with their interests merely because his own ideal for-
bids their pursuit, if *their* ideals permit the pursuit
of these interests.' (13)   It is clear that the concept of respect as non-interference is being used here,
and it would be possible to quote from other influential moral philosophers to make the same point.

This notion of respect, in the sense of refraining
from interference or regard for liberty, is the
central theme of Mill's 'On Liberty', and his main
principle expresses it as follows: 'the sole end for
which mankind are warranted, individually or collec-
tively, in interfering with the liberty of action of
any of their number is self-protection.   His own good,
either physical or moral, is not a sufficient
warrant.' (14)   Now what does Mill mean by 'self-protection' here?   To answer this, we must consider what
was meant above by 'unnecessary' when we said that
unnecessary interference with the liberty of persons is

wrong, and in the course of this discussion we can show
how liberty is related to equality and utility.

We have said that the principle of liberty declares
that we ought to be free to pursue objects of interest.
But since human beings tend to clash in their pursuit
of objects of interest it is obvious that complete
liberty is self-defeating. The principle of liberty
must therefore be combined with the principle of
equality, to produce the conclusion that each person
has an equal right to pursue objects of interest; in
other words, he may act at liberty to the extent that
every other person may do likewise. Thus, when Mill
speaks of 'self-protection' he means that it is legitimate to forbid a person to perform certain actions only
if it can be shown that his performance of them will
interfere with the liberty of others.

How does the principle of liberty relate to that of
utility? At first sight the answer seems to be that
liberty as governed by equality is the same thing as
the *negative* side of utility when governed by equality.
(The negative side of utility, as was explained at the
beginning of the chapter, consists in refraining from
interference in men's pursuit of their aims and in not
causing them pain or distress.) It may therefore seem
that the principle of liberty is not an *independent*
principle but simply an expression of one aspect of
the principle of utility.

It can be shown, however, that the principle of
liberty may conflict with the *positive* aspects of
utility as governed by equality. These positive
aspects stress the importance of achieving the maximum
satisfaction of interests, and for this to be possible
some degree of social co-operation is necessary. For
instance, with a system of rules based solely on social
harmony a person could be at liberty to seek medical
help when he was ill; but it is only in a society
with rules of co-operation that his seeking of medical
help is likely to be materially effective. In other
words, to have medical benefits it is necessary to have
rules governing, say, taxation, and these cannot wholly
be justified by the conception of social harmony but
require also the concept of social co-operation to
render their existence legitimate. Now such rules of
social co-operation infringe people's liberty to do as
they want, and we do in fact regard it as at least
debatable how far individual liberty ought to be restricted in order to develop a system of co-operation
in the interests of all. It is clear that there
should be rules enforcing co-operation on matters such

as health and hygiene, but how far beyond these matters
a government or official body is justified in imposing
further restrictions is a question which raises the
issue of socialism versus *laissez-faire* individualism.
It can be argued, for example, that the formal freedom
to enter a university or to be employed is of no value.
Freedom is worth having only if it is material, and it
becomes a material freedom only when it is guaranteed
by the state.   The costs of this guarantee, however,
are the restrictions with which anyone living in a
socialist state is familiar.   The price may be worth
paying, but the point is arguable.

But what does 'worth paying' mean here?   If the
principle of liberty is simply one aspect of utilitarianism, the issue between (say) socialism and *laissez-faire*
individualism amounts to no more than the question
whether the greatest happiness is in fact achieved by
not interfering with others and thus losing the benefits
of co-operation, or by co-operating with others and
thus losing the benefits of liberty.   Now it is sometimes held that interest is maximized by a *laissez-
faire* policy (though if we consider the need to meet
the demands of equality this is perhaps an implausible
view).   But very often the point at issue is not how
interest can be maximized.   Most people would hold
that it is worth *sacrificing* some measure of the general
interest for the sake of a high degree of individual
liberty.   Thus the problem usually concerns the *degree*
to which this should be done.

We can now see why the principle of liberty cannot
in the end be identified with the negative aspect of
the principle of utility.   If it is admitted that
the claims of liberty sometimes prevail over those of
utility, then liberty, like equality, must be an independent value - one which cannot be accounted for
solely in utilitarian terms.   It remains to consider
why we put this high value on liberty for its own sake.

We have said that to stress the importance of
liberty is to stress that the area of his life in
which a person is free of the restrictions of rules
must be as large as is compatible with the existence
of a similar freedom in the lives of others.   The
most plausible explanation of this stress is that we
all recognize that freedom from external compulsion is
necessary over a certain area of a person's life if he
is to develop those attributes which make him characteristically a person.   If a certain minimum freedom
of action is violated by external compulsion then the
individual will fail to achieve the level of self-

realization which makes him a person: at first failing
to express himself in characteristically human actions
he will in the end fail even to envisage these actions
as possibilities in his imagination.   The principle of
liberty is therefore the principle of respect for
persons expressed in a context where the importance of
self-realization is being weighed against that of
achieving an harmonious and co-operative society.

It may be objected that the principle of liberty cannot be connected with that of respect for persons by
insisting on the need for the human person to grow,
because there is much evidence that this growth takes
place in communities lacking in liberty.   For example,
in Scotland at the height of Calvinism there was little
room for the expression of inclinations and ideals in
the tight system of rules and regulations imposed by
the Calvinists.   Yet during this period, it may be
argued, there was no sign of the human personality
wilting away: on the contrary, it was a period of
fierce individualism and independence in Scottish
history.   Hence, it may be said that liberty is not
essential to the development of the human person, and
consequently that the principles of liberty and respect
for persons are only contingently connected.

In reply it can be argued, to begin with, that the
restraints of Calvinism were self-imposed by the Calvinists.   They were not the restraints of a secular
state imposed from the outside, but were rather vol-
untarily adopted, and do not therefore offend against
the principle of liberty.   It was by means of the
discipline of their restraints that Calvinists believed
they were realizing what made them truly persons.
Indeed, the importance of the principle of liberty to
Calvinists is brought out if we consider how much they
resented any interference with their liberty to be
Calvinists.   It is true that Calvin tended to impose
suffocating regulations even on those who did not
accept his beliefs, and that Calvinism stultified the
artistic and cultural life of Scotland for hundreds of
years.   But this merely supports the point that enforced rules not connected with the maintenance of
social harmony and co-operation kill human personality.
Where Calvinism did lead to the growth of the human
person its restrictions were freely accepted, and so
were not felt as restrictions: but where they were
externally imposed, and felt as restrictions, they did
not lead to the development of the human person.

A fuller discussion of what is meant by self-development must be postponed till Chapter III.   There, it

will be noted, it is presented chiefly in terms of the
way in which a man should respect humanity in his own
person.   This is indeed its chief importance.   But
we do have some duties to respect others' need for
self-development and others' self-respect.   Now these
duties are mainly duties to respect another's liberty,
as we have seen.   To try to contribute to a man's
self-development in some more positive way, by preventing him from indulging in the lower pleasures and
forcing him to indulge in the higher ones, is a self-
contradictory activity, as his own processes of choice
are an important aspect of his self-development.

Two qualifications should, however, be added to
this.   When we are dealing with children we consider
it legitimate to apply a certain amount of pressure on
them to follow self-developing pursuits; for example,
we think it right to compel them to be educated.   We
make an exception of children because we think they
have not got the knowledge and experience to make any
choice worthy of the name, and also because there are
some talents which have to be cultivated young if at
all, so that the adult's ability to make a valid choice
(one with plenty of possibilities) itself depends on
early restriction of liberty.

It might here be objected that if the restriction of
a child's liberty is permissible in this way, we cannot
speak of the *self-contradictoriness* of making a man
indulge in higher activities for the sake of his self-
development, as we did in the previous paragraph.
But we may restrict the child's liberty only if this
is in the interests of his own freedom later in his
life.   Thus we must not seek to indoctrinate him in
such a way that he cannot later genuinely choose
between one activity and another.   It might also
seem that what we have said about children would
justify an over-paternalistic attitude towards childlike adults (primitive peoples for example) or even
towards the less well educated who 'don't know what's
good for them'.   But the cases of the child and of
the childlike adult are not similar.   In the child we
are endeavouring to develop the potentiality for choice
in such a way that he can eventually take over.   In
the case of the childlike adult, however, we are not
envisaging a time when he can take over, but are
managing his life for him.   And it is the span of the
individual's life which counts - we cannot speak in
terms of the childhood of a race and use this metaphor
to justify treating its adults as children.

The second qualification is that we think that a

government ought to subsidize the arts where there is not enough private patronage for them to be self-supporting.   This involves using the money of those who are indifferent to the arts, and to that extent may seem to be an imposition of standards of worth-whileness on others.   But there is a difference between imposing worthwhileness and making it possible. Money spent on the arts by the government makes worth-whileness possible for the few who desire it, and in so doing increases the range of possibilities for all, including those who are not interested.   But the sums of money involved are too small to constitute an inter-ference in the pursuit of whatever the individual chooses for himself.   The Philistine would have a case against art subsidies only if he could plausibly main-tain that his contribution restricted his area of choice rather than enlarged it.

We have said that liberty is to be valued not only for the sake of its possessor's interests, but also with a view to his self-development and self-respect. In discussing this we have partly answered a question which might be raised: how far making another's ends my own involves treating all his ends on a par.   The answer seems to be that it is not for us to prevent him from pursuing ends just because we think them unworthy. But it may be legitimate to encourage some ends more than others.   This does not, however, deal with the special case of a man's moral ends.   Ought we not to regard these with special deference?

This is a very complex issue which we do not pro-pose to investigate in detail here. (15)   It arises most sharply when a man's moral convictions prevent us from carrying out some policy which we feel to be demanded on moral grounds.   Are we justified in trying to get him to do what he believes to be wrong, by threats or bribes, for example - in other words, trying to corrupt him?   Notice that this is not simply a question of taking his ends into consideration; rather the question is which of his ends should be regarded as paramount.   And the question is not answered by declaring that a man would *rather* be bribed than overcome by force in some way.   For even if in a given case this were his choice we can still ask whether such a preference is the right one, and thus again raise the question of the relative value of different types of end.

The conclusion of this discussion of liberty, then, is that ordinary moral views require us to modify the public morality of utility to make room not only for a

principle of equality but also for one of liberty,
and that the importance we attach to these principles
in each case can be explained only if we assume that
they are expressions of the basic principle of respect
for persons.

6   FRATERNITY

We have discussed liberty and equality at some length.
What (it may be asked) of fraternity, which is so often
linked with liberty and equality?   Is there such a
thing as a separate principle of fraternity?   The
answer seems to be that there is no one thing to which
the term 'fraternity' unambiguously applies. (16)   The
best we can do is to try to distinguish various possible
meanings of the word and show how they relate to what we
have so far said.
     First of all, then, the term 'fraternity' may be
applied to the policy of co-operation in the interests
of all which, as we mentioned earlier, is apt to conflict with individual liberty.   Thus we may say that
in a communist state the principle of fraternity is
exalted at the expense of that of liberty.   Coupled
with this may be a tendency to regard the community as
an entity over and above the individuals which compose
it, so that fraternity is held to demand the sacrifice
of the individual to some abstraction such as 'the
State'. (17)
     Now this notion as it stands may be illogical, but
at the same time it reflects a real deficiency in
classical utilitarianism with its exclusive concentration on the individual.   Thus writers like Mill do
not make clear that a community is not merely an
aggregate of individuals but has an institutional
structure.   How far this omission matters depends on
whether Mill is thinking simply in terms of the whole
of humanity from now to eternity as the field of
reference from which the majority is drawn, or whether
he is thinking rather in terms of present and future
members of a particular community (the British nation?)
which needs institutional definition to explain its
continuity.   If (as is likely) he is thinking of a
particular community then his account is deficient in
not explaining what constitutes a community such as a
state.   Those who think of the state as a self-sub-
sistent entity have merely erred in the opposite
direction.
     The word 'fraternity' is also used sometimes to

suggest something different in kind from a principle of
social co-operation.   It may stand for something more
like the *spirit* in which rules should be applied.   The
force of this comes out when we consider what happens
when the letter of the law is put into practice without
its spirit and we have 'working to rule' with all that
that implies.   Even granting that 'working to rule'
often means doing somewhat less than the rule indicates,
we can still appreciate that for efficient operation of
rules a certain 'spirit' is required which is something
more than an administrative matter, even if it is less
than an ideal of creative service.   This spirit
obviously involves a certain intelligence in the operation of rules, but more significantly it involves also
a certain humanity.

The principle of fraternity so understood has to do
with the need in society for a recognition of human
fallibility in the pursuit of common social objectives.
It does not refer to a set of rules but rather to a
willingness to be of service where there are no rules
and to a manner of enacting rules which speaks of the
consciousness of a common human predicament.   Such a
spirit may be called one of 'co-operation', but co-
operation in this context must be distinguished from
the social co-operation which was equivalent to
'fraternity' in the first sense.   'Co-operation' or
'fraternity' in this second sense covers a host of
detailed concepts concerned with our response to contingencies, with the quality of our enactment of social
roles and with the manner of our adherence to and
application of rules.   For instance, fraternity in
this second sense would cover concepts such as 'neighbourliness', 'tact', 'courtesy', 'discretion', 'give
and take'.   If we use the metaphor of social machinery
we may say that fraternity in the second sense draws
our attention to the need for oil.

So far, then, we have discussed fraternity as the
principle of co-operation and as the *spirit* of give-
and-take.   A third meaning of 'fraternity' is again
different in category.   'Fraternity' suggests above
all a *motive* for action, a devotion of a kind resem-
bling that felt to brothers but extended to the members
of some community to which one belongs.   In so far as
people in a community really are imbued with a feeling
of fraternity, they will not see restraints on liberty
in the general interest as restraints - in fact they
will not *be* such, but rather ways of bringing about
what the individual wants most.   This is the feeling
which communism hopes to foster in its members.   From

motives such as these, people in a democracy choose to
spend time in the service of others; and whereas it
would be an infringement of liberty to *make* them do
so, it is an exercise of liberty if they choose to do
so.

It may be asked whether 'fraternity' is the same as
'respect' or '*agape*'. The answer to this question
depends on the sense of 'fraternity' involved.   Where
fraternity is to be interpreted as a principle of
social co-operation (our first sense) it simply amounts
to another way of regarding one aspect of the principle
of utility.   As such it cannot wholly be explained in
terms of *agape* for, as we have seen, the principle of
utility is at best an imperfect crystallization of the
attitude of *agape*.   Fraternity in the second sense is
similar to *agape* in that both concepts refer to a
quality of response to people and situations which cannot be pinned down in precise rules.   But *agape* is,
of course, a wider conception than fraternity.   Fraternity in the third sense - a motive for action within
a community - may or may not be explicable in terms of
agape.   If kinship is acknowledged only within some
restricted group (of fellow-workers or the like) it is
not the same as *agape*.   But where fraternity can be
expressed by a saying like 'The whole world is my kith
and kin' it does seem to be the same as *agape*, where
agape is regarded as a motive for action.

7   CONCLUSION

In our first chapter we investigated the attitude of
respect for persons and suggested that it would give
rise to the fundamental principles of morality, and in
this chapter we have tried to show how this works out
in detail for public or social morality.   The theory
of utilitarianism seemed at first to reflect our
ordinary moral views since it suggested a detailed pro-
gramme for 'making the ends of others one's own' in the
life of a large and complex society.   It turned out,
however, that utilitarianism on its own provided only a
distorted image of ordinary views and we had therefore
to amend it to take into account the demands of the
principles of equality and liberty.   But the importance attached to the three principles of utility,
equality and liberty can be explained only if we say
that the principle of respect for persons is assumed.
Our contention that respect for persons is the ultimate
principle of morality is therefore justified to the

extent that the ordinary judgments of social morality
presuppose it.   Fraternity turned out to be not an
independent principle but (depending on its interpretation) a principle analysable in terms of utility or
of *agape*.

NOTES

1   J.S. Mill, 'Utilitarianism', London, Collins,
Fontana Library, ed. Mary Warnock, 1962, ch. 2,
p. 257.
2   Ibid., ch. 2, p. 276.
3   For a discussion of Deontology, see D. Daiches
Raphael, 'Moral Judgement', London, Allen & Unwin,
1955, ch. 3.
4   See J. Rawls, Two Concepts of Rules, 'Philosophical
Review', 1955.
5   Mill, op. cit., ch. 5, pp. 318-20.
6   For a discussion of the concept of desert, see D.
Daiches Raphael, op. cit., pp. 67-79.   Our whole
discussion owes a great deal to the chapter on
Justice in Raphael's book (pp. 62-94).
7   Aristotle, 'Nicomachean Ethics', Book V, ch. 3.
8   Raphael, op. cit., pp. 65-6.
9   Ibid., pp. 77-9.
10   See R.S. Peters, 'Ethics and Education', London,
Allen & Unwin, 1966, p. 128.
11   'Children and Their Primary Schools' (The Plowden
Report), London, HMSO, 1967, ch. 5, esp. p. 57.
12   Raphael, op. cit., pp. 73-4.
13   R.M. Hare, 'Freedom and Reason', Oxford University
Press, 1963, p. 178.
14   J.S. Mill, 'On Liberty', London, Collins, Fontana
Library, ed. Mary Warnock, 1962, ch. 1, p. 135.
15   For a discussion of this question, see W.G.
Maclagan, How Important is Moral Goodness?,
'Mind', 1955.
16   For a discussion of the concept of fraternity, see
R.S. Peters, op. cit., pp. 215-27.
17   Ibid., p. 216.   Compare also the passage quóted
earlier (p. 54) on justice and utility from
Raphael, op. cit.

8   Liberty, equality and fraternity

David Donnison

Governments of this country are being compelled to
formulate increasingly explicit policies about prices
and incomes, about the structure and growth of our
towns, and therefore about the distribution of this
world's goods among our people.   To do so they must
decide where they stand on some very old questions.
These questions - about liberty, equality and fraternity
- were much discussed by our forbears, but are now
obscured beneath the dust of a decaying liberal faith.
I shall try to shake the dust off some of these ideas
and show how they can be brought to bear on today's
problems.   This discussion will not conjure our confusions into miraculous consensus, but it may help us
to disagree more fruitfully.

POLICIES NEEDED

The British pride themselves on going about their
politics in a practical, unemotional way: 'unflappable'
was the word they coined to honour their most successful politician of recent years - the pipe and the
umbrella their leaders' chosen symbols.   Ask them
about their fundamental social and political beliefs
and they grow embarrassed, rather as their Victorian
forbears would have been if questioned about their
sexual mores: gentlemen don't discuss such things.
But we shall have to discuss them.
    The basic, if unspoken, social and political agree-
ments which make urban, industrial society governable
may be breaking up.   Workers in every trade and profession are growing more militant than ever before, and
Governments, it is clear, can only restore order to
the economy by formulating policies about incomes and

prices which command some support.   They must help us
work out the rules which determine who gets the gravy.
Otherwise there will be no gravy, for to decline this
responsibility and 'leave it to the market' will con-
sign us to galloping inflation or to unemployment.

Debates about poverty, urban squalor, race relations
and the deprivations which afflict economically back-
ward regions pose the same distributional questions in
spatial form.   *Where* is the gravy to go - the regional
premiums and investment allowances, the new motorways,
factories and houses?   Nationalists at regional level,
squatters and demonstrators at street level, are
teaching the nation that militancy pays.   The voters
have learnt that, on some occasions at least, Government can determine people's incomes (farmers', for
example), can regulate prices (house rents, for
example) and can decide where jobs are to go (in alumi-
nium smelters, for example).   Thus, paradoxically,
Governments' only hope of avoiding daily intervention
in such matters is to formulate more explicit principles
about the distribution of income, wealth and opportunities, and to seek public support for these principles.
To have no incomes policy will mean more strikes and
more inflation; to have no planning policies will
mean more protests, less action and less development.

If we shirk these tasks we should not assume that
we shall muddle through.   The people of this country
have shown they are as capable of racial conflict and
religious hysteria as their neighbours.   Their tolerant
political traditions may be the lucky and temporary
result of a conservative and reasonably prosperous
society, not its statesmanlike cause.

THE CONVENTIONAL WISDOM

Our Victorian forbears delighted in debating great
moral issues but we are ill-equipped for the task, as
the 1970 election - possibly the dullest in our
history - only too clearly showed.   Since inequalities
persist in every corner of our society most of us
must approve, or at least tolerate, inequality.   But
it would no longer be polite to say so.   Even the
most resolute defenders of hierarchy feel compelled to
assume an egalitarian guise: they argue, for example,
that the direct grant grammar schools should be pre-
served because they 'offer a valuable opportunity to
clever boys and girls from poor or culturally deprived
homes' (1) - despite the fact that the same publication

clearly shows that poor children are almost wholly
excluded from these schools.   This prudery - for that
is what it amounts to - does their opponents no good,
for it allows advocates of equality to shirk the
clarification of their own point of view.

When rational argument is lacking, people rely on
cliques to determine their loyalties and on stereotypes
to express their views.   Since they are largely unspoken, our attitudes and assumptions about equality
are difficult to pin down clearly, but I believe two
contrasting standpoints can be identified.   To summarise is inevitably to caricature them: no one,
perhaps, would wholly assent to every proposition in
either of the sets that follow.   The first, which
might be called the standpoint of the tough-minded,
economically oriented Right, goes something like this:

1   When policies are decided for this country, top
    priority should normally be given to economic
    growth.
2   Economic growth means growth in the goods and
    services produced by private enterprise.
3   The fruits of growth should reach people in the
    form of money incomes, because it is healthier,
    both for the individual and for the country, if
    people buy what they want with their own money
    rather than getting things free through the social
    services.
4   To succour the casualties growth leaves in its
    wake there must be some redistribution of incomes.
    This is brought about through the social services
    which confer most of their benefits on poorer
    people, at the cost of taxes levied mainly on
    richer people.
5   So far as the poor are concerned, our aim must be
    to raise their living standards to an adequate
    minimum from which they should be encouraged to
    make further advances by their own efforts.
6   The growth of the social services must wait on the
    growth of the private sector of the economy, for
    it is only from the surplus generated in this
    sector that the resources for their expansion can
    be found.
7   Greater equality of incomes may be morally desir-
    able, but it tends to be economically self-defeating
    because it is apt to be inflationary (the poor
    having low marginal propensities to save) and
    because it penalises the most productive, rewards
    the idle and thus frustrates growth itself.
8   The success or failure of individuals is largely

due to their psychological inheritance, cultivated
by will and character.   It is thus impossible to
create a much more equal society than the one we
now have.

The standpoint of the tender-minded, socially
oriented Left goes somewhat as follows:

1 When policies are decided for this country, top
   priority should normally be given to the equalisation of incomes and living standards.   That should
   be achieved by raising the standards of the poorest.

2 Equality is valued for essentially moral reasons:
   the more equal we become, the more civilised and
   compassionate will be our relationships with our
   fellow citizens.

3 Poverty does not mean failure to attain a fixed
   minimum, but exclusion from the continually rising
   standards of the country's middle income groups.
   Thus the problem of poverty can only be resolved
   by movement towards equalisation of rewards.

4 The main instruments for redistribution are the
   social services (here the tender-minded broadly
   agree with the fourth point in the tough-minded
   set of propositions).

5 Economic growth, which is valuable if it enables
   the country to move towards greater equality, consists partly of the growth of the social services.

6 It is healthier, both for the individual and for
   the country, to distribute many of the basic essen-
   tials of life according to need and preferably
   without payment, rather than through the market.

7 The success or failure of individuals is largely
   due to environmental influences, many of which
   society is capable of modifying.

In real life, people do not divide as neatly as
these formulae suggest.   At least three different
dimensions of attitude are involved - from tough- to
tender-minded, from economically to socially oriented,
and from Right to Left.   A man may talk about one
problem like a tough-minded, economically oriented
Leftist, and about another like a tender-minded,
socially oriented Rightist; and how he acts on either
may be yet another matter.   Nevertheless patterns of
belief much like these go far to shape British discussion of distributional questions.   And that is alarming because most of the factual assertions in both
sets of propositions are false.

The social services do *not* confer most of their
benefits on poorer people: indeed, some of the most
expensive of them - the education and health services

for instance - were never intended to.   The taxes
which finance them are *not* levied mainly on richer
people. (2)   The social services are *not* merely
parasitic upon the private sector of the economy:
some of them furnish an important part of the national
income, some instigate growth in the private sector,
and some are an essential part of the social infrastructure required for a thriving economy.   A more
equal distribution of income and wealth does *not*
necessarily frustrate economic growth: it is in the
wealthiest and most highly industrialised countries
that the pre-tax distributions of earnings tend to be
most equal.   The same countries also tend to spend the
largest proportions of their national incomes on social
services. (3)   Greater equality does *not* necessarily
make a society more compassionate and less conflict-
ridden: it sometimes has the opposite effects. (4)
     Many of our factual assumptions about Britain's
central social problems are mistaken or ludicrously
obsolete (some were truer when the Poor Law, financed
by taxes on property owners, was this country's largest
social service - but that was before 1870).   The
moral judgments which underpin arguments about these
problems are equally shaky.   Take the central question
of equality, for example.   Since most people seem to
agree that greater equality would be a good thing
(even if unattainable in practice) they should have
no difficulty in explaining why they want more
equality.

FRATERNITY, THEREFORE EQUALITY

It is to social philosophers of the Left that we must
look for an answer to this question - and first to the
pervasive influence of Richard Tawney.   One of the
latest American books on poverty still relies wholly
upon him; 'In this book we do not argue the reasons
why inequality should be reduced.   For one, it is
difficult to be more eloquent and moving than R.H.
Tawney'. (5)   That great and Christian teacher based
his case for equality upon man's need for fellowship.
'What a community requires, as the word itself
suggests, is a common culture, because, without it, it
is not a community at all....   But a common culture
cannot be created merely by desiring it.   It rests
upon economic foundations....   It involves, in short,
a large measure of economic equality....' (6)   Twenty-
five years later Anthony Crosland went further, saying

'if we want more equality, the case for it must rest on statements largely, if not entirely, unrelated to economic welfare'. (7)   Although economic arguments - about wasted talent, for example - do appear in it, most of his chapter on 'The Case for Social Equality' is devoted to sociological, psychological and moral argument about industrial conflict, personal envy and social justice.   The very latest statement from this quarter concludes on a similar note.   Lord Balogh advocates equality because 'without greater equality in consumption, that consensus of opinion will never be reached which is needed to safeguard the steady progress of this country'. (8)

Tawney was not the first to use these arguments. They appear much earlier in discussion of another type of equality: the equality of relationships between people who live and work alongside each other in a non-deferential society.   Ebenezer Howard echoed the utopian writers of a century and more when he condemned, in 1898, 'the large cities of today' because they were not 'adapted for the expression of the fraternal spirit', and called for 'garden cities of tomorrow' which would 'silence the harsh voice of anger, and ... awaken the soft notes of brotherliness and goodwill'. (9)

No civilised person could deride human aspirations for fellowship.   Without the good Samaritan's capacity to perceive strangers as sentient, suffering human beings, we have no way of making judgments about social policies: we literally do not know what we are talking about.   Brian Abel-Smith put the matter very clearly:

> If we abandon the market-choice criterion, how do we
> decide what to spend on welfare?   All I can suggest
> is a very homely way.   Take a cross-section of
> population, show them the standards in the Welfare
> State and then ask them the following questions.
> Would you let your mother go into this home?   If
> your husband had a nervous breakdown, would you
> like him to live in this mental hospital?   Would
> you let a child of yours go into this institution ...?
> And finally, if you don't like the look of the Wel-
> fare State, now you have seen it, would you be
> prepared to pay ... more ... to have it put
> right? (10)

These are the accents of Tawney who taught a whole generation that their fellow citizens were also their neighbours, and thereby laid the foundations on which the great social reforms of the 1940s were built. But it is an altogether different matter, and a

dangerous error, to rest the case for equality on man's
need for fraternity in Tawney's sense of 'a common
culture', or to say with Crosland that 'the first argument for greater equality is that it will increase
social contentment and diminish social resentment'. (11)
Societies that grow more equal may prove to be not
more, but much less, fraternal - at least for a time.
(Something like this appears to have happened in
Ulster.)   Liberals who lose their nerve at this discovery are apt to turn against equality, and liberty
too.
      Many brands of fraternity are much less attractive
than Tawney's.   There is a cosy, conservative brand,
which seeks protection from new ideas, disturbing
people and competition of all kinds; and there is a
harsh, authoritarian brand: *Ein Reich! Ein Volk!
Ein Führer!* was a call for fraternity of a sort.   A
free world will be full of conflict: it cannot be a
fellowship of friends, ruled by love, because the
search for friends soon degenerates into the exclusion
of enemies, the suppression of conflict and, ultimately,
rule by hate.

LIBERTY, THEREFORE EQUALITY

When the arguments for them are so unconvincing it is
difficult to see how egalitarian ideals came to be so
widely accepted - but much easier to understand why so
little is done about them.   Where did they begin?
      Some have traced the origins of British egalitarian
thinking to the Levellers of Cromwellian times.   But
the Levellers' plea was for political rights, not for
economic and social rights - 'the poorest that lives,
hath as true a right to give a vote, as well as the
richest and greatest' - and they would have excluded
from the franchise all 'servants' (or employees as we
would now say) 'because they depend upon the will of
other men and should be afraid to displease'. (12)
That would have left more than half the men in Britain
without a vote.   Serious advocacy of something we
would recognise as an equal society begins much later -
with the Utilitarians.
      In essays published in 1859 and 1861 John Stuart
Mill gave us the clearest and most comprehensive statement of the Utilitarian point of view.   By then the
doctrine was already in decline, encrusted with the
qualifications that ultimately bereft liberalism of
its cutting edge.   But the vigour of the original

faith still shines through his exposition.   Shorn of
the encrustations, this is what it amounted to:

1   A government which must decade what to do should
not look for guidance to history, religion, the
ruling classes, or some mythical social contract.
It should consider the consequences of the different
courses of action open to it, and the essential
consequences to ask about are those that affect
people.

2   People should, so far as possible, be enabled to
attain their own ends, for each of us 'is the
person most interested in his own well-being ...'
and 'with respect to his own feelings and circumstances, the most ordinary man or woman has means
of knowledge immeasurably surpassing those that can
be possessed by anyone else'. (13)

3   It is not enough to abolish monopolies and arbitrary
powers, and to extend political rights and religious
toleration.   We must also protect individuals from
'the tyranny of the majority' which may be exercised
not only 'through the acts of the public authorities' but also through 'a social tyranny more
formidable than many kinds of political oppression,
since ... it leaves fewer means of escape, pene-
trating much more deeply into the details of life,
and enslaving the soul itself'. (14)

4   When the interests of different people conflict, as
they often will, we should try to follow 'Bentham's
dictum, "everybody to count for one, nobody for
more than one"', for Utilitarianism 'is a mere
form of words without rational signification,
unless one person's happiness ... is counted for
exactly as much as another's'. (15)

5   This 'equal claim of everybody to happiness ...
involves an equal claim to all the *means* of happiness ...' (16)

6   Restrictions on liberty can only be justified if
they are necessary to protect other people's
liberties.

This philosophy is regularly shot full of logical
holes in lectures to first-year students (which seldom
offer anything half so interesting in its place).   My
concern is not with its moral logic, but with the mix
of ideas it presents.   Utilitarians sought liberty,
and *therefore* equality.   Bentham, their founding
father, was confident that the trinity of liberty,
equality and industrial progress went naturally
together: 'if the laws do not oppose [equality], if
they do not maintain monopolies, if they do not restrain

trade and its exchanges, if they do not permit entails,
large properties will be seen without effort, without
revolutions, without shock, to subdivide themselves by
little and little'. (17)

In its day this philosophy moved men to poetry and
to heroism.   In his poem on 'London' William Blake
gave us the most searing indictment of the inseparable
evils of oppression, inequality and human degradation
to be found in the English language.   Shelley was more
gaily savage about the capital 'Hell is a city much
like London' (18) - but as grimly aware of the injustices suffered by 'The Men of England'.   And when, in
'Prometheus Unbound', his 'Spirit of the Hour' pro-
claims man's release from these injustices it is to a
paradise of liberty, and *therefore* equality, that he
is admitted.

   ... thrones were kingless ...
   None fawned, none trampled ...

   ... the man remains
   Sceptreless, free, uncircumscribed, but man
   Equal, unclassed, tribeless and nationless,
   Exempt from awe, worship, degree, the king
   Over himself ... (19)

The poets of revolutionary liberalism and the capit-
alist creators of the industrial revolution were not
'really on the same side':   had they been, the poets
would not so often have died young, poor and exiled.
But they were inspired by a common intellectual and
spiritual tradition - a tradition more robust than our
own.

We set out from a world in which educated, liberal
people believed that economic and social progress
could both be achieved, and could only be achieved, in
a society that was both freer and more equal.   We
have arrived in a world where guardians of the conventional wisdom assert that there are inherent and
possibly insoluble conflicts between social justice
and economic growth, and between equality and freedom.
How did it happen?   It would take two centuries of
history to answer that question, and I can only offer
a few glimpses of the story.

THE DECAY OF LIBERALISM

Britain's industrial revolution took shape at a time
when Governments were, not occasionally but *usually*,
oppressive, incompetent and corrupt.   Thus liberals

who cared about freedom, dissenters who sought religious toleration, and capitalists who needed peace, prosperity and legally enforceable contracts, could all make common cause in demanding freedom, constitutional government and an end to arbitrary power.   As dissenters and capitalists gained rights and riches they shed the libertarian language in which they had clothed their demands, like other revolutionaries before and since. And when, from the Left, there eventually emerged the countervailing drive to control the excesses and rescue the casualties of ungoverned industrialism, this drive had to take the form of a reassertion of the rights of government over unbridled, profit-motivated, private enterprise.   These demands were voiced by Marxists, who did not greatly care about freedom, and by social democrats for whom the twin objectives of equity and public ownership became inextricably linked.   As its membership cards still testify, the Labour Party's aims are: 'To secure for the workers by hand or by brain the full fruits of their industry and the most equitable distribution thereof that may be possible, upon the basis of the common ownership of the means of production, distribution and exchange....'   In countries where industrial revolutions came after the political and administrative revolutions which made government constitutional, efficient and reasonably democratic, demands for social justice and equality were never so completely identified with the extension of public ownership and the social services, or so divorced from policies for economic growth.

By the time of John Stuart Mill, liberals were already losing their nerve.   He foresaw and dreaded the descent into democracy which lay ahead, like Niagara, down the stream of history.   Such fears could only be dismissed today by those who forget the terrible things that were to happen in Germany and Russia, and all that is still happening in many countries which are struggling to make the transition to parliamentary democracy.   But these fears, understandable though they were, repeatedly blunted the cutting edge of liberal thought.   Mill's own proposals for the franchise - a shameless attempt to rig the poll in favour of high-minded, professional people like himself - were a classic example of their debilitating effects.

Our brand of parliamentary democracy has meant that major steps towards greater equality have only been taken with the blessing of that middle-of-the-road opinion on which all our Governments depend;   and that

means during or immediately after major wars. These
wartime associations may explain why egalitarians
generally tend to carry with them a slight whiff of
rationing, puritanism and worse - all the things
Orwell so brilliantly evoked in '1984'. Thus the
pursuit of equality - once heralded by a trumpet blast
from the Spirit of the Hour - has been degraded into
a dreary matter of butter rationing, utility furniture
and municipal restaurants.

All sorts of less subtle corruptions have followed.
People calling themselves 'social-liberals' say they
'would resolutely oppose all social levelling and uniformity' (20) - thereby implying that equality and
uniformity are the same thing. Others have said there
must inevitably be a conflict between equality and
freedom. There are indeed cases - typically rather
trivial ones - where equality does amount to uniformity
and does eliminate freedom. If all schoolboys are to
be 'equally' dressed they must wear the prescribed
uniform and no other. In more important cases a
self-respecting independence, born of equality in human
relationships, is the essential basis both for freedom
and for variety. It is the social pressures imposed
by the hierarchies of an unequal society that restrict
freedom and variety, fastening William Blake's 'mind-
forg'd manacles' upon us.

For many purposes, the aim of 'equality of opportunity' has been substituted for equality. Most people
can spot inequalities readily enough when they see
them; but it is far harder to be sure whether we have
equality of opportunity - and if we do have it, the
comforting conclusion can be drawn that all remaining
inequalities must be the fault of those who fail to
seize their opportunities.

The old-fashioned demand for greater equality *of*
incomes, education, housing conditions and the like
has in many quarters given way to demands for greater
equality *for* negroes, women, Catholics and other
deprived groups. The new version often sounds
fiercer, but its implications are nowhere near so
radical. It suggests that negroes, women and
Catholics should be satisfied (as indeed some of their
leaders will be) when they secure their fair share of
positions among the bosses. We may applaud or join
such campaigns, but we should not delude ourselves
into thinking they are egalitarian. The rich and
powerful may eventually be recruited from slightly
different sources, but if the sources are good they
may be all the better equipped to maintain their
privileges thereafter. (21)

A REFORMULATION

The philosophical and practical difficulties of distri-
buting policies have baffled scholars and statesmen for
a very long time.   Properly speaking, they are not
problems (to which solutions can be found), they are
dilemmas (to which a more or less creative response can
be made).   But we would avoid the sillier muddles if
the egalitarian ideal could be extricated from the
debris of decayed liberalism and reconnected to the
ideas from which it originally sprang.

To formulate a new social philosophy, or rather to
reformulate an old one, calls for thorough analysis of
the economic and social systems to which it must be
applied, and the political institutions through which
it must be put into practice.   That is not a task to
be tackled from the armchair, or completed in a few
pages.   But after writing so unkindly about other
versions I should try to outline a better ideology than
those with which this essay began, and suggest directions in which it may lead us.

1   When policies are decided for this country, top
    priority should normally be given to the extension
    of liberty, particularly among the underdogs -
    those whose lives are most severely stunted by
    economic, social and political constraints.

This starting point commits us heavily to trusting
in people's capacity to choose better for themselves
than anyone else could choose for them (a faith that
will naturally be bitterly disappointed from time to
time).   It precludes the construction of utopias
because the future character of society cannot be
precisely forecast or planned: people will use their
freedom in unpredictable ways.   It is based on confidence that we can solve the practical problems which
arise when freedom produces chaos (such as the conges-
tion and pollution caused by the unforeseen growth of
motor transport) as it sometimes will.

2   To be freer, a society must be less deferential
    and less constrained by social hierarchies.   That
    means its distributions of status, living stan-
    dards and command over resources must become more
    equal.

An English-speaking country which may enter the
Common Market offers its people exceptional and growing
opportunities for migration.   Until we have international policies for incomes, our scope for modifying
the distribution of earnings will therefore be limited.
The scope for change will be greatest among groups

suffering (or gaining) from discrimination that owes
little to market forces - among some groups of women
and some racial minorities, for example.   But there
is greater scope for redistribution of wealth through
the fiscal system, and for redistribution of income
through family allowances and other social security
payments which could be much more effective instruments
for this purpose than they have yet become.   No one
can say such policies must fail, for they have not yet
been tried.   Until now, as a United Nations study
shows, 'incomes policies have been seen as one among
several possible instruments for countering the forces
of inflation, rather than as policies directly concerned with improving the distribution of income'. (22)
    We must take more trouble to ensure that social
services offered in kind reach everyone in a form that
really enables the deprived to seize the opportunities
they purport to offer.   Otherwise they will reinforce
the economic and social handicaps from which the under-
dogs already suffer - as has happened in education.
Recent research strongly suggests that early selection
and specialisation in our schools handicap the deprived
without benefiting the privileged. (23)   Other social
services may have similar tendencies to exclude those
who most need their help. (24)   But we must learn
far more about our society and the way it works before
the social services can be made into the liberating
and opportunity-extending instruments they could
become. (25)
3 We should ensure, wherever possible, that our towns
   grow in ways that make it easier, not harder, for
   people to seize new opportunities, and to encounter
   others of different ages, races, classes and
   incomes.
    We should not assume, with Ebenezer Howard, that
this will 'awaken the soft notes of brotherliness and
goodwill', or be discouraged if it does not.   Fraternity is desirable, but liberty is more important
still.   And where do people feel most free to experiment, to try new ways of doing things, and to be themselves: where are children most likely to take their
education further than their parents did: to take
jobs their parents would never have contemplated, to
work and save to buy better homes, and help their own
children get an even better start in life?   In
places where people are divided into rich and poor,
perched at the top and bottom of the ladders of opportunity, with no rungs between them (as in parts of
Kensington); in places where everyone stands on much

the same rungs of the ladder and an upward or downward
step compels people to break with family, friends and
neighbours (as in some of the Glasgow Council estates
and the plusher Surrey suburbs); or in places where
the steps to higher rungs in the labour market, the
income distribution, the housing market and the education system are all within easier reach (in Camden
perhaps, or in parts of Coventry and Reading)?

These questions are too complex to be answered con-
clusively: the springs of human aspiration and achievement run too deep and diverse to be described in simple
generalisations.   (Before we are tempted to vulgar
environmental determinism we should recall the fountain
of talent which has flowed from some of the one-class,
one-industry valleys of South Wales.)   But there is a
growing volume of evidence to show that aspiration,
attainment and mobility tend to be higher - liberty,
that is, becomes a reality - in mixed and pluralistic
societies where people are not segregated wholly amongst
their own kind. (26)

The economic and social influences working upon us
tend to have a mutually reinforcing character.   In
future the planners must ensure that vicious spirals
grow virtuous.   We should ask not merely whether the
slums are being cleared or whether schoolchildren grow
healthier - separate questions about different aspects
of life, directed to different public services.   We
should be asking whether the location and distribution
of housing ensure that the most deprived children
attend schools where there are good teachers, *and*
sufficient numbers of able and ambitious children to
make high attainment a feasible and respectable aspiration; *and* whether the opportunities for work and
leisure open to pupils from these schools are of a
kind to encourage high attainment; *and* whether public
transport and the location of housing and industry
give everyone access to these opportunities; *and*
whether family allowances, rate rebates, housing subsidies and other systems of income redistribution work
in ways that extend the aspirations of the deprived,
rather than restricting them; ... and much else
besides.   These demands will make the planners' task
more comprehensive, and much more difficult.

4   Liberty will not have been effectively extended
unless it provokes new demands and unlocks new
talents for meeting them.   For the extension of
freedom, the promotion of innovation, and economic
and social progress are all part of the same
process.

Our habit of divorcing economic from social progress,
and treating the latter as parasitic upon the former,
has made us more concerned about production than about
innovation, and more concerned about restraining inflation than about encouraging new and potentially
creative demands.   And that is very bad economics.
Jane Jacobs, (27) although she repeatedly underrates
the contribution of planners and the public services,
shows clearly that economics and sociology are only
different languages for discussing the same processes:
the brassiere was invented and mass produced, not in
countries where feminine crafts were most advanced, but
where women had high status, readier access to credit,
bigger incomes and greater self-confidence - on the
eastern seaboard of the United States.   We know from
our own experience that fifteen years after teenagers
secured (during the war) a bigger increase in incomes
than anyone else, we experienced a boom in young
people's music, consumer goods and tourism which was
largely created by young people themselves, both as
producers and as consumers.   (Imagine the opportunities
for innovation, growth and exports that a redistribution in favour of old people might one day create - in
new forms of housing? heating systems? holidays?
hearing aids ...?)
    If equality, freedom and economic growth tend to
go together, so do inequality, restraint and stagna-
tion.   But the British do not readily think in these
socio-economic terms.   When presented with a Report
proposing reforms of the public schools, they embarked
on an emotional orgy of dispute about class distinction,
fagging, flogging ... never pausing amidst the welter
of irrelevancies to note that a system which gave the
old boys of six schools two-thirds of the seats in the
cabinet and more than two-fifths of the directorships
of our most prominent firms is a singularly inefficient
way of choosing elites.   Not surprisingly, they proved
incapable of doing anything about the problem.   Jeremy
Bentham must have turned in his grave.
  5 Eventually it should be possible to sustain the
    process by which policies for the equalisation of
    income, wealth and living standards extend freedom
    and promote innovation and development which
    ensure the continuing economic growth that makes
    further progress towards equality possible.
    At the moment our wheels are firmly stuck in ruts
that lead in the opposite direction: slow growth,
repeatedly interrupted by economic set-backs, prohibits
movement towards equality which would be inflationary

in the short run.   Hence we preserve a divided and
deferential society, talent is wasted, innovation is
difficult, and the economy stagnates.

More would have to be said to explain this philosophy
properly, and far more must be learnt about the way our
society works before we can decide how much faith to
put in it.   Even then, many will reject it - and reject
it with greater conviction the sounder its assumptions
prove to be.   They do not want to turn the economy
round.   They fear that a society which grows too free,
too equal or too rich will become coarsened, congested
and quarrelsome.   And they may be right.   Freedom and
growth bring unforeseeable changes, and every change is
a kind of bereavement.   Their point of view is a respectable one which deserves to be more frankly stated.
It would provoke more productive argument about more
important problems than this country's political
debates customarily deal with.

NOTES

1 Second Report of the Public Schools Commission,
   'Points of Disagreement', London, HMSO, 1970, vol.
   1, p. 120.
2 See The Incidence of Taxes and Social Service Benefits in 1965 and 1966, 'Economic Trends', no. 172,
   February 1968, HMSO, which suggests that all forms
   of tax together take remarkably similar proportions
   of the income of rich and poor.   Alan Peacock and
   Robin Shannon (The Welfare State and the Redistribution of Income, 'Westminster Bank Review',
   August 1968) argue that the evidence does not
   justify so simple a conclusion, but give no support
   to the conventional assumptions outlined above.
3 See Harold Lydall, 'The Structure of Earnings',
   Oxford University Press, 1968; and J. Frederic
   Dewhurst et al., 'Europe's Needs and Resources',
   London, Macmillan, 1961.
4 See W.G. Runciman, 'Relative Deprivation and Social
   Justice', London, Routledge & Kegan Paul, 1966.
5 S.M. Miller and Pamela Roby, 'The Future of Inequality', New York, Basic Books, 1970, p. vii.
6 'Equality', London, Allen & Unwin, 1931, p. 41.
7 'The Future of Socialism', London, Jonathan Cape,
   1956, p. 190.
8 Thomas Balogh, 'Labour and Inflation', London,
   Fabian Tract No. 403, p. 61.
9 'Garden Cities of Tomorrow', London, Faber, 1965,
   pp. 146 and 150.

10 Whose Welfare State? in 'Conviction', ed. Norman
    MacKenzie, London, MacGibbon & Kee, 1958, p. 68.
11 'The Future of Socialism', p. 205.
12 See C.B. Macpherson, 'The Political Theory of Pos-
    sessive Individualism, Hobbes to Locke', Oxford
    University Press, 1962, chap. III.
13 'On Liberty', London, Dent, Everyman edition, p.
    133.
14 Ibid., p. 68.
15 Ibid., p. 68.
16 'Utilitarianism', Everyman edition, p. 58; my
    italics. People's happiness, Mill says, must be
    'supposed equal in degree (with the proper allowance
    made for kind)' - a qualification which led him to
    emasculate Bentham's original doctrine. Their
    equal claims to the means of happiness were like-
    wise subject to limits, but 'those limits ought to
    be strictly construed'.
17 Bentham, Principles of the Civil Code, 'Works',
    1843, vol. i, ch. xii; quoted in 'Equality', p.
    133.
18 'Peter Bell the Third', Part the Third.
19 'Prometheus Unbound', Act II, lines 131 and 193.
20 Ralf Dahrendorf, 'Essays in the Theory of Society',
    London, Routledge & Kegan Paul, 1968, p. 214.
21 For a revealing and far more thorough treatment of
    the language of egalitarian debate, see Brian
    Barry, 'Political Argument', London, Routledge &
    Kegan Paul, 1965.
22 UN Economic Commission for Europe, 'Incomes in Post-
    war Europe: A Study of Policies, Growth and Dis-
    tribution', Geneva, 1967, ch. 1, p. 1.
23 For a cross-national study of these questions see
    Torsten Husén, ed., 'International Study of Achieve-
    ments in Mathematics', New York, Wiley, 1967.   For
    a more detailed study of the workings of the
    British system see T. Christie and A. Griffin, The
    Examination Achievements of Highly Selective
    Schools, 'Educational Research', vol. 12, no. 3,
    June 1970.
24 But see Martin Rein (Social Class and the Health
    Service, 'New Society', 20 November 1969) who shows
    that the poor probably get more medical care than
    the rich under a nationwide, free health service.
    The unanswered question is whether this advantage
    matches their, presumably greater, medical needs.
25 Although the positive discrimination recommended in
    the Plowden Report ('Children and their Primary
    Schools', London, HMSO, 1967) for schools in the

most deprived areas would make a start in this
direction, the Plowden Committee frankly recognised
that it knew very little about the criteria and
methods for such policies.

26   For a discussion of some of this evidence and an
important new contribution to it, see B.T. Robson,
'Urban Analysis: A Study of City Structure',
Cambridge University Press, 1969.

27   See 'The Economy of Cities', London, Jonathan Cape,
1970.

9   Who is my stranger?

R. M. Titmuss

1

In this chapter we return to the theme of 'the gift'.
In an earlier one (Chapter 5), setting out a typology
of donors, we drew attention to the similarities and
dissimilarities between the blood gift in modern
societies and forms and manifestations of giving and
gift-exchange in primitive societies. The social and
economic aspects of gift-exchange as a universal phenomenon offer material, as Lévi-Strauss has said, for
'inexhaustible sociological reflection'. No one has
done more to provoke such reflection than Lévi-Strauss
himself, especially in his book 'The Elementary
Structures of Kinship'. (1)

Both Lévi-Strauss and Mauss, in analysing materials
from an immense range of culturally diverse societies,
are tempted from time to time to speculate about the
relevance of the rules and functions of giving in
such societies to present-day institutions in the
West. Mauss was eventually led to see modern forms
of social security, expressing 'solicitude or co-
operation', as a renaissance of 'the theme of the
gift'. Had he been born later he might well have
explored comparatively the concept of socialized medical care as exemplified by Britain's National Health
Service or the principles underlying systems of voluntary blood donorship. When he was in his seventies,
blood transfusion services were in their infancy;
today, they are practically universal and world demand
for blood is estimated to be growing at a much faster
rate than adult population growth, economic growth and
other physical indicators. (2) What seemingly lags
far behind this imperative demand from medical science
in most countries - and especially in the United States

and Japan - is the rate of 'social growth' in the form
of adequate numbers of voluntary donors.   This refusal
to give without immediate reward could be interpreted -
if translated into the context of the primitive societies
studied by Mauss - as a 'refusal of friendship and
intercourse'.

Lévi-Strauss had comparative pictures also in mind in
deploying examples of gift transactions in the West.

In North American society, which often seems to seek
the reintegration into modern society of the very
general attitudes and procedures of primitive cul-
tures, these occasions (festivals) assume quite
exceptional proportions.   The exchange of gifts at
Christmas, for a month each year, practised by all
social classes with a sort of sacred ardour, is
nothing other than a gigantic *potlatch*, implicating
millions of individuals, and at the end of which
many family budgets are faced with lasting disequil-
ibrium ... even in our own society the destruction
of wealth is a way to gain prestige. (3)

These and other examples drawn from both complex and
traditional societies indicate that the personal gift
and counter-gift, in which givers and receivers are
known to each other, and personally communicate with
each other, is characterized by a great variety of
sentiments and purposes.   At one end of the spectrum,
economic purposes may be dominant as in some forms of
first-gifts which aim to achieve a material gain or to
enhance prestige or to bring about material gain in
the future.   At the other end are those gifts whose
purposes are predominantly social and moral in that as
'total social facts' they aim to serve friendly relationships, affection and harmony between known individuals and social groups.

Within all such gift transactions of a personal
face-to-face nature lie embedded some elements of moral
enforcement or bond.   To give is to receive - to compel some return or create some obligation - either in
the form of a similar or different material gift or in
the overt expression of sentiment, pleasure or pain,
manifested in physical acts of behaviour on the part of
the recipient.   No such gift is or can be utterly
detached, disinterested or impersonal.   Each carries
messages and motives in its own language.

Both Lévi-Strauss and Mauss - and other anthropologists - have sought to show that exchange in primitive
societies consists not so much in economic transactions
as in reciprocal gifts, that these reciprocal gifts
have a far more important function in these societies

than in our own, and that this primitive form of
exchange is not merely nor essentially of an economic
nature but is what Mauss called 'a total social fact',
that is, an event which has significance that is at
once social and religious, magic and economic, utilitarian and sentimental, jural and moral. Dalton concluded from a survey of the literature that economic
theory, developed to analyse the structures, processes
and problems of market-organized industrialism, was
not relevant to primitive economies. (4)

Tönnies in his classic study of European societies,
'Gemeinschaft und Gesellschaft' (strangely neglected by
the French anthropologists) developed what he called the
'Fellowship Type' in Gemeinschaft-like relationships.
Gift-exchanges in such community oriented societies
were, he argued, essentially mutual depending on equality of knowledge or volition in performance. By contrast, Gesellschaft-like relationships (in which
economic man was dominant) were governed by the principle, *Do, ut des* (I give, so that you will give).
'What I do for you, I do only as a means to effect
your simultaneous, previous or later service for me.
Actually and really I want and desire only this.   To
get something from you is my end; my service is the
means thereto, which I naturally contribute unwillingly.' (5)   Strong elements of compulsion,
dominated this type of gift relationship which,
according to Tönnies, often had as its purpose a desire
for status, power or material gain.

But in our societies, argued Lévi-Strauss, the proportion of goods transferred according to the gift-
exchange modalities of primitive societies is 'very
small in comparison with those involved in commerce
and merchandising.   Reciprocal gifts are diverting
survivals which engage the curiosity of the anti-
quarian ...'. (6)   The examples he gives - whether
they are regarded as 'survivals' or not - relate to
physical objects all of which have utility;   they are
bought and sold in the market.   They involve the
use of money which could have been put to other purposes and which might have been more (or less) profitable to the giver.   Other writers, like Schwartz and
Veblen, discuss the psychology of the gift in the context of economic commodities being used as vehicles and
instruments for realities of another order.   Thus,
such gifts presuppose some element of calculating
'economizing' behaviour.   In so far as these forms of
gift-exchange in modern societies are partly or mainly
economic in form or intent then it could follow that

certain kinds of action or behaviour often regarded as primarily social might be considered to be primarily economic in intent.   Like Blau, this would lead us to apply the principles of marginal utility analysis from economics to exchange in social life. (7)

Whatever the general validity of these theories concerning gift-exchange relationships of a Gesellschaft-like type they entirely neglect large areas of gift actions and behaviour in both personal and impersonal contexts which do not involve physical objects, which are difficult or impossible to price and quantify in economic terms, and which, while involving an act of giving, carry no explicit right, expectation or moral enforcement of a return gift.   If it were possible to apply to such actions the metaphysical concept of utility it would be found that they are not processes, relationships or things which generally people want to acquire, possess or buy.   They have no exchange value.

Yet, as we have argued in this study, social gifts and actions carrying no explicit or implicit individual right to a return gift or action are forms of 'creative altruism' (in Sorokin's words). (8)   They are creative in the sense that the self is realized with the help of anonymous others; they allow the biological need to help to express itself.   Manifestations of altruism in this sense may of course be thought of as self-love. But they may also be thought of as giving life, or prolonging life or enriching life for anonymous others. That they may, incidentally, create economic wealth by sustaining life is subsidiary in conception, conduct and objective.

We speak here, of course, of those areas of personal behaviour and relationships which lie outside the reciprocal rights and obligations of family and kinship in modern society.   We are thus chiefly concerned - as much of social policy is - with 'stranger' relationships, with processes, institutions and structures which encourage or discourage the intensity and extensiveness of anonymous helpfulness in society; with 'ultra obligations' which derive from our own characters and are not contractual in nature. (9)   In the ultimate analysis it is these concerns and their expression which distinguish social policy from economic policy or, as Kenneth Boulding put it, '... social policy is that which is centred in those institutions that create integration and discourage alienation'. (10)

2

In an earlier chapter we pointed out that the gift of blood had certain attributes which distinguished it from many other forms of gift and in a series of propositions we described these attributes. Most if not all of them are not to be found in any total sense in the forms of gift-exchange analysed by Lévi-Strauss, Schwartz, Blau and others which, interpreted structurally, lead to the elaboration of marginal utility models. Such models or theories of market exchange are, we suggest, irrelevant to an understanding of the place of blood in modern systems of medical care.

As we have explained earlier, in reflecting on the nature of medical care and its associated social and psychological elements we were eventually forced, by a process of logical inevitability, to more concrete generalizations and to ask whether the blood transfusion services and the use and distribution of human blood should be treated as a market consumption good. From an affirmative answer much could flow; the implications could extend to affect our thinking over wide areas of social policy and what are conventionally called 'the social services'. Hospitals, nursing homes, clinical laboratories, schools, universities and even, perhaps, churches would no longer be protected by laws or common conventions of 'charitable' immunity; they would be exposed to the forces of economic calculation and to the laws of the marketplace.

Blood transfusion services were selected as material for a case study on a comparative basis to illumine the problems of social policy in general and medical care in particular. The reasons for this selection were explained in Chapter 1. But other areas of gift-relationships in modern society might have been chosen for detailed examination from a large and expanding social policy territory of stranger relationships and transactions of a non-economic character. Some indications of this territory, actual and potential, of a 'caring community' in Britain were given in the Seebohm Report: 'This new department (of social service) will, we believe, ... enable the greatest possible number of individuals to act reciprocally, giving and receiving service for the well-being of the whole community'. (11)

We could, for example, have taken for study the giving role of the patient as 'teaching material', and as research material for experimentation and the testing of new drugs and other diagnostic and therapeutic measures. Millions of people in Western societies

every year are expected to give themselves, without
price or a contractural reward, in these situations.
Moreover, measured in terms of time and numbers, the
demand is increasing.   To qualify as a doctor in
Britain, it is probable that the average medical
student now needs access to or contact with in one
form or another some 300 different patients.   This
contribution from patients to the training of a professional élite will be substantially higher when the
recommendations of the Royal Commission are fully
implemented. (12)   They are no longer 'charity'
patients and could not in the 1970s, whatever the
future of the National Health Service, be treated as
such.   Should their contribution to medical education,
therefore, be paid on market criteria?

At present, patients as strangers are asked or
expected to behave as givers on the unspoken assumption
that they may benefit;   sometimes their consent is
sought;   sometimes they are simply informed;   often
nothing is said. (13)   Their willingness to be 'taught
on' and to give of themselves, physically and psychologically, is presumed.   It is taken for granted in
the name of research, the advancement of medical
science, society's need for doctors, the better
training and more rapid progression of doctors professionally and financially and, ultimately, for the good
of all patients irrespective of race, religion, colour
or territory.

Gift transactions of this type between strangers -
at present unpriced in non-market situations - are by
no means unilateral transfers.   Patients may benefit
immediately more from contact with medical students
than with consultants.   Doctors in teaching roles
give more to patients than a strict definition of their
duties may warrant.   But the benefits of teaching,
experimentation and research - often inextricably
mixed up - mostly accrue in the long run.   They are
not immediately a 'return gift' to the individual
patient.   While there may be 'fall-out' benefits they
are not at once obvious to the patient.   Among medical
students, doctors ascending career ladders, research
workers and scientists, however, the connections are
more obvious and more personal.   As individuals they
expect to benefit in the short run from these gift
transactions.   The benefits to patients mostly accrue
in the long-run;   they further the well-being of some
future collectivity of patients.   If old age pensioners
with chronic bronchitis put to themselves the Hobbesian
question - why should men do other than act to their

own immediate advantage? - they might start charging
for the gifts they make which are more likely to benefit
future cohorts of chronic bronchitics.

All personal service professions in an increasingly
professionalized world are becoming - like medicine -
more dependent on other people to further their professional aspirations.   Sociologists need co-operative
field and control material; psychologists need laboratory volunteers; psychiatric students need the
mentally ill; social workers-to-be need clients;
various professional groups within and without the
pharmaceutical industry need healthy volunteers as well
as diseased patients for drug trials; student teachers
need pupils, and so on.

Considered individually as examples of stranger
relationships, more people are expected to contribute -
to give - to serve the interests of other people.
There is in all these transactions an unspoken assumption of some form of gift-reciprocity; that those who
give as members of a society to strangers will themselves (or their families) eventually benefit as members
of that society.   More often than not, however, such
donors are in captive situations; the transaction cannot, therefore, be considered to be spontaneously
altruistic in its most attainable form.   There is,
nevertheless, a vague and general presumption of a
return gift at some future date, but a gift that may
not be deliberately sought or desired by the individual
concerned - as with voluntary blood donors.   Few people
when well wish to be ill; few people desire operations,
blood transfusions, inpatient treatment or social care
from social workers.   More and more instruments of
social policy are in action requiring, as scientific
knowledge advances *pari passu* with professionalization,
these acts of 'voluntaryism' which carry with them no
wish for return acts or return gifts.

This is but one brief illustration of a number of
social policy areas in which gift transactions take
place and which might have been developed at length as
case studies in this book.   Another unexplored area of
a different type - though also containing elements of
altruism and self-interest - relates to the institution
of foster care.   At present we know little about the
attitudes and motivations of foster parents and about
who gives and who receives in systems of child care
outside the family.   It would seem that foster care is
in Britain an essentially working-class institution. (14)
Why do not the middle classes participate to the same
extent?   Is this another area of unquantified redistri-

bution because foster parents though receiving payment
are not rewarded on market criteria?   Or because - as
Sir Denis Robertson once said - love is a 'scarce
resource'? (15)   In the interests of society as a
whole this resource is needed if the children concerned
(as well as society) are not to suffer harm immediately
and in the future.   In this area also we might have
raised questions about foster parents and the gift of
foster care of a similar nature to the questions asked
about the characteristics and motives of blood donors.

Or, to take one other example, we might have explored
the gift transactions of Regional Eye Banks under the
National Health Service in the prevention and reduction
of blindness.   At one such bank, the South Eastern
Regional Eye Bank, 448 eyes were donated in 1965 - a
number that had been steadily rising. (16)   Because
the supply of donated eyes is much less in other
countries without a National Health Service than it is
in Britain, 73 of these 448 corneas were exported as
free gifts to India, Jamaica, South Africa, Singapore,
Turkey, Hong Kong and other countries. (17)   Should
human eyes, bequeathed by donors or given by relatives
to unknown strangers, be treated as a consumption good
and sold to the highest bidders?   These are not just
idle theoretical questions as experience in the United
States and other countries has shown in recent years in
the expanding area of organ transplantation. (18)

3

'Modern social welfare' wrote Wilensky and Lebeaux, 'has
really to be thought of as help given to the stranger
not to the person who by reason of personal bond commands
it without asking.   It assumes a degree of social distance between helped and helper'. (19)   The degree will
vary from the social distance separating the patient
from medical students engaged in examining, feeling and
questioning to that of blood donors who do not know and
can never see the recipient of the gift.

The givers in these relationships - whether captive
or altruistically voluntary - may themselves be harmed
by the act of giving.   Blood donors can be harmed - in
rare cases mortally - by giving.   Patients can be
harmed, physically and psychologically, by giving themselves, willingly or unwillingly, knowingly or unknow-
ingly, as teaching material.   So can pupils, clients,
foster parents and many other categories of people in a
variety of 'giving' social policy situations.   There

are risks to the giver as well as to the receiver in these social gift transactions.

Welfare propositions in economic theory rest to a large extent on an often unexpressed ethical proposition - the 'Paretian optimum'. Any change is for the better as long as nobody is worse off and at least one person is better off, each in his own estimation. But in the whole area of social gift-relationships this proposition is inapplicable. Givers are in no position themselves to evaluate gains and losses to themselves or to others. Professional arbiters decide but they, in turn, can seldom estimate as individuals the gains and losses for either the givers or the recipients. Their interventions are transitory and episodic; they seldom know the ultimate outcome. Those economic theorists who in assuming God-like mantles apply the Paretian optimum to increasing areas of social transactions have been blinded by their own calculus. In their blinkered pursuit of economic arithmetic they and those who follow them endanger society's unmethodical knowledge of the living man.

While physicists have increasingly been yielding theoretical territory many economists have been claiming more. In a remarkable book 'The World View of Physics', first published in English in 1952 Von Weizsäcker had this to say:

Yielding step by step to the pressure of new data, scientists have given up more and more completely the presupposition that classical mechanics or a theory modelled on it is valid for the whole of nature. Instead the attempt is made to develop an independent theory of the phenomena not apprehended by classical mechanics and, conversely, to understand classical mechanics as a 'limiting case' of the new theory, i.e. as the result of its application to a definite, restricted field of inquiry. (20)

Ethical considerations are, as we said earlier, also endangered when scientific, technological and economic considerations are uppermost. Concrete illustrations of this danger - particularly to captive donors - are increasingly being provided by those engaged in the world of medical science. (21) One example was given in earlier chapters of the use of plasmapheresis techniques by the pharmaceutical industry in the United States. Many others could be drawn - if this were a full-length survey - from what the 'British Medical Journal' described in 1963 as the 'alarming rate of increase in experiments on human beings'. (22) But two examples - relevant to this case study of human blood - must suffice. (23)

The first relates to a study of hepatitis infection undertaken at a University College of Physicians and Surgeons in the United States and reported in August 1969. (24)   Earlier studies by other investigators had shown that a serum factor, hepatitis antigen, was specifically associated with viral hepatitis.   The university investigators tested 2211 units of blood of which 16 were found to contain the antigen.   These 16 units of blood were transfused into 16 different patients.   A control group of patients received blood which did not contain the antigen.   Of 12 surviving recipients of blood containing the antigen 9 (75 per cent) developed hepatitis.   The incidence of hepatitis in recipients of antigen-negative blood was 5.8 per cent (4 of 69).   'Our observations', said the authors, 'indicate ... an impressive correlation between the presence of hepatitis antigen in donor blood and the development of hepatitis following transfusion'.   The question raised by this investigation is whether in the light of the findings of earlier studies blood containing the hepatitis antigen should have been transfused to patients.   It is assumed that these patients and/or their relatives were informed of the possible risks involved.

The second example concerns an experimental study, reported in 1967, which took place at Willowbrook State School, Staten Island, New York, an over-crowded institution containing some 6000 mentally retarded patients predominantly children.   Those in the experiment were children aged 3 to 10 years of age 'whose parents gave written consent after being informed of the details, potential risks, and potential benefits of the investigation'. (25)   No information was published about the actual methods of the consent procedure and how it was carried out.

The purpose of the experiment was an attempt to elucidate the origins of serum hepatitis and to evaluate the possibility that there are several immunologically distinct types of the disease.   The institution had a history of endemic infections.   This in part was said to be a justification for the experiment.   Groups of these children were in a series of trials exposed to hepatitis.

Scientific lessons were, of course, learnt for the benefit of society from these studies of mentally retarded children who participated as givers.   As the 'Journal of the American Medical Association' commented: 'these recent studies ... represented an important contribution to our knowledge of hepatitis that would have

been impossible without the judicious use of human
beings in carefully controlled experimental studies'. (26)

Judicious means justify the ends; a plea made more
urgent by the increasing commercialization of blood in
the United States and the increasing use of 'derelict'
and Skid-Row populations as a source of blood. It is
doubtful whether this experiment would have taken
place had social policy considerations dominated the
supply and distribution of blood rather than the
economics of the market. (27)

In these expanding fields of human experimentation -
as with plasmapheresis programs - virtually all the
strangers who give, by inducement, for money or in
captive situations, are poor people; the indigent, the
deprived, the educationally handicapped, the socially
inadequate (in and out of prisons and other institutions), and all those described by an American sociologist as 'inept' in advancing a hypothesis that modern
economic systems 'utilize the inept more efficiently'. (28)

How some of the 'inept' in captive prison situations
have been utilized for the presumed benefit of society
in clinical trials undertaken for profit by an American
drug corporation was described in Chapter 8. Among
those who were utilized, some died and some were dis-
abled. These are the human cost facts that can be
and were counted but what cannot be assessed are the
moral effects on all those who were involved, in one
form or another, in this and similar experiments which
'utilize' the poor and the inept; physicians, prison
staff, prisoners, technicians, administrators and
officials of the pharmaceutical companies involved,
and many others. What effects do such experiences
have on their values and on their attitudes and behaviour towards the 'inept' in society? The ethical
consequences - or disvalues - of market experiments of
this kind extend far beyond the biological damage
actually done to those who are utilized.

What is also a fact that could be counted - if
anyone thought of counting - is that in the United
States and certain other Western societies poor people
and those classed as 'indigents' are the providers of
most of the teaching and research material needed to
sustain the fabric of medical systems. Many American
teaching hospitals are facing a crisis in the 1970s as
the relative proportions of indigents in the locality
decline. The rapid growth of profit-making hospitals
(referred to in Chapter 8) is likely to accentuate the
shortage of 'clinical material' for teaching and

research - with consequential effects on the American
output of doctors.   The corporations who operate these
hospitals have decided not to treat 'indigent' or
'charity' patients and not to provide emergency,
obstetrics or paediatric departments 'which, traditionally, are money-losers in hospitals'. (29)

With rising standards of living the availability and
number of poor charity patients would also have presented problems in Britain but the advent of the National
Health Service saved the situation as it brought in
after 1948 millions of Health Service potential
'teaching cases'.   Even so, some element of discrimination is still practised in favour of some private
patients.   They are not required or expected to the
same extent to make stranger gifts for the eventual
benefit of society at large - just as the rich of New
York and Chicago write cheques for blood bills without
thought of tomorrow or the social direction of their
society.

4

We have continually in these discussions of gift relationships asked the question: who gives and why?   In
this chapter we have placed these same questions in a
much broader social service context.   An essential
corollary is the further question: who in fact benefits
from all these unpaid social transactions?   Do the
poor benefit proportionately as much or more in relation
to their social and medical needs as the rich for the
gifts they make in the interests of science, of medicine, of the medical and other professions and of
society?   What return gifts does society make?

In the preceding chapter we discussed certain social
costs arising from the wastes, shortages, inefficiencies,
unethical practices and hazards involved in the American
commercial blood market.   We concluded that despite
the difficulties of measuring such costs in money terms
a disproportionate part was borne by poor people, the
sick and the handicapped.

In this chapter we have extended the discussion of
costs and benefits to encompass a far wider area of
social policy.   An economic statistician, specializing
in cost-benefit analysis, and looking at the scene with
the aid of quantifying spectacles might see this whole
area of social gift transactions as a great and growing
redistributive process favouring - in some societies -
the rich and the privileged;   a process, moreover,

stimulated by advances in science and technology, by
the growth of professionalism and the personal service
occupations, and by systems of buying and selling
medical care and other social services through which
gifts are received but are not returned in kind or
money. (30)

Could our statistician then, pursuing further and on
a comparative basis this statistical fantasy, bring
together and merge, in an immense series of tables, all
his social redistribution data with the conventional
income and wealth data available for Britain, the United
States and other countries?   Is it not possible that
the results would show for some economic and social
systems large flows of total redistribution from the
poor to the rich?   In other words, would not the social
gifts from the economically poor more than outweigh the
combined effects of progressive taxation and the cash
transfers of social welfare programs?

However many computers were provided for our statistician, and whatever advances were made on 'theories
of public goods' developed by Samuelson (31) and others
he would, in the end, have to confess to failure.   The
task would be beyond him because, in the first place,
most of the hard facts about the beneficiaries of services in kind are missing.   To take the case of blood
transfusions again, no national data exist for any
country in the world which show the distribution of
blood recipients by sex, age, social class, income
group and other characteristics.   There are certain
indications - particularly in the United States - of a
positive relationship between the incidence of blood
transfusions and the utilization by higher income
groups of certain sectors of medical care services. (32)
But none of the studies that have been made in the
United States and Britain are comprehensive in scope
and analysis.

The sample survey in 1967 of some 3800 blood donors,
reported in Chapter 7, suggested that the families of
higher income/social class groups received proportionately more blood than the families of lower income/
social class groups.   This survey was, however, from
the viewpoint of estimating the beneficiaries and
benefits of blood transfusions on a limited scale.   We
have to conclude, therefore, that even in this relatively small area of social policy our statistician
would not be able to answer on a national basis the
question: who receives blood?

Nor could he even begin to answer some of the more
metaphysical and distributive questions that have re-

curred again and again in this book.   He would not,
for example, be able to identify and evaluate all the
'externalities' or 'disvalues' in the total redistributive process.   What implied money values would he
place on the human lives saved and lost, on sickness
induced and prevented, even if he had all the demographic data?   What prices would he expect medical
students, doctors and many other professional aspirants
and groups to pay for the right to treat people as
teaching, learning, research and scientific experimental material?   What allowances would he make for the
external costs of malpractice and counter-malpractice
claims as more areas of stranger-relationships became
subject to the laws of the marketplace?   What profit-
ability value would he accord to a spirit of altruism
in society today and in the future, its absence or its
presence as an element of free choice for individuals?
How would he cost the consequences to a society in
which people, by simply writing cheques for blood, say
'I need no longer suffer from or experience a sense of
duty, of obligation, of responsibility for strangers'?
How then would he quantify the costs of violence?

   All this is not pure speculation.   There is growing
disquiet in the United States, Japan and other countries
with expanding commercial blood programs that such programs are driving out the voluntary system.   Insurance
companies are said to be stifling the spirit of giving
and thereby harming society by selling policies which
provide for cash reimbursement of the cost of blood
transfused.   The pharmaceutical industry, in developing commercial plasmapheresis programs, is similarly
under criticism for encouraging among the public at
large the notion that dollars can substitute for blood.
Even the President of the American Medical Association
was led to say in 1968 '... money payments for blood
can destroy the motivation of the family and friends
to replace the blood and could result in the creation
of many "semi-professional" donors who would contribute
too frequently, to the detriment of their own health.
It also would increase premiums and rates for this
portion of insurance plans; would tend to commercialize
what have been community-spirited voluntary contributions; and could affect the amount of blood available
in time of national catastrophe'. (33)

   Such externalities cannot be measured in statistical
or monetary terms.   As Edgeworth once said in another
context: 'We cannot *count* the golden sands of life; we
cannot *number* the "innumerable smiles" of seas of
love'. (34)

It is here that we can discern some of the fundamental distinguishing marks of social policy which differentiate it from economic policy. Because it has continually to ask the question 'who is my stranger' it must inevitably be concerned with the unquantifiable and unmethodical aspects of man as well as with those aspects which can be identified and counted. Thus, in terms of policies, what unites it with ethical considerations is its focus on integrative systems: on processes, transactions and institutions which promote an individual's sense of identity, participation and community and allow him more freedom of choice for the expression of altruism and which, simultaneously, discourage a sense of individual alienation.

This book, centring on gift relationships, is an attempt at measurement in respect of one such institution. It has also advanced three inter-related theses. First, that gift-exchange of a non-quantifiable nature has more important functions in complex, large-scale societies than the writings of Lévi-Strauss and others would suggest. Second, the application of scientific and technological developments in such societies, in further accelerating the spread of complexity, has increased rather than diminished the scientific as well as the social need for gift relationships. Third, for these and many other reasons, modern societies now require more rather than less freedom of choice for the expression of altruism in the daily life of all social groups. While this requirement has been argued primarily on social, ethical and biological grounds it is also justified on scientific and economic criteria.

5

To end this chapter we move from abstract generalizations about gift relationships and unanswered questions about social redistribution to report concretely on some blood donor responses in England. We end, therefore, on an individual note by quoting what some donors had to say about their motives for giving when they took part in the questionnaire survey in 1967.

First, however, we have to repeat a few warnings scattered throughout this book and offer some general observations.

The assumption should not be drawn from the comparative material presented in this study that, in terms of moral values, there is anything particularly unique or meritorious about the British people in their commitment to and support of a voluntary blood donor program.   In many other countries beside Britain and the United States there are countless numbers of voluntary community donors.   If asked, there is no reason to doubt that many would respond by expressing similar sentiments of altruism and reciprocity.   What we cannot write about (apart from a few countries) are their numbers, proportions, characteristics, representativeness, and so forth.   But just because we have presented a mass of facts about voluntary donors in Britain and few facts about voluntary donors in many other countries there must not, we repeat, be thoughts about chosen people.   In any event the blood donor, however he is classified by type (see Chapter 5), represents only a minority in a total eligible population.

Nor must it be concluded from what we have written that all is well with all British social institutions and distributive welfare systems; with, in short, the 'social condition of Britain'.   As a corrective, perhaps for some who may err in interpretation, it needs to be said that the themes pursued in this book are linked to the issues of social justice raised in the author's 'Commitment to Welfare' and 'Income Distribution and Social Change'.

What is unique as an instrument of social policy among the countries we have surveyed is the National Health Service and the values that it embodies.   Attitudes to and relationships with the National Blood Transfusion Service among the general public since 1948 can only be understood within the context of the Health Service.   The most unsordid act of British social policy in the twentieth century has allowed and encouraged sentiments of altruism, reciprocity and social duty to express themselves; to be made explicit and identifiable in measurable patterns of behaviour by all social groups and classes.   In part, this is attributable to the fact that, structurally and functionally, the Health Service is not socially divisive; its universal and free access basis has contributed much, we believe, to the social liberties of the subject in allowing people the choice to give or not to give blood for unseen strangers.

Of course, in probing the deeper human motives for giving and return-giving, for altruism and self-love, it would be facile to suggest that socialized medicine was wholly responsible.   We have not said that at all. What we do suggest, however, is that the ways in which society organizes and structures its social institutions -

and particularly its health and welfare systems - can
encourage or discourage the altruistic in man; such
systems can foster integration or alienation; they
can allow the 'theme of the gift' (to recall Mauss's
words) - of generosity towards strangers - to spread
among and between social groups and generations.
This, we further suggest, is an aspect of freedom in
the twentieth century which, compared with the
emphasis on consumer choice in material acquisitiveness,
is insufficiently recognized.   It is indeed little
understood how modern society, technical, professional,
large-scale organized society, allows few opportunities
for ordinary people to articulate giving in morally
practical terms outside their own network of family
and personal relationships.

We have from time to time in asking questions about
gift relationships employed the words 'motives' and
'motivation'.   Their use may have promised too much.
We did, however, a long while ago - in Chapter 2 - draw
attention to the association of blood, its possession,
inheritance, loss and transfusion, with religious
beliefs, theories and concepts of race, kinship, ances-
tor-worship and so forth and its many symbolical
properties.   The very thought of blood touches the
deepest feelings in man about life and death.   Consequently, we said, any attempt to study individual
motives for giving or not giving blood would face
some extremely demanding conceptual and analytical
problems.   In any event, we concluded, these could not
even be formulated until we had the basic facts about
the social and demographic characteristics of a sample
of blood donors.

In Chapter 7 and Appendix 4 we presented an analysis
of the facts derived from the pilot study in certain
areas of England for some 3800 donors.   We shall not
attempt to repeat the findings here.   As regards that
part of the questionnaire which asked about reasons
for giving blood, we expressed our hesitations about
the value of such questions and the difficulties of
interpreting the responses.   Hence, the analysis of
the results in Appendix 6 was undertaken in a relatively
straightforward manner; no attempt is made to speculate widely and deeply, and no statistical tests of
significance adorn the tables.   The analysis is
chiefly confined to a classification of the answers to
question 5 under fourteen main heads.   The generally
uncomplicated way in which this question was answered
does not justify a complicated motivational analysis.

These fourteen heads are set out in Table 38 along

with the proportions of donor replies judged to fall in
one or other category.   We now provide below some
examples of individual replies to illustrate each
category of answer to Question 5 ('Could you say why
you *first* decided to become a blood donor?').   They
were selected because they seemed to express more
vividly different categories of replies than many
stereotyped answers like 'Because I want to help to
save lives in hospital'.   A purely random selection
would have been less interesting.

1   Altruism (26.4 per cent of answers)

The great majority of answers in this category expressed
in general terms a desire to help:
   'Knowing I mite be saving somebody life' (single
   woman, aged 40, power press operator, £10-15 a
   week, 10 donations).
   'Anonymously, without financial reward to help
   others' (married man, aged 34, no children, insurance
   claims official, £20-30 a week, 23 donations).
   'You cant get blood from supermarkets and chaine
   stores.   People them selves must come forword, sick
   people cant get out of bed to ask you for a pint to
   save thier life so I came forword in hope to help
   somebody who needs blood' (married woman, aged 23,
   no children, machine operator, £15-20 a week [chief
   earner, electrician] 4 donations).
   'No man is an island' (married man, aged 36, two
   children, foreman maintenance fitter, £30-50 a week,
   21 donations).
   'I thought it just a small way to help people - as a
   blind person other opportunities are limited'
   (married man, aged 49, no children, piano tuner,
   £30-50 a week, 26 donations).
   'I felt it was a small contribution that I could
   make to the welfare of humanity' (married man, aged
   45, four children, bank manager, £30-50 a week, 26
   donations).
   'A desire to help other people in need' (single man,
   aged 51, road labourer, £10-15 a week, 11 donations).
   Some donors singled out for help the Health Service
in its various manifestations:
   'Just to help the Hospitals' (married woman, aged
   61, two children, husband retired, £10-15 a week, 45
   donations).
   'At the age of 18 I decided that it was a good thing
   for anyone capable and healthy to donate blood for

the good of other people and the advancement of medical science' (married woman, aged 28, three children,
husband carriage serviceman [railways], £10-15 a
week, 12 donations).
'I get my surgical shoes thro' the N.H.S. This is
some slight return and I want to help people'
(married man, aged 53, one child, insurance agent,
£15-20 a week, 20 donations).
A small proportion of donors specified those who
should be helped:
'To help babies that are borne with bad blood'
(married man, aged 23, one child, skilled boot polish
worker, £15-20 a week, 12 donations).

2 Gratitude for good health (1.4 per cent of answers)

'Because I am fortunate in having good health myself
and like to think my blood can help some-one else
back to health, and I felt this was a wonderful service I wanted to be part of' (widow, aged 63, four
children, widow's pension, less than £10 a week,
25 donations).
'Briefly because I have enjoyed good health all my
life and in a small way it is a way of saying "Thank
you" and a small donation to the less fortunate'
(married man, aged 53, two children, retired police
officer now welfare officer, £20-30 a week, 11
donations).
'To me it is a form of thanking God for my own good
health' (married woman, aged 64, two children,
clerk, £20-30 a week [husband also a clerk], 47
donations).

3 Reciprocity (9.8 per cent of answers)

In Chapter 7 we showed the proportions of donors who had
themselves received transfusions. Many of them gave
this as the reason in filling in the questionnaire:
'After being told that my own life had been saved by
transfusions - childbirth. Determined to repay'
(married woman, aged 46, five children, husband
toolmaker, £20-30 a week, 6 donations).
'To try and repay in some small way some unknown
person whose blood helped me recover from two operations and enable me to be with my family, thats why
I bring them along also as they become old enough'
(married woman, aged 44, three children, farmer's
wife, more than £50 a week, 8 donations).

Over 40 per cent of those whose answers were classified under 'reciprocity' referred to transfusions
received by relatives or friends:

'Some unknown person gave blood to save my wifes
life' (married man, aged 43, two children, self-
employed window cleaner, £15-20 a week, 56 donations).

'A young niece died from Luekemia after having
several transfusions which prolonged her life a
little.   After discussing this with a friend who
was already a donor, I went along with her to the
next session' (married woman, aged 59, one child,
husband sheet metal worker, £20-30 a week, 12
donations).

'My husband aged 41, collasped and died, without whom
life is very lonely - so I thought my blood may help
to save some-one the heart ache I've had' (transfusion received by husband before he died) (widow,
aged 47, one child, school meals service cook, less
than £10 a week, 16 donations).

Another substantial group of donors gave blood
because they thought that in the future they or a member
of their family might need it:

'Someone in my family may one day need blood, I would
like to think that someone will be there then, so I
give mine knowing that some unknown person will be
eternally grateful' (married woman, aged 28, no
children, industrial chemist [husband motor mechanic],
£20-30 a week, 13 donations).

'I have a motor Bike and someday I may need blood to
help me, so why shouldnt I give mine to help someone
who may have had an accident' (married man, aged 50,
two children, waterman textiles, £15-20 a week, 4
donations).

4   Replacement (0.8 per cent of answers)

These were donors who thought that someone in the family
should give blood and who said that they were replacing
a member who could not - or could no longer - donate:

'My mother was a donor for a number of years and when
she died in 1958 I decided to carry on in her place'
(married man, aged 49, five children, bricklayer,
£20-30 a week, 16 donations).

'When my wife was refused as donor due to anaemia I
stepped in' (married man, aged 63, one child, bus
driver, £15-20 a week, 23 donations).

'My son was killed on the road, he was a Blood Donor
and I knew they did their best to save him and

because I know he would be pleased I am carrying on
as long as I can to help someone I hope' (married
woman, aged 63, four children, husband timber
sawyer, £10-15 a week, 19 donations).

5   Awareness of need for blood (6.4 per cent of answers)

All donors in this category said that they gave blood
because they had become aware of the need for it.   The
circumstances in which they recognized need varied
considerably:
'Being in the construction side of building you see
many people hurt and it makes you feel as though you
have done a little bit to help' (married man, aged
25, no children, scaffolder, £30-50 a week, 3
donations).
'Owing to the nature of my work I feel the need to
give to the unfortunate people who require blood
after an accident.   Having seen so much lost in the
course of my work I thought my health could stand
helping others' (married man, aged 49, three children, ambulance driver, £20-30 a week, 23 donations).
'A sister had to receive five pints after an illness
and I realized how much benefit could be had by receiving blood from a donor' (married woman, aged
62, three children, husband company director, £30-50
a week, 17 donations).
'After seeing a bad accedent I thought it was the
best way I could help' (single woman, aged 22,
upholstress, father rubber tyre header, £20-30 a
week, 5 donations).
'In order to help maintain the supply of blood so
urgently needed at all times' (married man, aged 59,
three children, postman, £10-15 a week, 10 donations).

6   Duty (3.3 per cent of answers)

The distinction between 'Altruism' (Category 1) and
'Duty' was extremely difficult to draw.   There were
the donors who said quite simply that they *wanted* to
help other people;   there were donors who said or implied
that as a matter of conscience, or duty or feelings of
guilt they *ought* to help other people.   The difference
in these responses - if there really is or could be a
difference - may well lie in the accidental choice of
words by individual donors.   But, as we said earlier,
there is no justification for reading more into these

responses about motives than appears on the surface of
language.   Hence, the classification into categories
was undertaken on the basis of what people actually
wrote on the questionnaire.   Some examples of 'duty'
answers are:

'Sense of duty to the community and nation as a
whole' (married man, aged 31, three children, charge-
hand fitter, £15-20 a week, 7 donations).

'My conscience - having served 5 years on active
service in the war (1939-45) helping to destroy life,
and during this period my wife was receiving blood
to save her life, it occurred to me, after demobili-
zation, that I could at least ease my conscience'
(married man, aged 52, 1 child, clerical officer
civil service, £20-30 a week, 58 donations).

'Feelings of guilt at receiving so much in life and
giving so little' (single woman, aged 60, school
teacher, £20-30 a week, 20 donations).

'Primarily to "conform" with teenage contemporaries -
desire "to be of service" to others was a secondary
reason' (married man, aged 37, two children, contracts engineer, £20-30 a week, 26 donations).

'During the war I was afraid I would be considered
too old to help my country.   Giving blood, as I
started to do then, was just a balm to my pride.   I
was called up late for service, which restored my
pride.   Afterwards I just carried on donating.
With other voluntary jobs I have undertaken, I have
just felt the job was there, and I was available.
Other jobs were in trade unions or political parties.
I have never thought "Why should I do it? I'll leave
it to someone else".   I have thought "Why should
not I do this?"   I am not a do-gooder, at least, I
don't feel like one nor think like one' (married man,
aged 62, three children, compositor, £15-20 a week,
28 donations).

'I am a father of two, and feel that if I, or any of
mine ever need blood, they have a moral right to it.
It is an obligation of a father' (married man, aged
55, two children, motor mechanic, £15-20 a week,
33 donations).

'I have been a mental patient (PSYCOPATH) and I have
always tried to help people.   Also I tried to
commit suicide by stabbing myself and a transfusion
saved me' (single man, aged 19, labourer, £10-15 a
week, 2 donations).

7 War effort (6.7 per cent of answers)

In comparison with the preceding category, most of the
answers classified here were fairly straightforward.
Naturally, they all came from donors over the age of
40:

'During war service in the WAAF I was made aware of
the need to give blood to help injured servicemen and
civilians and afterwards I realized that it was also
necessary in peace time' (single woman, aged 45,
bank clerk,£20-30 a week, 40 donations).
'Came unscathed through 1939-45 war; felt "owed"
something' (married man, aged 43, three children,
chief establishment assistant local government,
£30-50 a week, 30 donations).
'1941. War. Blood needed. I had some. Why
not?' (married man, aged 47, three children, sales
representative, £20-30 a week, 10 donations).
'I first gave blood during the last war to try and
help save people from the results of war to which I
am very strongly opposed - prefer to preserve life
as against destroying it' (married woman, aged 53,
one child, part-time actress and housewife, £30-50
a week, [husband television producer], 20 donations).

8 The Defence Services since 1945 (5.0 per cent of
answers)

This category, partly associated with the preceding one,
comprises donors who said that they first gave blood as
members of the Services. Some of the answers indicate
that the respondents became donors at least partly
because of certain benefits, e.g. 48-hour passes, being
excused drill, etc. Other answers suggest that the
act of donating was not entirely voluntary; that there
were, as we discussed in our typology of donors, external pressures 'to volunteer'. However, the majority
of donors placed in this category did not specify either
benefits or pressures; the most usual wording employed
took the form 'I answered an appeal for blood while in
the Army.' Some illustrations of the responses of
donors in this category who whatever the reasons given
for the first donation had continued to donate are:

'Gave blood when in the services (seemed a good way
to get out of an afternoons duties!). Later there
was a general appeal for blood where I live'
(married man, aged 37, two children, sales office
manager, £30-50 a week, 9 donations).

'It was a good excuse for a good cup of tea and the
afternoon off duty whilst serving in the Navy'
(married man, aged 42, three children, maintenance
engineer printing, £30-50 a week, 49 donations).
'Request for voluntary donors whilst serving in
Forces' (married man, aged 41, no children, sales
representative, £20-30 a week, 6 donations).
'Told to volunteer in RAF! Subsequently as a
civilian happened to pass a blood donor session (not
well advertised) and called in on spur of moment'
(married man, aged 41, two children, local government
clerk, £30-50 a week, 36 donations).

9   Rare blood group (1.1 per cent of answers)

The general idea expressed in this type of answer was
that the discovery that they were in a rare blood group
was instrumental in the donor deciding to give blood.
Such answers further imply that because one's blood is
rare or unique there is a particular responsibility to
make it available to others who may need it.   To learn
also that one has in one's make-up some element of
'uniqueness' may contribute to feelings of self-respect
as well as to acts of giving.
    'My blood is fairly rare - this I did not discover
    until I had had my twins (4th pregnancy).   I now
    have six children which is most unusual because of
    my group.   Maybe my blood may help some other
    mother.   I give blood in gratitude for my good
    fortune' (married woman, aged 42, six children,
    school teacher [husband also school teacher, £30-50
    a week], 20 donations).
    'Curiosity first.   Then continued when I discovered
    I had a rare blood group.   I like to think that a
    life may be saved by my blood' (married man, aged
    53, two children, engineering toolmaker, £15-20 a
    week, 25 donations).
    'My mother is of a rare blood group and I thought
    perhaps I would be.   I was not, but felt my blood
    would still be needed' (married woman, aged 23, no
    children, hairdresser [husband advertising art
    director, £30-50 a week], 10 donations).

10   To obtain some benefit (1.8 per cent of answers)

These were fairly straightforward answers the great
majority of which were concerned with benefits to the

donor's physical health; nose bleeding, regular health
checks, learning one's blood group, etc.   A few donors,
however, introduced more complex reasons:
'From being a boy I had suffered from constant nose
bleeding and since I became a donor I have not had
a single nose bleed' (married man, aged 43, two
children, newsagent, £30-50 a week, 17 donations).
'I wanted to do something to convince myself I was
18 and I always wanted to be a blood donor - snob
appeal' (married woman, aged 20, no children, donor
attendant blood transfusion service [husband car
fitter £15-20 a week] 6 donations).

11 Personal appeal (13.2 per cent of answers)

In this category were placed the answers of donors who
said that they had been influenced to give blood by
encouragement, requests and appeals on a personal basis:
'A workmate convinced me of the need for more donors'
(married man, aged 35, one child, form grinder/miller
[machine tools], £20-30 a week, 20 donations).
'A pretty young nurse walked round the factory I was
working in' (married man, aged 41, three adopted
children, development engineer [pressure diecasting
non-ferrous], £30-50 a week, 17 donations).
'Coerced by my husband as I was rather apprehensive'
(married woman, aged 35, two adopted children, husband teacher technical education, £30-50 a week, 16
donations).

12 General appeal (18.0 per cent of answers)

These were mainly short answers by donors who said that
they had been influenced by a general appeal:
'I heard the appeal on the BBC' (married woman, aged
61, three children, husband old age pensioner, less
than £10 a week, 16 donations).
'On seeing TV Advert I thought what great help to
patients it could be, with so little effort by giving'
(married man, aged 45, 1 child, builder's manager,
£20-30 a week, 7 donations).
'I became a donor when the Unit came to the firm at
which I worked, and ask for donors because of a
shortage of blood' (married man, aged 42, six children, glass furnace operator, £15-20 a week, 19
donations).
'I read the notice the appeal for donors in the

Putney Hospital waiting room' (widower, aged 56, five children, manager [cleaning], £20-30 a week, 7 donations).

13   Miscellaneous (5 per cent of answers)

All types of answers occurring less than twenty times in the whole of the sample were put in this category. They varied greatly, ranging from the obviously frivolous to serious essays of a personal nature:

'To get a good cup of tea' (married man, aged 24, one child, store-keeper [lock and door closers], £15-20 a week, 4 donations).

'I went along to hold my husbands hand' (married woman, aged 39, two children, husband shop manager [grocery], £15-20 a week, 32 donations).

'No money to spare. Plenty of blood to spare' (married man, aged 35, two children, painter and decorator, £15-20 a week, 19 donations).

'After seeing fellow hitch hikers in Greece selling their blood for a few pounds a pint to raise some money for food. It made me realize what a good system the voluntary system is' (single man, aged 23, industrial chemist [abrasive wheel industry], £15-20 a week, 2 donations).

14   More than one type of answer (0.9 per cent of answers)

Some donors gave answers which included more than one of the categories we have employed in the analysis in Appenidx 6. Most of them seemed to recognize that the decision to give blood is often a complex process and that, consequently, they could not distinguish a single or predominant motive:

'I feel that with blood it would have to be used for the purposes it was given, no deductions for administrative purposes like so many Charity Organizations. Blood is something which could not come out of the rates. I have also now become a car driver and know that I use a dangerous weapon. And as a hypochondriac who has not visited a doctor for illness for some 7 years I felt that I would like to have some sort of blood test and felt sure, rightly or wrongly, that if I became a donor my blood would go through a test of some kind - at least I would know I had blood' (married man, aged 33, no children, company secretary, £30-50 a week, 2 donations).

'My group is rather rare. I drive every day, I see
blood on the road every week. One day it may be
mine. With that cheerful thought one may regard
donating as an investment' (single man, aged 25,
advertising copywriter, £20-30 a week, 4 donations).
'It is in my estimation, a good way to keep a half
yearly check on my own health. The thoughts of my
own children at some time needing a donor's blood'
(married man, aged 40, two children, foreman building maintenance, £20-30 a week, 4 donations).

This is what some of the donors had to say in their
own words about their reasons for giving. The vividness, individuality and diversity of these responses add
life and a sense of community to the statistical gener-
alities in Appendix 6. To speculate further about the
psychology of these relationships would require not only
depth interviews and a larger sample but, maybe, the
insights of a Freud, a Jung and a Lévi-Strauss.

All we can do is to call attention to the facts and
the donors' own statements. Over two-fifths of all
the answers in the whole sample fell into the categories
'Altruism', 'Reciprocity', 'Replacement' and 'Duty'.
Nearly a third represented voluntary responses to
personal and general appeals for blood. A further 6
per cent responded to an 'Awareness of Need'. These
seven categories accounted for nearly 80 per cent of
the answers suggesting a high sense of social responsibility towards the needs of other members of society.
Perhaps this is one of the outstanding impressions
which emerges from the survey.

NOTES

1 C. Lévi-Strauss, 'The Elementary Structures of Kinship', revised edition (ed. R. Needham), London,
Eyre & Spottiswoode, 1969.
2 'Proc. Conf. American Association of Blood Banks',
Los Angeles, 1966.
3 Lévi-Strauss, op. cit., p. 56.
4 G. Dalton, Economic Theory and Primitive Society,
'American Anthropologist', vol. 63, February 1961.
5 F. Tönnies, 'Community and Association' ('Gemeinschaft und Gesellschaft'), translated and supple-
mented by C.P. Loomis, London, Routledge & Kegan
Paul, 1955, pp. 20-1.
6 Lévi-Strauss, op. cit., p. 61.
7 P.M. Blaue, 'Exchange and Power in Social Life', New
York, Wiley, 1964.

8   P.A. Sorokin, 'The Ways and Power of Love', Boston,
    Beacon Press, 1954.
9   For a philosophical discussion of 'ultra obliga-
    tions' see G.R. Grice, 'The Grounds of Moral Judge-
    ment', Cambridge University Press, 1967.
10 K.E. Boulding, The Boundaries of Social Policy,
    'Social Work', vol. 12, no. 1, January 1967, p. 7.
11 'Report of the Committee on Local Authority and
    Allied Personal Social Services', Cmnd 3703, 1968,
    p. 11.
12 'Report of the Royal Commission on Medical Education
    1965-8', Cmnd 3569, London, HMSO, 1968.
13 For an explanation of the problems of defining
    'true' or 'informed' consent see 'Medical Research
    Council, Annual Report 1962-3', Cmnd 2382, London,
    HMSO, 1964 and M.H. Pappworth, 'Human Guinea Pigs',
    London, Routledge & Kegan Paul, 1967.
14 See R. Parker, 'Decision in Child Care', London,
    Allen & Unwin, 1966, especially pp. 68-9, and R.
    Dinnage and M.L. Kellmer Pringle, 'Foster Home Care -
    Facts and Fallacies', London, Longmans, 1967.
15 D. Robertson, 'Economic Commentaries', 1956, p. 154.
16 Personal communication, Sir Benjamin Rycroft and
    P.V. Rycroft, December 1966 and see also G.E.W.
    Wolstenholme and M. O'Connor, ibid., pp. 43-50.
17 New eye donors in Britain were being registered at
    a rate of about 1000 a month in 1965 ('Report of
    the Central Health Services Council for 1965',
    HMSO, 1966).
18 For an informative discussion of the ethical and
    legal problems of organ transplantation see G.E.W.
    Wolstenholme and M. O'Connor, ibid.
19 H.L. Wilensky and C.N. Lebeaux, 'Industrial Society
    and Social Welfare', New York, Russell Sage, 1958,
    p. 141.
20 C.F. von Weizsäcker, 'The World View of Physics',
    London, Routledge & Kegan Paul, 1952, p. 69.
21 Western scientific medicine appears to be making
    increasing use of two 'captive volunteer' groups
    for research and experimental purposes, 1, primi-
    tive peoples in Africa and South America, 2,
    prisoners in the United States and South Africa.
    The main area of research interest in relation to
    the first group is coronary heart disease and its
    reported connection with diet (one of the major
    health preoccupations of Western man).   Many
    studies involve the provision for a short period of
    comprehensive medical care.   When the research
    facts have been collected medical care is withdrawn

(see, for example, A.G. Shaper and K.W. Jones,
Serum-Cholestrol in Camel-Herding Nomads, 'Lancet',
ii, 1305, 1962).   As regards the use of prisoners,
see references in this book to plasmapheresis;
A.J. Davis, 'Trans-Action', December 1968 (des-
cribing extensive laboratory experiments in
Philadelphia gaols) and Wolstenholme and O'Connor,
op. cit.

22 'Brit. Med. J.', editorial Ethics of Human Experimentation, 6 July 1963, p. 1.

23 For more documentation and references to some 200
papers see Pappworth, op. cit., and letter to
'Brit. Med. J.', on the ethics of liver transplants,
7 June 1969, p. 631.

24 D.J. Gocke, H.B. Greenberg and N.B. Kavey, Hepatitis
Antigen, 'Lancet', ii, 248, 1969.

25 S. Krugman, C.P. Giles and J. Hammond, Infectious
Hepatitis, 'J.A.M.A.', vol. 200, no. 5, 1 May 1967,
p. 365.

26 'J.A.M.A.', Editorial, vol. 200, no. 5, 1 May 1967,
p. 407.

27 'In initial trials of any new agents, the investi-
gator must be genuinely open-minded concerning the
possibility that the drug is worth a trial and that
it may be as good as, or perhaps better than, one
or more of those already available.   Strong convictions for or against its value in the treatment of
a disease can render it unethical for him to use or
withhold the agent under trial or to use a placebo;
in this case he should not undertake the investigation' ('Principles for the Clinical Evaluation of
Drugs, Report of a WHO Scientific Study Group',
World Health Organization, Tech. Rep. Ser., 1968,
no. 403, p. 6.

28 W.J. Goode, The Protection of the Inept, 'Amer. Soc.
Review', vol. 32, no. 1, February 1967, pp. 5-19.

29 'Wall Street Journal', 13 October 1969.

30 In Britain, private patients who find the National
Health Service uncongenial are not charged for blood
received from the National Health Service.

31 See, for example, P.A. Samuelson, The Pure Theory
of Public Expenditure, 'Review of Economics and
Statistics', XXXVI, 1954, Diagrammatic Exposition of
Theory of Public Expenditure, op. cit., XXXVII,
1955, and Aspects of Public Expenditure Theories,
op. cit., XL, 1958.

32 Two of the main American sources of medical care
utilization data are: 1, 'Vital and Health Statistics Data from the National Health Survey', National

Center for Health Statistics, Public Health Service, U.S. Department of Health, Education and Welfare, 1960-9 and 2, Commission on Professional and Hospital Activities, 'Medical Audit Program Reports', Ann Arbor, Michigan, 1963-9.   Sources of data for England and Wales are the 'Report on Hospital Inpatient Inquiry' for 1961 and 1966 and 'Annual Report of the Ministry of Health', Department of Health and Social Security and General Register Office.   See also J.N. Morris, 'Uses of Epidemiology' (2nd edn), Edinburgh and London, Livingstone, 1964.

33   M.O. Rouse, Blood Banking and Blood Use, 'Transfusions', vol. 8, no. 2, March-April 1968, p. 106.

34   F.Y. Edgeworth, 'Mathematical Physics', London, Kegan Paul, 1881, p. 8 (original italics).

10   The concept of community

John Benson

The term 'community' in the title cannot be said to
mark off a clear topic for discussion.   It is used in
ordinary speech and in the semi-technical vocabulary of
sociologists in a wide variety of applications and in
different, and sometimes seriously ambiguous, senses.
Its relations to and overlap with other terms in the
same conceptual region, such as 'society', and 'association', are far from clear.   To take 'community' and
'society';   sometimes 'society' is taken to refer to the
most inclusive groupings, the most extensive collecti-
vities felt to be marked by a significant degree of
unity and integration, while 'community' is taken to
refer to particular sub-divisions of such inclusive
societies: regions, cities, national and racial groups,
religious denominations, neighbourhoods, and so on.
With this distinction we have a very wide sense for
'community', for it is obvious that these various
groupings are marked off by quite diverse principles of
classification, and one may question whether they have
any significant features in common.   At any rate it
is clear that in this sense a community is a part of a
wider social whole.   But there are other uses of the
two terms, not obviously illegitimate, in which this
is not so.   'Community' may be used to refer to any
group, large or small, whose members live together in
such a way that they share, not this or that particular
interest, but the basic conditions of a common life; (1)
and 'society' to refer to the institutional organisation, political, legal, and economic, which may or may
not be a feature of such groups.   Again 'society' may
be used as a generic term and 'community' as a specific
term denoting societies characterised by particular
kinds of relationship (e.g. 'face-to-face', or sympathetic as opposed to contractual) between the members.

An example of this use is the distinction between
'community' and 'association' derived from Tönnies'
analysis of *Gemeinschaft* and *Gesellschaft,* supposedly
fundamental types of social relationship providing a
way of classifying actual social groupings.

There are then at least these three senses of
'community' which, even if not severally very clear,
are pretty clearly different.   Of course their areas
of application overlap, but this is just where the
danger lies, for though the word may apply in two or
all of its senses to the same thing it does so by
virtue of different criteria and says very different
things depending on the criteria which are held to
justify the application.

One further possible ambiguity should be mentioned,
which is rather different from those considered so far,
which consist in the currency of different *descriptive*
senses of 'community'.   'Community' is often used
with strong evaluative and emotive force, commonly
signalled by the use of such intensifying adjectives
as 'real' and 'genuine'.   When people talk about 'real
community' they are not referring to an objectively
definable type of social structure so much as to a
vaguely sensed quality of common life which is felt to
be valuable and is assumed to depend for its existence
on a specific type of social structure (such as the
self-contained village).   It may be unfair to label
this an 'ambiguity' since many words have both descriptive and evaluative meaning without confusion being
engendered.   But it is important to keep separate the
two kinds of meaning so that one may be clear about
which descriptive features of a social grouping are
relevant to the value-judgments that are made of it.
This is particularly important when the descriptive
content is itself variable, as we have seen is the
case with 'community'.

It would be useful, though perhaps tedious, to
elaborate these distinctions, so far only broadly indicated, and to examine in detail the concepts involved.
But before this kind of clarification can get very far
it seems to me necessary to discuss something more
fundamental, namely the notion of 'the social' or 'the
communal' as something essentially characteristic of,
and peculiar to, the life of human beings.   Is there
anything to be said in general terms about what constitutes a 'common life'?   It might be thought that
the answer to this question is 'no'.   To distinguish
and classify various different groupings that are found
to exist involves the analysis of different ways in

which individual human beings may be related to one
another and act *vis-a-vis* one another.   These relationships and patterns of interaction are so various and
constitute such widely different kinds of group-life
that it may seem naïve essentialism to look for a common
factor, for some special bond which ties a man to his
fellows in whatever kind of social whole he may be a
member.   It has been urged against the classical political philosophers that they went wrong in looking for
some such essential social bond and that this search
naturally led to such quasi-historical myths as the
social compact or to the dubious metaphysics of supra-
individual wills and social 'organisms'.   However, I
don't think that they did go wrong so obviously.   What
they did - or some of them at any rate - was to give a
misleadingly concrete, in some cases quasi-historical,
expression to the attempt to specify *formal* conditions
for the existence of a human political community.
Part of what Rousseau was saying in 'The Social Contract', to mention one instance, was that a political
community in which it makes sense to distinguish between
legal and illegal actions by citizens or governments
must be a body of individuals each of whom recognises
as binding on himself rules which are for the common
good and not, at least directly, for his own good.
This is a formal condition in that it does not say anything about the content of the rules or about the
institutional machinery by which they are formulated.
Whatever criticisms may be made of this formulation it
is not hopelessly nebulous.   The point of citing this
example is to show that the attempt to give a general
account of the most basic presuppositions of social
life does not necessarily lead to answers that are
vacuous or unilluminating.

What I mean to attempt then is to give in outline a
similarly formal account of what it is for a collection
of individuals to have a common life (at this level of
generality it makes little difference whether one
calls this 'social' or 'communal').   In this case the
account will be formal in the sense that it will not
say anything about the specific kinds of relationship
that can characterise human societies, though it will
be an attempt to answer the question what it is that
makes a relationship a human social relationship.

We are inclined to talk about animals having a
social or communal form of life when we find species
that are not only gregarious but whose collective
existence involves differentiation of function and
interdependence of individuals performing different

functions.   As a definition this is too broad, for it
would cover animals which come together to mate but are
otherwise solitary.   Two further conditions need to be
added.   First it seems necessary that to have a social
life individuals must form groups that have some degree
of continuity; a mating pair that breaks up immediately
the mating is completed does not satisfy this condition.
Second, the individuals must be dependent on others in
some identifiable group in a reasonably high proportion
of their activities and for some substantial portion of
their life-span; this condition would exclude animals
which, say, formed packs on infrequent occasions for
hunting, but were otherwise solitary.   Interdependence
of individuals performing different functions, however,
seems to be the most central feature, and the one which
is so striking in the collective behaviour of certain
species, such as the bee, and in them invites comparison
with the social life of human beings.   But this feature,
even with the addition of the other necessary conditions
mentioned, would not be enough to characterise the human
form of social life.   What more needs to be added?   It
seems obvious that what is necessary is that the distribution and performance of functions should be not merely
de facto but should be governed by rules or norms.

To perform a function is to act in certain definite
ways in specific types of situation, but to perform a
function in a human society is to act in ways appropriate to certain types of situation *because of* the
type of situation one is in, where the 'because' is
the agent's and not merely the observer's.   So, for
example, a bus conductor who issues a ticket in response
to a passenger's demand is not automatically responding
to a stimulus but is acting for a reason, namely that
he has been asked for a threepenny, or whatever it may
be.   If asked why he issued the ticket when the
passenger asked for it he might well say: 'Well,
that's what I'm paid for.'   That is, acting on such
requests, accepting them as reasons for acting in a
certain way, is what the job consists in.   There is
of course the different question of why this man has
this particular job, the answer to which would have to
invoke a second level of rules, those governing the
recruitment to roles in a society.   I am concerned
with the rules that operate within the role, which define
the character of the role.   In the case of the bus
conductor this normative definition of the role is
obvious enough, and may be explicitly set down in his
terms of employment.   There are obviously many roles
of which this is not true, but which are defined by

rules that are not set down at all, for instance those
of a friend, or a son, or a host.   To use the term
'role' in such a wide sense is in need of justification
and of some qualification.   It depends perhaps on what
is no more than an analogy, if a strong one, between
such institutionalised roles as those of the bus conductor, the professor, and the income-tax inspector,
and the more private, commonly less formal, 'capacities'
in which a man may act in relation to other people.
The rules governing the former are no doubt more explicit and more precise; but the latter are just as much
governed by what is expected and what is recognised.
A son is expected to show his parents a particular
kind of respect, to help maintain them if necessary
and so on.   A friend is expected, among other things,
to be willing to give and receive confidences and to
help in difficulties.   There is a significant sense in
which talk of rules is appropriate here.

It can be illuminating to think of society as a network of roles, institutionalised and non-institution-
alised, of many different kinds, each regulated, indeed
constituted, by a set of rules.   Each person's conception of his society consists in the knowledge that he
has of the network of roles, in his knowing what is
expected of him in the roles he occupies and what to
expect of others in theirs.   S.F. Nadel, who brilliantly developed this approach to the description of
societies, puts this as follows:

> ... each actor in his role knows about all the other
> roles from which his own differs in some manner,
> and is guided by this knowledge in his own actions.
> We might say he carries a role map of his society
> in his head, indicating the way in which his role
> fits in amongst others.   This map need only be a
> rough one, though one sufficiently accurate to show
> the boundaries between any actor's role and relevant
> others - similar, as it were adjacent, roles or
> perhaps opposed ones.   So that a 'father' will act
> in full knowledge of how his position compares with
> that of an 'uncle' or 'teacher'; a 'doctor', of
> how his right to the confidences of his patients
> compares with that of a 'friend' or 'priest'; and
> so forth. (2)

It might be as well, before going further, to guard
against two misinterpretations to which this account
might be subject.   The first is that to talk of society
as a network of roles might be thought to imply that
human action in a social context falls into a rigid,
stereotyped pattern.   But no such inference need be

drawn.   Few, if any, roles can be specified in terms of a set of rules which specify completely determinate actions for specific situations, the entire range of possible situations being explicitly and exhaustively set out in the rules.   No one could give an exhaustive list of actions that ought to be performed by a friend in all the various situations that might arise in the course of a relationship.   One must operate rather with a number of 'rules of thumb' that apply to situations of fairly common occurrence (such as being asked for a loan), and for the rest with much more general rules that call for interpretation to apply them to particular situations.   But there must be some criteria by which it can be decided that an action is or is not a friendly one, and unless there were general agreement about these, no one could begin to know how to be friendly.   One would not know how to be unfriendly either.   For one thing which the recognition of roles summing up, however loosely, normal ways of behaving does, is to make intelligible certain kinds of departure from them.   There is no real opposition between a description of a society in terms of roles and recognition of individual purposes.   The framework of roles is the context in which individual purposes and actions become intelligible.

The second misinterpretation would be to suppose that the rules defining social roles are all moral rules.   By and large, however, such rules do not prescribe what the occupant of a role must do on pain of being immoral.   For instance, one of the things that may be expected of me as the friend of another is that I should lend him five pounds.   He has more reason to expect me to lend him the money than someone else who is not his friend, and I have more reason to lend it to him than I would have to lend money to a stranger or casual acquaintance.   It would be appropriate for me, as his friend, to lend him the money, but this is not to say that I am under an obligation.   Here it may be objected that the 'appropriateness' in question has at least a moral flavour; I might be thought mean if I refuse the loan, and this would be a moral appraisal of the action.   But it is easy to think of instances in which even this kind of moral significance is absent;   if I drink his whisky or allow him to drink mine, both, in their ways, are acts of friendship.

Both of these misinterpretations derive from an oversimple notion of what a rule (or a 'norm' in the jargon) is, and the next task must be to indicate some of the kinds of rule that are relevant to the understanding of human action.

Hindu ideas about pollution explain why the blows which were struck were not simple assaults, but were also attacks on a fundamental moral principle, governing the relationship between clean caste and untouchable. This ritual relationship is now seen as one part of a complex in which political and economic interests are also involved. [The *Pans* have no representation on the village council and only own such property as their masters choose to give them.] The blows now appear not only as an offence against all village morality, but also as an attack on the established political order of the village. Given that the rituals of untouchability symbolise also political inferiority, these assaults were tantamount to a revolution. (7)

What gives sense to an interpretation of this sort is that it is in terms of the way in which actions of this kind are understood by the participants. Reference to Hindu ideas about untouchability and to political and economic institutions helps to explain what happened because these things are incapsulated in the actions themselves. The distinction between rules of action (requirements and permissions) and rules of meaning is needed here, for the assaults are not in accordance with the 'norms' of society and yet are clearly significant. In any society there is common agreement about what actions mean, not merely common agreement about what should or should not be done in specified situations. Because of this it is possible to 'say' things with actions, and particularly to say unusual, unconventional, even defiant and revolutionary things, and be understood. It is because a description of society in terms of roles involves reference to rules of this kind that such a description does not imply that the behaviour of social beings is stereotyped and invariable, but rather lays bare a framework within which both conventional behaviour and innovation become intelligible.

I must now try to bring to a focus this rather long discussion of different types of rule. I suggested that an account can be given of society in terms of the roles that individuals occupy and the way in which these roles are related to one another. From this point of view society is thought of not as a collection of actual individuals interacting with one another in various complex ways, but as a system of roles that can be occupied by many individuals, and of which many can be occupied simultaneously by a single individual. The model does not deny that in one obvious sense it is

precisely individual people who do constitute society.
But it offers a way of speaking about the modes of
behaviour through which individuals come to constitute
a society, and which remain relatively constant while
the agents themselves are replaced in the course of
time.   Nor is the model unduly artificial, for it is
already implicit in the way in which people actually
characterise their relationships with others.

When one proceeds to examine what is involved in the
notion of playing a role and the way in which a man is
related to others in his various roles one finds the
fundamental place occupied by rules, since a role can
only be defined in terms of the mutual expectations of
the role-player and those towards whom his actions in
the role are directed.   'Expectation' is here more
than a psychological term, but is normative, and corresponding to the expectations of others are the rules
that guide the agent in playing the role.   An account
of society in terms of roles therefore necessarily
involves the notion of common agreement about rules.
For a role is constituted by a set of rules and moreover
a role exists not by virtue of its occupant's recognition of the rules only, but also by virtue of their
recognition by others.   A collection of individuals
can be said to have a social existence, a common life,
to the extent that there exists among them a consensus
about the rules that define the various roles that
individuals can occupy.   This consensus should be
understood in terms of the account I have given of the
different kinds of role.   It involves agreement not
only about what actions are required or permitted in
particular roles, but also about the significance of
various kinds of action.   A society is a collection of
people who have the same ideas about what is involved
in being a father, or a doctor or a friend, and so on
through the indefinitely long list of recognised
activities.

Such an account avoids both an individualistic
analysis of society, according to which individuals
take part in a co-operative enterprise in the pursuit
of individual ends which are prior to the social relationships that they enter into, and the view of society
as an organism, individuals having their being only as
parts of a whole.   On the sort of accounts that I have
been giving there is no need to ascribe anything like
purposes to social wholes that cannot be analysed in
terms of individuals and the relationships between
them, and yet the fact that we can ascribe actions,
intentions, and purposes to individuals is owing to

the existence of a common understanding of what constitutes various kinds of action.

In giving an account of what is essential the idea
of a common life I have said nothing directly relevant
to the question of how societies or communities may be
individuated, i.e. what sorts of collection can usefully be regarded as social entities.   It will follow
from my account that some principles of individuation
will be more important than others; neither geographical unity nor the existence of a single political
system for instance would by itself be an important
criterion in the absence of agreement on other rules
concerned with family and group life and personal
relationships.   Similarly it is conceivable that two
groups of people might have distinct territorial loca-
tions, distinct political and perhaps economic institutions, and yet have the same language, or languages
with similar conceptual structures, the same family
structure, the same ideas about love and friendship and
so on, and so constitute a single society by virtue of
this agreement.   (However, it must be admitted that
it is difficult to say in general to what extent such
elements can be dissociated from one another; there
are conceptual as well as causal links between them,
which would need to be analysed in detail.)   The
notion of society being constituted by consensus also
has implications for what can be regarded as an autonomous group.   If one thinks of the tightly knit and
self-contained group that the family can be one may be
tempted to suppose that it constitutes an autonomous
social unit.   But however self-contained and inward-
looking it may be, a family is part of a society that
contains it not only in the sense that its members will
have some relationships with people outside the family,
and so will occupy other roles besides those of kinship,
but also in the sense that the 'norms' which define
kinship roles exist by virtue of a consensus that is
wider than any single family.   In this way even what
may be thought of as personal, as distinct from social
relationships, such as friendship, are dependent on
such a consensus about the modes of behaviour appropriate to them.

This last point enables me to bring my account into
relationship with the influential notion of community
(*Gemeinschaft*) developed by Tönnies, which can all too
easily lead to a kind of sociological sentimentalism.
Gemeinschaft is characterised by a close bond of
sympathy between the members, mutual trust, shared
sentiments and beliefs, non-contractual co-operation in

the carrying out of common tasks.   *Gesellschaft* relationships by contrast are those into which people enter
on the basis of 'I give, so that you will give', the
prototype of which is barter or exchange;   societies
based on such relationships are impersonal and individualistic.   The distinction is an important one, and
Tönnies is alive to the fact that human society cannot
be understood 'as an arrangement of convenience, based
on contract, into which individuals enter as independent beings with certain interests which they seek to
further by means of mutual services.   To be able to
enter into such relationships people must already have
the institution of promising, or a common understanding
of some gesture as an undertaking to perform, and this
already constitutes a social relationship.   Further,
although Tönnies sees *Gemeinschaft* as originating in
blood-relationships, he regards the community of mental
life as 'the truly human and supreme form of community',
and emphasises the way in which language is the necessary means by which a common understanding is brought
about.

     Even so, the sharp dichotomy between community as
involving deep personal involvement and commitment, and
an impersonal kind of association based on the rational
(calculative) will, and the application of this dichotomy in classifying social groups, can be misleading.
For the examples of *Gemeinschaft* societies are the
family, the neighbourhood unit (agricultural village or
city) and the fellowship of friends.   These are the
paradigm cases, and there is a twofold danger in presenting them as such.   We may be persuaded to think of
any large-scale society as a mechanical contrivance,
hostile or at best indifferent to human values, and
having nothing to do with genuine human relationships.
And to the extent that we are persuaded of this we may
lament as an irreparable loss, or try to create arti-
ficially, the small face-to-face community, in the
belief that it is only in this kind of social environment that the sorts of norm can be developed that give
significance and purpose to the projects of the individual.   To accept these ideas is to beg too many
questions.   It is to beg important empirical questions
about what kinds of social organisation are and are not
compatible with the personal satisfaction of the individual and the development of satisfying personal
relationships.   But it is also to beg a different kind
of question, for it is to suppose that the community
which is creative of the rules defining social roles
and relationships is identical with the particular group

which may be the setting of an individual's main
interests, activities and relationships.   The purpose
of my contribution has been to indicate that these are
different senses of 'community', and more particularly
to develop the notion of a community as creative of
rules.   This may be said to be an invisible community, but it is no less real for that.

NOTES

1 This definition of 'community' (though not the definition of 'society' immediately following) is given
   by R.M. MacIver and Charles H. Page, 'Society, an
   Introductory Analysis', London, Macmillan, 1950,
   p. 8.
2 S.F. Nadel, 'The Theory of Social Structure', London,
   Cohen & West, 1957, p. 58.
3 G.C. Homans, 'The Human Group', London, Routledge &
   Kegan Paul, 1951, p. 123.
4 Ibid., p. 124.
5 Nadel, op. cit., p. 27.
6 Homans, op. cit., p. 123.
7 F.G. Bailey, Two Villages in Orissa, in 'Closed
   Systems and Open Minds, the Limits of Naïveté in
   Social Anthropology', ed. Max Gluckman, Edinburgh
   and London, Oliver & Boyd, 1964, p. 64.

11

The function of
social work in society
A preliminary exploration
Peter Leonard

---

1   INTRODUCTION

The purpose of this paper is to explore some questions
concerning the philosophical and political basis of
social work.   This exploration will involve questions
about the nature of knowledge as well as the nature of
society and is based upon the conviction that unless
social workers are prepared to examine some fundamental
theoretical problems, the study of the activity of
social work will continue to be reduced to issues of
technological effectiveness.   Such a reduction is
characteristic of much of the work undertaken in the
field of social policy study, where concentration is
given to specific social problems, such as housing,
education and employment, but little effort given to
discovering the interaction between them as a whole,
and their relationship to basic economic and political
structure.
  The reasons for the reluctance to come to grips with
theoretical questions which raise as problematic
assumptions which are usually taken for granted, are
not difficult to discover.   Principally, this reluctance arises from a distaste for theoretical discussion
which results from the fact that social work is developing largely within a positivist, empiricist tradition.
This tradition insufficiently emphasises that social
facts have a dual nature, that they exist both in themselves and in the conceptualisations of those who
observe them.   Even psychoanalysis has striven to
maintain its place within the empiricist tradition,
and so it has sealed off, Habermas suggests, (1) fuller
exploration of the problematic nature of 'facts'.   A
concern with the 'practical', the applied and the specific, which takes the 'common-sense' definitions of

social institutions as given, avoids the necessity of facing the problem that definitions of social reality are highly ideological.

As a first step in examining the function of social work in society, we shall discuss some problems associated with the definition of social situations with which social workers are concerned. This discussion, in Section 2, will rest heavily on the work taking place in the sociology of deviance, (2) and particularly on the debate which is being conducted on the place of phenomenology in the social sciences. (3) Having looked at the problematic nature of social facts and their implications, we shall, in Section 3 be able to move to a consideration of the function of social work in society from the point of view of different definitions of society and of the place of social work within it. Here I shall draw especially on the work of sociological theorists (4) in examining alternative models of society and of social work. Finally, in Section 4 we shall examine the implication of our theoretical discussions for the practice of social work.

2 DEFINITIONS OF SOCIAL REALITY

A central problem for the social worker is how to understand the meaning which the client gives to his social situation. The social worker assigns some meaning of his own to this situation, but how does he take account of the client's meaning? The empiricist tradition in social science suggests that if subjective interpretation, *verstehen* is to be allowed, then it is simply an intervening variable relating observable stimulii to observable reactions. The problem, as Hindess (5) suggests, is that 'if the actor acts in terms of meanings, of his definition of the situation, these meanings are never, as far as the social scientist is concerned, directly observable. Yet the scientist must refer to these meanings in order to account for the actions which he observes.'

In so far as the social worker attempts to base his understanding on social science knowledge and approaches, he faces a similar problem. A social relationship has to be understood from a number of viewpoints. (6) First, there is the understanding of the participants themselves, who know the relationship from the *inside;* then there is the understanding of others outside the relationship to which it appears as an environmental fact; finally there is the social worker himself who

tries to understand both the participants' subjective
perception and the others'perception of the social
relationship and then adds to it his own account.   The
point is that we are not here discussing observable
facts, but second order constructs made by someone
before the consciousness of a social relation arising
exists.   Schutz (7) argues that 'the constructs of
the social sciences are ... constructs of constructs
made by the actors on the social scene, whose behaviour
the social scientist has to observe and to explain in
accordance with the procedural rules of his science.'
In attempting to understand social reality, social
workers like social scientists are bound to get further
and further away from direct experience as they give
attention to a particular social action, try to control
and use it, and typify and over-simplify the experience.
Such a typification is essential to study and diagnosis, for the social worker's concept of the experience
is sharpened, but it may also be false.   In other
words, the social worker does not have a true account
of observed behaviour as though he had seen it in the
head of the client; the social worker has a typification which may be clear but wrong.   Equally, of
course, in the client's interpretation of his own
action there is the possibility of false consciousness, a point to which we shall return later.

Once we acknowledge the problematic nature of the
social worker's (and others) interpretation of reality,
we can no longer accept, without question, the given
definitions of social situations and social problems
which are presented by the major institutions of
society.   In constructing any kind of model of
society, for example, what has to be taken into account
is how the various elements in the model come to be
defined and evaluated.   Because of this subjective
element, we can recognise that people may disagree as
to the nature of the social world in general and the
social relations in which they are involved in particular.   Disagreement about the nature of the social
world begins from the very concept 'society'.   We may
use the concept to refer to people, things and activities within a given geographical boundary and suggest
that people's behaviour can be explained, in part, in
terms of being members of a society organised in a
particular way.   However, it is possible to move from
this point to a perception of society as something
which *causes* behaviour, as if society were separate,
mystical, and over and above people, things and activities.   Thus, although men created society, definitions

of society have developed which suggest that society
created men.   Such definitions of our social world
personify things, the arrangements of society, and reify
persons, reducing them to the status of things.   The
personification of society and the reification of
persons, which summarises what Marx meant by alienation, prevents the individual in society, whether social
worker or client, from understanding the actual sources
of influence and power which affect his behaviour and
beliefs.   The politician who talks of 'the national
interest', and the social worker who talks of 'being
responsible to society', are both suggesting definitions
of the social world which involve mystification.

In a critique of role theory in Western sociology,
Urbánek, the Czech sociologist, shows that reductionist
definitions of man may be accepted because men feel
powerless, are alienated from each other and themselves,
and therefore experience a false consciousness of their
social situation.   Urbánek writes as follows:

Reduction of man to an average, to a bearer of common
social qualities, roles and masks, to an impersonal,
outward, shared and forced character is ... the product of the evolution of that period of history....
Thus man, although he is the unconscious author of
his own life's drama, exists first of all as an
actor of a role, where the conditions, relations,
circumstances and institutions, though created by
himself, are prescribed to him almost fatally and
irrevocably. (8)

The problematic nature of definitions of social reality
are especially evident when one examines the definition
and treatment of 'social problems' by government and
other services.   The established approach is based
upon a reified model of society in which it is assumed
that people are bound to the state by a common set of
values and that social problems and deviancy are an
aberration which has to be eliminated.   It is assumed
that the population as a whole is healthy and integrated
and keep to the rules because they reflect a central
value system.   Problems arise with individuals and
groups because they have been inadequately socialised
into society's norms, due, for example, to family
breakdown which prevents the individual from incorporat-
ing appropriate social values into his superego.   Some
individuals are seen as lacking the opportunity to
benefit from what society offers and may then engage
in 'senseless', 'meaningless' and 'irrational'
behaviour.

Some members of society are seen as mentally dis-

ordered in some way, either as a result of environmental
factors, or because of inherent, biological factors, or
a combination of both.   In either case, such people,
the source of many social problems, are seen as not
being responsible for their actions, for they are
'maladjusted', 'psychopathic', 'schizophrenic' or
'immature'.

We can see immediately that such an approach ignores
the problematic nature of the definition of social
problems and of the conflict of perceptions which may
exist as between the problem individual and others.
Nor is it clear that the problems which some individuals
experience stem fundamentally from physical, mental and
environmental factors over which they have little control.   Also, many individuals internalise values which
they perceive, albeit through false consciousness, as
legitimate but who, through personality factors, are
unable to respond to the demands made upon them.
However, the liberal, humane, therapeutic approach of
the established services fails to take account of the
possibility of a conflict of values based upon radically different definitions of social reality.   People
with 'problems' are often seen as not understanding
what has or is happening to them and of needing help to
accept the definitions of their social situation which
social workers, in particular, can provide.   One of
the major problems of this established, consensus
approach to social problems is that it denies the
meaning which those with problems, especially the
deviants, place on their own actions.   The 'real'
causes have to be discovered and actions themselves
are deprived of meaning.   Theft, for example, is not
seen as possibly expressing value conflict over the
ownership of property; alternative norms are often
seen as the absence of values due to personality
failings.   Ultimately, the deviant and other clients
of the social services, are viewed as essentially
lacking freedom of choice and, in the best empiricist
tradition, as determined by physical, social and psychological factors, and hardly ever by their own
intentions.   Those who operate the services, including
social workers, tend to see *themselves* as determined
in their actions not only by internal and external
forces, but by their intention based upon their definitions of social reality.   In this way many clients
of the social services are deprived of a moral status
which social workers claim for themselves.

This discussion of definitions of the social world
is not intended to suggest that a full phenomenological

approach to social work and social problems is the answer to our difficulties. Schutz (9) argues that the individual is free, that his acts proceed from spontaneous activity, that these acts are determining, not determined, and that we can only study conceptual models, not real people.

An approach which gives much pre-eminence to subjective meanings ends up as a highly individualistic and psychologically reductionist view of the world. Sociologists who have been heavily influenced by phenomenology, such as Becker (10) and Goffman, (11) emphasise the importance of social interaction in small groups in developing self-images and face a similar danger of reductionism, where social phenomena are reduced to views of the situation held by individual participants. Rather than swallow phenomenology whole, social workers should welcome the critique with which it confronts the established social sciences and might, in part, emulate the approach which Matza suggests is incumbent on those who recognise the importance of the subjective view:

> It delivers the analyst into the arms of the subject who renders the phenomenon, and commits him, though not without regrets and qualifications, to the subject's definition of the situation. This does not mean that the analyst always concurs with the subject's definition of the situation; rather that his aim is to comprehend and to illuminate the subject's view and to interpret the world as it appears to him. (12)

The social worker cannot, however, stop where Matza, a sociologist, stops. He must view subjective meanings, liable as they are to false consciousness, as one determinant of behaviour alongside others and he must take action to intervene in social situations. It is the problem of social work intervention within a context of conflicting definitions that leads us to examine alternative models of society and social work.

3 MODELS OF SOCIETY AND SOCIAL WORK

The preceding discussion has emphasised the importance of recognising the range of definitions of social reality which may exist, definitions which reflect the social position and consciousness of the individual and which may be an integral part of the ideology of a social group. The definitions of social reality which we are now going to examine are models of society and

the function of social work as perceived within the
context of these models.   A model, in the social
sciences, is a general orientation to some social
phenomenon usually by analogy from the natural sciences
or technology (as, for example, in organic and mech-
anistic models) whose purpose it is to provide a framework within which theories can be tested.   Thus, from
the scientific stance, one does not ask of a model
primarily whether it is true or false, but whether as
a general orientation it fits the major features of the
phenomenon and is a fruitful source of theory
development.

However, models of society, as we have seen, define
important social arrangements, are concerned with
power and its legitimation and cannot, therefore, be
seen simply as value-free scientific statements.   It
is important to recognise that the implicit models of
society which lie behind statements about the nature
of social problems and the role of social work in
meeting them, are ideologically charged;   they are
value-laden definitions of social situations.   How are
we to choose between these definitions?   Are personal
authenticity and political commitment our only guide?
Goldmann suggests that there is something more:

> Once the conscious or unconscious effect of value
> judgements on scientific theories is recognised,
> the problem of the criterion of truth is raised.
> Must a sociology of knowledge lead to relativism?
> Are all ideologies of equal value, at least, as far
> as the search for truth is concerned;   and is the
> choice of one over another only a matter of indi-
> vidual preference?...   Viewed in terms of their
> effect on scientific thought, different perspectives
> and ideologies do not exist on the same plane.
> Some value judgements permit a better understanding
> of reality than others.   When it is a question of
> determining which of two conflicting sociologies
> has the greater scientific value, the first step is
> to ask which of them permits the understanding of
> the other as a social and human phenomenon, reveals
> its infrastructure, and clarifies, by means of an
> immanent critical principle, its inconsistencies
> and its limitations. (13)

Goldmann argues, and this paper is based upon a
similar viewpoint, that on the criterion of its understanding of ideologies, the Marxist orientation provides a better definition of social reality than
others.

We now turn to specifying some alternative models of

society and of social work having already made reference
to one such model.   This model has a long pedigree in
conservative social theory (14) and is based upon an
organic analogy in which society is conceived as a
system of interacting parts which are cemented together
by a common set of values.   In this *consensus* model of
society, social institutions are prior to individuals,
the major purpose of society is to secure social order
and this is achieved largely by the imprinting of
values through the socialization process.   Institutions
and values are seen as essentially man-received rather
than man-made.   This reified model of society, in
which common interests bind diverse social groups to a
set of values which legitimate the authority of the
central elites, is the basis of Western representative
democratic theory.   Such a model is also the basis,
often unacknowledged, of an *integration* model of social
work.   Because, in the final analysis, the interests
of the individual and society are the same, social work
is able to function in the interests of all individuals
and groups in society.

The focus of social work within this model is the
resolution of conflict and tension, the mutual adjust-
ment of the individual and his environment within
certain limits, and the socialisation of deviant individuals and groups into the common value system.
Social work with 'multi-problem' and 'inadequate'
families, for example, focuses on rehabilitation and
good child-rearing practices.   Whilst within this
model emphasis tends to be placed on defining problems
in terms of the pathology of individuals and groups,
there is place also for community development which
lays stress upon self-help as a means of integrating
values and encouraging citizenship.   The approach to
deviance of all kinds is liberal and compassionate,
for deviants are not 'bad', but are to be pitied as
unfortunate, disadvantaged or ill.

The integration model of social work is the model on
which the established services are largely based.
Social work is seen both as an agent of social control
in the interests of society as a whole, and of social
change within the limits demanded for the maintenance
of social order and the major social institutions.
The mainstream of social-work literature has reflected
this integration model, though without reference to
the model of society on which it is based.

The critique of the consensus model of society
involves the outlining of an alternative model of
society and enables us to add three further social-work

models to our typology.   We have already argued that
the reified view of society is mystifying; it masks
the fact that major social groups in society, especially
those centrally involved in the means of production,
have different interests and these are frequently
expressed in different values.   The consensus model
in particular fails to take proper account of the differential distribution of power in society.   The main
features of a *conflict* model of society, which stands
as the major alternative, are outlined by Rex (15) in
the following way:

1. Instead of being organised around a consensus of
values, social systems may be thought of as involving conflict situations at central points.   Such
conflict situations may lie anywhere between the
extremes of peaceful bargaining in the market place
and open violence.

2. The existence of such a situation tends to produce not a unitary but a plural society, in which
there are two or more classes, each of which provides a relatively self-contained social system for
its members.   The activities of the members take
on sociological meaning and must be explained by
reference to the group's interests in the conflict
situation.   Relations between groups are defined
at first solely in terms of the conflict situation.

3. In most cases the conflict situation will be
marked by an unequal balance of power so that one
of the classes emerges as the ruling class.   Such
a class will continually seek to gain recognition
of the legitimacy of its position among the members
of the subject class and the leaders of the subject
class will seek to deny this claim and to organise
activities which demonstrate that it is denied
(e.g. passive resistance).

A significant point about this conflict model of
society is that it provides a definition which includes
an account of the ideological distortions which both
the ruling class and the subject class may be involved
in.   The ruling class may propose a definition of
society based upon a consensus model and thereby try
to legitimate its dominant position by reference to
common values and goals - the 'national interest'.   The
subject class may either resist such ideological distortion by proclaiming its conflicting interests, or
by false consciousness come to accept the legitimacy
of the ruling class.   Marcuse (16) argues that the
ideological hegemony of the ruling class has been established largely because the working class, especially in

the United States, has been won over by relative
affluence.

Two other points are worth noting about this model.
Conflict may be institutionalised through the political
parties and through trade unions and employers' associations; it then operates through arriving at a
consensus as to the rules by which the conflict will be
conducted. The conflict model may be applied to any
social system and from the point of view of social work
we may identify as a subject group or underclass those
in society who form a large proportion of the clientele
of the social services - the poor, the unemployed, the
deprived and the deviant. This underclass may, of
course, have little consciousness of its collective
interests and may be particularly vulnerable to ideological distortion which suggests that their social
situation is a 'natural' one, or due to their own
inadequacy, or that radical alternatives may be 'worse'
than the present injustice.

The conflict model of society presents the social
worker with a dilemma. Once a reified view of society
is abandoned social work can no longer be seen simply
as balancing individual against society interests.
As major social classes have different interests and
are engaged in a struggle for power and legitimacy, so
social work has to operate within this context especially as it directly affects the underclass clientele
of the social services.

The conflict model, like all sociological models, is
an abstraction which is bound to simplify and distort
reality to some degree, and would need to be differentially applied to particular societies. In addition,
it has been sketched here only in broadest outline.
Nevertheless, the model suggests that there are three
possible broad functions for social work in society,
those of controller, adversary and mediator.

The *control model* of social work is appropriate when
social work is clearly operating predominantly in the
interests of the ruling class and its institutions.
The ruling class, whether a majority or minority in
society, uses social work primarily to contribute to
the protection, expansion and legitimation of its
power. The social services will be provided for the
subject class and its casualties in order to improve
the health and social functioning of the labour force
and mitigate the extreme effects of structural inequality. Social work is especially important in legiti-
mating the values of the ruling class by its emphasis
upon the socialisation process. Social work aims, in

other words, at re-education of the underclass clientele
who are seen as irresponsible and immature.   The subject class as a whole may be seen as aggressive and
inadequate and needing more socialisation, as
Eysenck (17) suggests in his discussion of working
class psychopathy.   The dividing line between deviant
acts and political acts may be difficult to draw, as in
Rhodesia and the Soviet Union.   Above all, if social
work is to operate in the interests of the ruling class
then its social control functions will be to the fore.

The *adversary model* of social work may be applied
to a situation where social workers are operating in
the interests of the subject class or at least the
underclass clientele of the social services, and in
opposition to the ruling class.   In the extreme case
where a revolutionary war is in progress the subject
class may, as in Angola and Mozambique, develop its
own health and social services and provide some forms
of social work.   In the United States, Black communities may develop their own network of welfare services.
In other situations, such as in Britain, where overt
class struggle is less pronounced, the adversary model
is difficult to apply to highly professionalised and
institutionalised social work.   Voluntary, fringe
social service organisations working on behalf of
deviant groups such as drug-takers may function as
adversaries and so, at times, may other social workers,
covertly, with individuals and community groups.
Social workers trying to operate to this model have no
commitment to the existing social order.   Their
primary tasks, with the individual and the family, may
be seen as 'working the system' in the clients'
interest, and combating false consciousness and ruling-
class definitions of social situations by sharing a
diagnosis with the client which sharpens his consciousness of his underprivileged position and urges his
involvement, where appropriate, in social and political
action.   In working with community groups such as
Claimants Unions, direct action, confrontation and sub-
version would be the most favoured approaches.
Deviancy will be re-defined in terms of value-conflict
and its political implications emphasised in the way
that Taylor (18) suggests in the following passage:

> ... unless our conception of the criminal is that
> of someone fighting against the fundamental interests
> of a society we admire, we should surely seek to
> redirect his aggression, his anger, into political
> channels.   Our therapy, our concern should surely
> be to raise consciousness of the possibilities for

external change and not to insist on the necessity
for internal personality change.   Here is a large
group of predominantly working-class people who
refuse to take quietly a society which steals from
them products of their labour, which insists that
they undergo periodic bouts of unemployment, that
they live in inadequate houses, which ensures that
their children will be processed through an educational system in such a way as to be only suitable
to perform a similar depressed and alienated role in
society.   We hear a lot about the fatalism of the
working-class, about lack of consciousness, but when
we find a group of individuals who are taking a hand
in determining their life chances we tend to treat
them with no more than a rather condescending liberal
humanitarianism.

Finally we come to the *mediation model* of social
work.

In this model social work recognises a fundamental
conflict of interests between ruling and subject class,
and works towards institutionalising that conflict by
mediating on behalf of the underclass clientele of the
social services.   Pressure group activity in the
Fabian manner, such as Child Poverty Action Group,
where the object is to achieve change by influencing
the rulers, will be characteristic of this model.
Considerable emphasis will be laid on the advocacy role
of the social worker with individuals, groups and
communities, especially with regard to 'welfare rights'.
Social workers will favour both universal social services in order to gain positive discrimination in the
interests of underprivileged groups.   Social workers
within this model will tend to have a conditional,
though reluctant, commitment to the existing social
order.

4   IMPLICATIONS FOR SOCIAL WORK PRACTICE

The purpose of the theoretical discussion in this paper
has been to demonstrate that in order to clarify the
functions of social work in society it is essential to
explore the various definitions of social situations
relevant to these functions which will be held by all
the participants, including clients, social workers,
administrators, and politicians.

The implication of this for social work is that the
social worker's task is to place his own definition of
social situations, with the value judgments that these

imply, alongside definitions drawn out from clients and
others in the social services.   In attempting the very
difficult task of revealing and understanding the
client's subjective meanings, the social worker may
draw not only upon the current work in the sociology of
deviance which lays stress on identifying the client's
intentions and the value orientation implicit in the
intention, but also on recent developments in psychoanalysis.   As Rycroft, (19) among others, has suggested, psychoanalysis may not be a causal theory at all,
but a semantic one in which the client's psychic situation is explained through helping him to understand
it and give it meaning.   At the same time, however, we
need to give more systematic attention to social
workers' typification of social situations, and particularly the part which social workers play in the process of labelling deviants and other clients.   One
step in this direction is renewed emphasis on the fact
that social workers' subjective meanings are important
in their work and that they are to be understood not
simply in terms of psychic processes, but also for the
light they throw on ideological orientations.

The four models of social work which we have outlined have suggested that the functions of social work
can be seen in terms of *integration, control, adversary* and *mediation* tasks.   In reality, of course, the
functions of social work are much more diverse and
complex than a simple model allows.   However, apart
from elaborating and refining this preliminary work
deriving from a Marxist sociological perspective, we
can use the models to increase our understanding of
the possibleddefinitions which the participants in
social-work situations may develop.

In discussing these models with social workers, it
becomes evident that some perceive themselves as con-
trollers, adversaries *and* mediators, depending upon
the particular situation in which they are placed.   In
part, this is due to the problems which these roles
present to social workers.   Given the established
organisational and political context of most of social
work, consistent adversary roles are very hard to maintain and often become no more than evening, off-duty
activities.   At the same time, it is important to
recognise that work involving the meeting of physical
and psychological needs of individuals and families
can hardly be seen as inconsistent with ideological
commitment to the adversary role of social work.
Participation of clients in the social services, the
aim of the mediator in social work, will be seen as

ultimately unsatisfactory by those committed to the
adversary role: client *ontrol* must be the eventual
goal and participation may be simply a means diluting
the conflict between the subject class and the ruling
class.

Mediating roles, especially in severe conflict
situations, such as those existing in Ulster, can also
be difficult to perform, for as Goffman (20) puts it,
the discrepant role of mediator is like 'a man desperately trying to play tennis with himself.'

If we use these social work models as a framework
to examine the perceptions of the participants in social
work as to its function, we can see how divergent they
can be.   It is not difficult to imagine a situation
in which a social worker in a local authority is working closely with a client trying to obtain for him
various financial benefits.   The social worker sees
his role as a mediating one, for though he is a tough,
determined negotiator he is only working for that to
which the client is strictly entitled and he believes
that the existing organisational structures can be
improved to provide better services.   The chairman of
the Social Services committee, however, sees the social
worker as a trouble-maker and his perception is that
the social worker is operating in the adversary role.
The client has another perception; to him the social
worker is a part of an indifferentiated 'them' and his
well-meaning attempts are seen as ineffectual and not
directed strongly to getting what the client wants -
adequate housing.   To him, then, the social worker is
essentially a controller.   Finally, the Director of
Social Services, whilst he is also inclined to see this
social worker in the adversary role, wishes that he
would take the role of integrator working for a consensus which he believes is possible between all of those
involved in the social services.

Clearly, this is simply a preliminary suggestion of
the range of possible perceptions of a social work
activity;   substantial work needs to be done in order
to explore this more adequately.

NOTES

1 J. Habermas, 'Knowledge and Human Interests', London,
   Heinemann, 1972.
2 See, for example, S. Cohen (ed.), 'Images of
   Deviance', Harmondsworth, Penguin, 1971;   J. Young,
   'The Drugtakers', London, Paladin, 1971;   E.

Rubington and M. Winberg (eds), 'Deviance, the Interactionist Perspective', London, Macmillan, 1968.

3 See: A. Schutz, Concept and Theory Formation in the Social Sciences, in 'Sociological Theory and Philosophical Analysis', ed. D. Emmett and A. MacIntyre, London, Macmillan, 1970; B. Hindess, The 'Phenomenological' Sociology of Alfred Schutz, in 'Economy and Society', vol. 1, no. 1, 1972.

4 See: J. Rex, 'Key Problems of Sociological Theory', London, Routledge & Kegan Paul, 1968; A. Gouldner, 'The Coming Crisis of Western Sociology', London, Heinemann, 1971.

5 Hindess, op. cit., p. 16.

6 See: J. Rex, Sociological Theory and Deviancy Theory, paper presented at British Sociological Association Annual Conference, 1971.

7 Schutz in Emmett and MacIntyre, op. cit., p. 12.

8 E. Urbánek, Roles, Masks and Characters: A Contribution to Marx's Idea of the Social Role, in 'Marxism and Sociology', ed. P. Berger, New York, Appleton-Century-Crofts, 1969.

9 Schutz, op. cit.

10 H. Becker (ed.), 'The Other Side', London, Collier-Macmillan, 1964.

11 E. Goffman, 'The Presentation of Self in Everyday Life', New York, Doubleday Anchor, 1959.

12 D. Matza, 'Becoming Deviant', New Jersey, Prentice-Hall, 1969, pp. 24, 25.

13 L. Goldmann, 'The Human Sciences and Philosophy', London, Jonathan Cape, 1969, pp. 50-2.

14 See Gouldner, op. cit.

15 J. Rex, 'Key Problems of Sociological Theory', p. 129.

16 H. Marcuse, 'One-Dimensional Man', London, Routledge & Kegan Paul, 1964.

17 H.J. Eysenck, 'Sense and Nonsense in Psychology', Harmondsworth, Penguin, 1968.

18 L. Taylor, The Criminologist and the Criminal in 'Catalyst', no. 5, Summer 1970.

19 C. Rycroft (ed.), 'Psychoanalysis Observed', London, Constable, 1966.

20 Goffman, op. cit.

12

The art and science of helping

Alan Keith-Lucas

When I was first asked to talk to you about helping,
my immediate thought was, 'What have I, a social worker
and a teacher of social work students, to do with these
people who are skilled in quite different things,
things about which, to tell the truth, I know practically nothing at all?' But I really do have something,
despite all that I do not know. For this matter of
helping people is wider than any profession. What
little I can add to it has already been taken up by
groups of ministers, welfare workers, probation
officers, guidance counsellors, Alcoholic Anonymous
members, doctors studying character change and Deans of
Students in our colleges. There does seem to be a
common core, whether the help that one gives is in the
form of money, advice, counselling or instruction,
which is, of course, only common sense, since people are
people whatever their problems and what all these professions are asking is basically the same thing. The
teacher, the preacher, the social worker, the consul-
tant, the agricultural expert, the marriage counsellor,
the home demonstration agent are all saying to those
they work with, 'Let me help you to change. Let me
help you do something different. Let me help you
begin to cope with whatever is making it hard for you
to succeed'.
It is not surprising then that there should be the
beginning, at least, of a little knowledge about how
people can be helped. The surprising thing is rather
that this beginning of knowledge should have been so
little regarded - that we should have, in our universities and colleges, no curriculum in helping; that
there should be so little common understanding of the
problems and methods of helping, of even the basic
principles that underlie this science and art. For,

despite the intuitive helping that some people seem to
be able to do without, it seems, being taught, the vast
majority of people go about helping most casually,
confident somehow that if one only knows one's subject
and gives the right kind of advice one has done all
that one could, and that if the person we're helping
doesn't take that advice, or do what we want him to,
it is his plain and obvious fault.   He's either
stupid, or idle, or obstinate, or weak, and he ought to
be punished for it - either by not getting any help, or
by being starved, or shamed, or made to do what's right
by some process or other - the law, or our inherent
authority, or the pressure of public opinion, or argument, or having us take over his thinking for him, or a
thousand different ways of putting pressure on him.
Fortunately we have dispensed with the whip, at least
for adults, the branding-iron and the gallows as aids
in the helping process, although all were used in the
past.   But one would have thought that our many fail-
ures should have shown us that something else was
wrong, that we had not somehow got hold of some basic
principles, that there was more to it than that.
     What, then, have we failed to see?   I would like to
start with two statements that may seem extremely simple
but lie, I think, at the heart of the matter.   The first
is that *all helping* - all real helping, that is, the
sort that really induces change - *takes place within a
relationship.*   And a relationship is a two-way thing.
It matters as much what I put into it as what the other
fellow does.   What may go wrong with helping may be as
much my fault as the helper, as it may be on the part
of the helped.   The second is that *people rarely
really want to be helped.*
     This may sound like a strange statement, especially
if one enlarges it, as I will, to include wanting to
learn.   It's true of course that many people profess
an eager desire to learn.   Others appear not only to
ask for help but to demand it as if it were their right.
But what these people profess to want, ask for, or even
demand, is not real help or learning at all.   It is
help on their own terms - help that will not force them
to change in any way.   It is in fact a way of warding
off any real offer of help, a way of going through the
motions, of pretending to oneself, of placating the
gods, even, rather than really getting help.
     Perhaps we could understand this better if we looked
a moment at what it takes really to ask for help.   It
takes:
     1 a recognition that there is something wrong, and

that one cannot do anything about it by oneself, without taking help, that is.

2 a willingness to confess this weakness to another, to let him know what one really is.

3 a willingness to let him advise one, to have some power over one's life, and

4 finally, a willingness to risk the unknown - to give up one's present situation, however intolerable this may be, for some unknown that may look better but may actually turn out worse.

I would add here, as an aside, and not to try to convert anyone, but to make this process clearer and perhaps to explain why I believe this to be something very basic indeed, part of what men actually are and not a psychologist's invention, that the Church, which is also concerned with help, has long known this process. It gives its elements different names - repentance, the recognition that one is a sinner and needs God's help to do any different; confession, submission and finally faith - the evidence of things unseen. And anyone who has had the experience of asking help from God may have a little inkling of how difficult this entire process really is. In addition, to ask help from a human being is even harder than to ask help from God. One has better reason to trust Him than one has to trust another man.

Is it surprising, therefore, that people will do almost anything to prevent themselves from being helped? Is it surprising that many of them refuse to admit their real need, that they demand help from us on their own terms, that they find ways of neutralising our help? My students do it to me, and I expect your clients do it to you. One of the best ways, incidentally, of doing this is to agree with a great deal of literalness with what the helping person wants - to follow his advice blindly, and then be able to show him that what he advised did not work. Some of you, to be honest, will do this with what I have to say to you today and it will work to show me up. Another way is to go through all the motions yet somehow, somewhere, to miss the really important point, the thing that really matters - just as one of the best ways of not getting help from God is to go to church, to sing all the hymns, to be busy in 'church work' and never permit the essential message to get across.

Those simple statements lead us to a number of others, the first of which is the realisation that *what prevents people changing is in fact, basically, fear* - the fear of change, the inability to risk. It is this

which makes people refuse to do what in all common sense,
what anyone else can see, ought or even has to be done.
It is what makes people obstinate, hostile, weak or
stupid or any other word we like to use to illustrate
this paralysis.   While there may be a few people who
quite genuinely do not *know* what to do - and, of course,
quite a lot of knowledge that can be helpful in deciding what to do - the basic problem is not generally
lack of knowledge.   It is fear of putting that knowledge to work.   The person who is so often thought of
as 'content with low standards' is often not that at
all.   He is by no means content.   But he is afraid to
act on his discontent, for fear that it will cost him
what little contentment he has.   Maybe his is a real
fear; fear of failure, of unemployment, fear of not
being able to compete, and in a depressed area like
parts of West Virginia I would suspect that many of
these fears are real.   Sometimes the fear is unrealistic, and this is where helping can begin.   For helping
could in fact be described as a process of establishing
the kind of relationship that can help exorcise fear.

It follows again, I think, that helping ought to be
understood *as something that it is impossible for one
man to give to another*.   It's not a commodity, a
thing.   Even where material things are part of the
help, such as in public assistance or surplus commodities, the help lies not in the thing but in the way that
it is given.   And this help cannot be given.   *It can
only be offered*.   The kind of relationship can be set
up that makes it possible for growth and change to take
place, but you or I, or the greatest social scientist
on earth, cannot ensure, cannot even predict that it
will take place.   We can only clear the way, make it
possible for it to do so.   And if it won't it won't.

This brings us then to another principle - that
help depends upon choice.   Now, this is a difficult
word, because there are two kinds of choice in this
world.   There is the kind of choice that we exercise
when we decided to wear a blue suit or a brown, or go
for a walk or watch TV.   And there's another kind of
choice, that may or may not have anything to do with
the choice of what we do in the purely material sense.
This is the choice to do one of the three things when
we are up against a problem that we can't manage by
ourselves - the choice between accepting the problem
and getting help for it, or fighting it blindly, or
doing nothing at all, escaping from it, pretending even
that it isn't there at all, hoping that it 'will go
away'.   This is the really essential choice that every

man has, and which will determine what he does with his
life.   Sometimes, as doctors know, it is the thing
that will, in fact, decide whether he lives or dies.
The best word that I know for it – and again you must
bear with me if I make reference to another framework
of understanding to illustrate my point – is the word
that the Church uses, 'commitment', to describe this
kind of choice.

We don't know too much about it.   But we do know a
little, I think.   One thing that we do not know is
where it comes from.   It isn't heredity.   The power
to make a positive choice turns up in the most unlikely
people.   It isn't environment, either.   Good heredity,
good environment may contribute to the ability to make
a positive choice, but there is an unknown factor
which upsets our most careful predictions.   One thing
we do know, however, is that it has little to do with
choosing to do what one likes.   It was this misunderstanding, this confusion about the meaning of choice,
that led so many people to put their eggs in the
basket of 'permissive' helping, of 'non-directive techniques', of giving the impression that all would be
well if people didn't have to obey laws or even moral
commands – a misunderstanding that has given my profession and many others the reputation of being soft
hearted and soft in the head as well.   It has, as a
matter of fact, little to do with freedom in the ordinary sense of the word.   It can, and must, be exercised
by a prisoner in jail, a public welfare recipient on an
inadequate grant, as well as by an executive at his desk.

We know also that it cannot be made by anyone else
than oneself.   A positive choice – which is, of course,
what all of us want – cannot be made, it cannot even be
too passionately wished by the person offering help.
It doesn't come from being exhorted, or persuaded
(except in the special religious sense of the word), or
shamed, or encouraged, or praised.   It has nothing to
do with reason.   One can't argue anyone into it.   One
doesn't do it because someone else wants one to do it.
All that someone else can do is to make it more possible
that the choice we dare to make is the forward-looking
one, the one that will really solve our problem instead
of fighting it or ignoring it.

We know something else, too.   This is a paradox, a
problem, for it goes against our instinctive way of
wanting to help people.   But the truth is that the
positive choice – the choice to accept the problem and
do something about it, *is possible only if a person is
free to do exactly the opposite, to deny it, to fight
against it.*

Intellectually this may not be too hard to see.   Man
cannot choose to be good unless he can also choose to be
bad.   To take another religious example, if God had
compelled man to be good he would not be good at all.
Again, man cannot choose to live fully unless he can
also choose (or accept) death.   He would never dare
get up in the morning.   Nothing is gained without risk
and to say 'Yes' sincerely always means that I could
have said 'No'.   We recognise this when we speak
slightingly of the 'yes-man' - for of all people the
yes-man can never really say 'yes'.

But this truth is terribly hard to recognise in
practice.   We so much want the man we are helping to
make the *right* decision, to choose independence and not
dependence, to take our excellent advice, to learn what
we have to teach him.   Even to recognise the possibility
that he may choose the wrong seems like treason to us.
Perhaps we work for an agency whose whole purpose is to
improve our client's lot.   How can we freely tell a man
that he is free not to improve.

And yet he cannot choose to get well unless he can
choose to be ill.   He cannot be pushed or forced or
even gently manipulated (one of the strongest forces I
know of) into choosing to improve - not if we want a
real decision.   This is the mistake that so many of us
make time and time again - churches, courts, protective
agencies, teachers and consultants.   I would not like
to have to confess to you how many students I have
failed because I could not let them fail - but, clear
as I am on the matter, I am tempted every time.

Perhaps I can make the point clearer by exploring a
little further what is meant here by the opposite, or
negative choice.   By this I do not mean merely a
failure to choose the good (or the supposed good).
That is what happens when we try to *make* someone into
something that he has not chosen to be, and he fails to
live up to expectations.   It is utterly defeating.
But there is always a negative choice - even a kind of
failure - that in itself is a choice and that has something of triumph about it.   It is the choice, the
determination, not to do what is expected of one, not
to have anything to do with this kind of help.   'It is
the decision to 'go it alone' or 'to take the consequences'.   And being free to make this choice does not
and cannot ever mean being spared these consequences.
It is this, that man, if he is to be helped, must
always be free to do - even to 'curse God and die'.
And we, and even our cherished values, are not, of
course, God.   What we think of as the wrong choice may

for another person be right.   Even if it cannot be,
the choice must still be there.   The risk must be
taken.   And the person who makes the wrong choice is
much closer to help than he who makes no choice at all.

Another way of looking at this is to liken the
human predicament to a trolley.   This trolley has an
engine that tends to move it in the direction that it
both needs and wants to go - the very same direction
that we, too, would want it to go.   Some trolleys do
not move.   They overcome minor obstacles, and sometimes, big ones, too.   But some are held by a spring,
pushing in the other direction - a spring of fear, of
anger, of shame, of hopelessness and despair.

Now our natural reaction on coming across this
trolley is to give it a push.   Perhaps we do move it
a little.   But if it really has a spring this movement
is at the cost of a tightening of its coils.   If we
relax our pressure, or perhaps turn away to try to push
another trolley awhile, the spring will recoil.   The
trolley is then less far on even than when we started.
And in any case our pushing will become harder hour by
hour.

The sensible thing, of course, is to get at the spring
and uncoil it.   This is why it is usually true that
*people need a great deal more help with their negative
feelings than with their positive.*   They need to look
at their negative feelings, to examine them, to discover
their weaknesses.   Their positive feelings usually get
a lot of support.   They are acceptable and everyone
can weigh in with reassurance, hope, or praise.   It's
their negative feelings with which they must struggle -
their fears, their doubts, their hates, their despair.
And this cannot be done, some psychologists and some
preachers to the contrary, by pretending that the
negative feelings are not there.   They are.   The man
who exhorted us to 'accentuate the positive and eliminate the negative' may have discovered a rule of social
intercourse, but he never had to help people in real
trouble - which is why the extroverted, Pollyanish kind
of helper who always wants to keep things pleasant is
sometimes more harmful than helpful.

It follows therefore, fourthly, that *the helping
relationship must be one in which negative feelings can
be expressed without fear of blame, anger, sorrow or
loss of face.*   This means in turn that it cannot be a
relationship of superior and inferior, saint and sinner,
wise and foolish, judge and judged, or even their
modern equivalent, adjusted and unadjusted.   These
things may objectively be true, or society may have

given one pair the responsibility to act as if they were
true, as in the case of a judge or a teacher.   But as
helped and helper struggle together to understand, to
come to a point where the helped person makes his essential choice, they must struggle as equals either of
whom could have felt and thought like the other.   This
is what we mean when we use the rather glib phrases
such as 'respect for human dignity' and 'accepting
people as they are'; that both helper and helped are,
for all their difference, fallible and imperfect
creatures who, if not capable of the particular weaknesses in question, are capable of many others.   One
of the greatest helpers of delinquent children I ever
knew, when I asked once how he was so able to have children share with him their real hopes and fears, said,
'Because I could be a criminal too'.

A number of other conditions that make possible the
commitment to change more or less follow from these:

First, *the relationship must be centred entirely on
the interests of the person served*.   It cannot be
centred in the helper's need to be liked or to control
or even to satisfy his own conscience.   It cannot
immediately be centred on any other good, such as the
good of society, the honour of one's department or
school, public morality, justice or fair play, although
once real help is given these generally will be added
to it.   This is a frequent mistake - to try to kill
two birds with one stone, and miss them both.   The
helped person's need is antecedent.   It must come
first.

Even more so, of course, helping cannot be centred
on goals of the helper's own - his desire to succeed,
or to be thanked, or to control another's life, or
satisfy his own conscience.   These are the things,
often subtle, that prevent us helping another, and it
takes sometimes a great deal of self-discipline and
personal insight to be sure that they do not get in the
way.   They crop up in the most unexpected places.   I
know myself that the kind of people that I find hardest
to help are those whom I dislike the most, against whom
I have to fight, and those whom I like the most, the
people whom I want to like me, whom I can't bear to see
suffer, whom I want to protect.

Second, *helping must deal with real things*, however
unpleasant they may be.   A doctor who refused to consider cancer of the anus because he was afraid of cancer
or he preferred to ignore the bathroom would be no
doctor at all.   So help with social problems must deal
with what is really there - with real sorrow, real hate,

real sin, and real despair.   It cannot deal with false
reassurances, with polite evasions, with 'pie in the
sky'.   And it must deal with them here and now.   It
cannot, as in a case I read lately, assure a woman
that she ought to be able to get support from an
absent husband and do nothing about the fact that her
gas and heat were to be turned off that afternoon.

Then again, *it must be based on trust; on the belief
that man can be helped, however wayward he may seem.*
I say this in contradiction to what seems to me the
trend in the social sciences today, which progressively
appears to see man as sicker and sicker and needing
more and more control and advice from his stronger
fellows.   But this kind of trust is necessary if one
is to stand by the whole process of helping.   Often
this is very difficult.   Man's first choices in the
process of finding himself again are often apparently
negative and are in any case quite unpredictable.

And finally, and proceeding from this, the helping
person needs not only courage - and plenty of that;
any idea that helping people is a sissy undertaking is
entirely wide of the mark - not only knowledge, not
only self-understanding, but an entirely different
virtue, which Christians call humility - and perhaps
there isn't another word.   I don't mean by this short-
changing oneself, or being hypocritically modest.   But
I do mean facing the real facts.   I do mean being
clear with oneself that one doesn't know what is right
for another person.   One is extremely lucky if one
knows this for oneself.   I do mean understanding that
however much one can feel and think with and for
another, it is his problem and not yours.   You don't
have to face what he is facing.   You may think that
you have, or are, but you don't know.   One of the most
dangerous kinds of helpers, or teachers, is the one who
has solved a problem and has forgotten what it cost him
to do it.   He expects everyone else to be able to
solve it as he did.   He gets impatient when the other
finds it harder than he remembers that it was for him.
And I do mean knowing that you will never know;   that
the more you think you know, the less you can really
claim to know, the more you will find that there are
factors not dreamed of in your philosophy, the less
certain you will be that you really have the answer.
For man is not a mechanical being who will someday be
known in all of his depth and breadth and height.   He
is a living soul.

So far, perhaps, you will have the feeling that most
of what I have said is negative.   Perhaps all I have

done is to tell you how not to help.   I hope that it
does not feel like that - but this is a difficult
subject, and one that needs a lot of self-discipline,
of knowing not what to do.   I am going to end my
talk, however, by suggesting three principles that do,
I believe, lie in a very positive way the very core
of help.

These three principles are a Trinity.   By that I
mean they are triune.   No one is effective without
the other.   They cannot be separated.   I won't conceal from you also something that you don't have to
believe - that they are actually reflections of another
Trinity of which we have heard - far-off, faint reflections, but nevertheless the three ways in which God
comes to us.   But that is not how I learned them, and
you don't need to make the connection, for they are
very real and practical things in themselves that
exist wherever man is helped.   They have technical
names - Reality, Empathy and Support - but I like to
try to bring them to life by putting them into the
natural language that we use when we are talking to
people.

Let us look at them in such terms.   So expressed
they come out this way:

(Reality) 'This is it'.

(Empathy) 'I know that it must hurt, or that it is
difficult'.

(Support) 'I am here to help you if you want me and
can use me'.

The first principle - reality - we discussed a few
minutes ago.   Let me see, however, if I can give it a
little more depth.   It means all that we said then -
not pretending that a problem doesn't exist, not taking
it away from a person, not disarming him about it, so
that he has no way of dealing with it.   It means not
giving false reassurance.   But it also means respect-
ing a person enough to share the truth with him.   It
means not being over-protective.   As you may know, my
principal work is with children in institutions, and I
have seen far more children - yes, children, not
adults - hurt because people wanted to protect them
from life, or the truth, or the consequences of their
actions than I have from facing them with these things.

Reality also means not being indirect.   For some
reason or other consultants, teachers, and social
workers, more than anyone else have gained the reputation of being rather wily birds who 'work round things',
who tread like Agag, who don't come out with the obvious
truth but are 'tactful' or 'considerate'.   These words

can be good ones, of course, but all too often they
describe the person who gently manipulates another,
who tries to get him subtly to do what the helping
person wants and thinks that he thought it up himself.
And all too often what this means is that the helping
person doesn't want to face the truth himself.   It is
not a bad adage to say that the fear of the unknown is
much worse than fear of the known - that the truth,
told with love, will set you free.   I could give you
many examples from my work;   I am sure that you can
find them in yours.

   Empathy is the second requirement.   'I know that
this must hurt'.   It is not too common a gift.   All
too easily it, or she, becomes confused with her much
less difficult sister, Sympathy, and sometimes even
with her puffed-up stepsister, Pity.   Let's see if we
can distinguish the three - for sympathy can be destructive, and pity is nearly always so.

   Empathy is an act of compassionate understanding.
It says, 'I can understand how you feel, and feel it
with you in a limited way, but I don't feel that way
myself'.   It maintains an essential difference between
the helper and the helped, and it is indeed this difference, set in the framework of the likeness, that
provides the means of help.   Empathy feels *with* a
person.   Sympathy feels *like* him.   To take a rather
flippant example, suppose a man tells you that he cannot
stand his wife.   The empathic person says, and means,
'I can understand how hard this makes your daily life.
I cannot judge, for I am not you, but with this feeling
you have for her what do you feel that you can do?'
Sympathy, on the other hand, would say, 'Oh, I know
how you feel, exactly.   I can't stand my own wife
either'.   This, of course, leads nowhere.   And pity
would say, 'Oh you poor, poor fellow, to have to live
with a wife like that.   I'm glad that mine is a wonderful girl.   Why don't you come and eat with us sometimes
and see what married life can be like'.

   One of the problems one frequently finds in trying
to help people to help is that when one describes a
person who is in trouble, perhaps has behaved badly,
has at least negative feelings, is angry, bitter, caught
up in lust or any other ill man is heir to, the helping
person fears that if he tries to understand he will
increase the other's weakness.   He will be condoning
wrong.   You hear it said over and over again, 'Sympathy
would make it worse.   It doesn't do to sympathise with
such people.   You can have too much sympathy, you
know'.   The very term 'bleeding heart' applied to

those who try to help is a reflection of this fear.
And if it's sympathy we're talking about, the objectors
are right.   One can have too much sympathy for another.
Sympathy does condone.   It does encourage the weakness.
It is, on the whole, a weakness.

But empathy comes from strength, not weakness.   It
is strong because, though it never judges, though it
strives to understand, it never condones.   It maintains its difference.   It is what my friend meant when
he said, 'I could be a criminal, too', and everyone
knew that he wasn't.

Empathy, too, is not a passive virtue.   It doesn't
mean just listening to someone's troubles, and empath-
ising with them, helpful as this may sometimes be.   It
is a positive act of the imagination, and properly used
breaks through even hidden defences.   I think perhaps
we can see this best if we go back to our trolley dia-
gram.   We said, rather blithely, that the sensible
thing to do is to uncoil the spring.   But what - and
this so often happens - if the spring is enclosed in a
tight casing of shame, of refusal to face the truth?
What if the person can't tell us about it and so help
us to get it uncoiled?   Then the one key may be that
act that we are trying to describe - imaginative empathy,
trying to know what the casing must look like from the
inside.   Even the statement, 'It must be hard not to be
able to talk about it' may be the thing that starts the
talk.

Empathy is the part of our Trinity that deals, of
course, with negative feelings, that encourages their
expression, that works with them in the here and now.
Support is its further dimension.

Support is both tangible and intangible - material
and in feeling.   We know that because we use the word
in both ways in our common speech.   We may support
someone through money, or gifts, count him as a depen-
dant on our income tax, or we may also give him what we
call 'moral support', which is, unfortunately, not
deductible.   But let's not ignore the importance of
material support.   One of the worst misunderstandings
about helping that I know, since it is so subtle, is the
down-grading of material means of support in favour of
counselling or advice.   It is tremendously important
that material support be sound - that, for instance, a
relief budget is enough to live on and not something to
starve on, or struggle desperately along on, or something on which one cannot count, so hedged around is it
with uncertainty.   It is important that the means of
doing things are there.   There is a type of helper who

considers practical helping somehow below his dignity and there are programmes which exist, I think, sometimes, only to conceal the fact that people don't have enough to eat.   There is even a theory around that if people have something to count on then they will never grow, or change - but the reverse is actually true. Only as people have something to rely on do they become free to change.

For every person who is dependent because help is too easy to get there are two or three who become dependent because they have never been freed from the necessity of clinging to everything they can get.   There used to be a description of certain men as being of 'independent means' - and the men really were independent.   They were really free to make something of their lives.

But moral support is also important.   The key to it is in the word 'here'.   'I am here to help you if you want me and can use me'.   The last is important, too. One cannot force help on another.   But so is the first - I am here.   Whatever you do, I will not desert you.   I may not be able to help you through this agency, of course, but I will respect your decision, will still be concerned about you.

None of these three is easy to give.   We'd all like to avoid reality.   We do find it very difficult to let people talk out their real feelings, particularly when these feelings are hostile (and of course particularly when the hostility is directed towards us).   We all feel like quitting on someone who won't, as we say, help himself.   This is why, I think, helping is both a science and an art.   It is a science - there are principles, even, though I don't like the word, 'techniques', but it takes a human being, a highly disciplined human being who is at the same time natural and full of feeling, to put this science to work - and this is what true professionals are - not people who simply know how, but people who have made this know-how part of their very being itself.

As I said when I started, I know nothing of your particular line or work.   What I have said may not be relevant, but I doubt it.   You deal with people.   You are one of the many new helping professions that have come into being in this century, more or less.   If I have spoken a foreign language, I hope that there are among you enough good translators that it may be of some use to you.

NOTE

This talk was given in 1964 to a conference of agricultural field agents and home demonstration workers in West Virginia, USA.

13   Knowing by living through

Dorothy Walsh

Many philosophers, of recent years, have emphasized the
asymmetry of self-ascription and other-person-ascription
of certain psychological characteristics.   How is this
view concerning asymmetry to be understood?   Is it to
be understood as constituting a challenge to the doctrine of philosophical behaviorism, in that cases of
self-ascription provide an exception to the application
of behavioristic methodology, or can the view be interpreted as constituting a challenge in a more ambitious
sense?

It is the purpose of this paper to argue for the
following claims.   1 What is chiefly characteristic of
self-knowledge in certain cases is not privacy of knowledge or certainty of knowledge but manner of knowing.
2 This manner of knowing is capable of extension to our
knowledge of others, even though it is less reliable in
such cases.   3 Therefore what we need to recognize is
not an exception to the application of behavioristic
methodology but, rather, the possibility of an alternative, noncompetitive, method for the understanding of
persons.   This may be called humanistic knowledge as
contrasted with scientific knowledge.   Humanistic knowledge is knowledge as realization, that is, the realization of the qualitative character of some actual or
possible lived experience.

1

Let us first of all consider the doctrine of philosophical behaviorism.   The essential claim is that statements
about mental events or conditions can be interpreted as
statements about overt behavior, or as statements about
dispositional tendencies to behave in certain ways.

However much philosophical behaviorism may have been
motivated by the desire to avoid dualism in favor of
an emphasis upon mind-body unity, yet the manner in
which this unity is understood - the emphasis on
behavior - is, I believe, testimony to the continuing
influence of the earlier doctrine of logical positivism.
Logical positivism, we may remember, was characterized
by a special regard for science.   It does not take much
reflection to see that the program of behavioristic
interpretation is admirably adapted to bring knowledge
of persons within the sphere of scientific inquiry.
The task of philosophy is to clear away the misconcep-
tions or verbal confusions that might seem to present
impediments to such inquiry.

Now, as to this, I think it should be said that the
behavioristic program of interpretation is a *possible*
program, and, moreover, the appropriate program for
scientific inquiry.   Scientific psychology must be
behavioristic.   If a person in pain reports that he
is in pain, a scientist may attend to that report, he
may regard the report as a suggestive clue, or as partial evidence for something, but he cannot rest on it.
This is not because the scientist is a highly skeptical
fellow given to entertaining doubts about whether a
person in pain is in a position to know that he is in
pain, or given to doubts about the veracity of speakers.
It is because the only way he can use the pain report
is to treat it as he would treat nonverbal pain behavior
such as grimaces or cries.   Let us remember that a
necessary requirement for a scientific statement is its
membership in a connected scientific discourse.   Within
the domain of a scientific discourse there must be paths
of transition from any one part to any other part, and
unless pain report is treated as pain behavior it cannot
be related to nervous system behavior.

The psychologist, as scientist, need recognize no
exceptions to the application of his scientific methodology.   The question, therefore, is not whether a
behavioristic interpretation of mental statements is a
possible interpretation.   It is.   And the question is
not whether persons can be objects of scientific
inquiry.   They can.   The question is whether those
who endorse philosophical behaviorism are justified in
the belief that this program of interpretation is not
simply *a* program but *the* program.

A proper respect for the enterprise of science is
compatible with the recognition of the importance, in
our personal and social life, of non-scientific modes
of knowledge.   If you are ambitious to achieve a more

adequate understanding of stars or of volcanoes you cannot do better than acquaint yourself with the most up-to-date scientific account, but if you are ambitious to achieve a more adequate understanding of persons, it is not the case that science has the same claim to your attention.   This is because we *are* persons.

2

Let us now turn to the consideration of the claim concerning the asymmetry of self-ascription and other-ascription of certain psychological characteristics. It should be obvious that the use of the word 'psychological' here implies or suggests nothing whatever about the science of psychology.   It is important to keep this in mind because the example most commonly cited to bring out the claim concerning asymmetry is the example of pain.   Every psychologist will say that pain is a sensation, and, from the point of view of scientific psychology, he is perfectly correct.   Whether or not something is to be classified as a sensation is not at all a matter of how it is experienced; it is a matter of whether we can specific a sense organ such as free nerve endings.   Thus, from the point of view of scientific psychology, apprehension of color and apprehension of pain are both cases of sensory response. However, if we turn to the consideration of *how things are experienced* - the phenomenology of experience - the situation is different.   Pain is experienced as phenomenally subjective; it is 'in me.'   Color is experienced as phenomenally objective; it is 'out there.' This is why, if we trust simply to the direct deliverance of experience, putting aside any beliefs we may entertain as a consequence of scientific inquiry, it seems perfectly plausible to say: 'There may be unseen colors but there cannot be unfelt pains.'   Now the uprush of anger and the euphoria of elation are experienced as phenomenally subjective, and this is why if we find it natural to say: 'When I am in pain I know I am in pain,' we shall also find it natural to say: 'When I am angry (or elated) I know I am angry (or elated).'

I do not wish to deny that, for certain purposes, it may be useful to recognize that pain is a sensation, anger is an emotion, and elation is a mood.   Even from the point of view of the phenomenology of experience the difference between anger and elation can be relevant in that anger is experienced as directed towards something.   We cannot be aware of anger

without being aware of something else.   We cannot be
'just angry' as we can be 'just elated'·or 'just in
pain.'

Now the claim concerning asymmetry of self-ascription
and other-ascription of certain characteristics is
usually presented as the claim that self-ascription has
a certainty that we cannot assume in the case of other-
ascription, in short, I cannot be mistaken about 'I am
in pain' though I may be mistaken about 'He is in pain.'
But what, exactly, does this mean?   Why can I speak so
authoritatively about my own pain?   Some philosophers
wish to say that self-knowledge in such a case, is non-
inferential and noncriterial.   Accordingly, they hold
that the question: 'How do you know you are in pain?'
is a senseless question.   The only answer that can be
given is: 'I just do.'   But the question: 'How do
you know?' need not be interpreted as a question that
asks for evidence; it can be interpreted as a question
that asks about manner of knowing.   So interpreted, the
question has an answer and the answer, I suggest, is:
'I know that I am in pain by living through the pain
experience.'

There is a difference between experiencing in the
sense of living through, and experiencing in the sense
of simply being aware of.   We can be aware of a color,
but we would not normally speak of living through the
experience of apprehending a color.   Accordingly,
lived experience is something more than just experience.
No doubt, anything experienced is experienced by someone, but lived experience is personal experience.   If
I know that I am in pain by living through the pain
experience, I know more than that I am in pain, I know
more than the pain, I know what it is like for me to
suffer this pain.   My pain, my anger, my elation, my
memory of my childhood, my religious conversion, and so
on, are mine.   Our sense of personal identity is
closely bound up with the sense of ownership, the
sense of 'myness.'

Because of the individuality of persons and the
uniqueness of their life histories, there is a sense in
which my lived through experience cannot be identical
with yours.   Nevertheless, there can be similarity.
When someone says: 'I know what your experience must
be like.   I too have undergone, lived through, that
kind of experience,' he is claiming that there is a
kind of understanding common to those who have lived
through a certain kind of experience and not shared by
those who have not.   Consider the common remark: 'You
don't really know what it is, unless and until you've

experienced it.'   The claim is that no amount of informational 'knowledge about,' no matter how reliable, can
be a substitute for understanding by undergoing, by
participation, by living through.   The former can be
described as knowledge from without, the latter as knowledge from within.   It is not a question of which is
better.   They serve different purposes;   they afford
different kinds of understanding.

3

Since I wish to claim that the kind of knowing from
within, knowing by living through, which we have of
our own experience, is capable of extension to the
experience of others, it will be necessary to draw
attention to our human capacity for self-transcendence.
We can transcend ourselves and see ourselves as 'other,'
and we can transcend ourselves and enter into the situation of another.   Let us consider these in turn.
    Some philosophers wish to say that statements such
as, 'I am in pain' or, 'I am angry,' are not based on
observation.   It is understandable that they should
wish to say this, for there would be something odd
about the request: 'Look and see whether you happen to
be in pain, whether you happen to be angry.'   Also,
when I am angry (or in pain) I know this without undertaking some particular act of looking or peering or
scrutinizing.   But though it is proper to say: 'I
don't have to observe myself to know I am angry,' we
should *not* say: 'I never observe myself being angry.'
If we say this latter, we say something that is not in
accordance with experience.   Consider the following
recital of events.
    'Before I had my interview with him I realized that
I might get angry, and I was fully aware of how unfortunate this would be.   Accordingly, I resolved not to
get angry.   But, alas, as the interview progressed, I
was aware that I was getting angry.   I kept telling
myself not to get angry, but I was unable to prevent
this happening.   With helpless frustration I watched
myself getting angrier and angrier.'
    It is to be noted here that the frustration is a
response to the state-of-affairs of me-being-angry, and
this means that we must distinguish between the phenomenal self (the angry self) and the spectator self who
witnesses the activity of the phenomenal self.   I-and-
myself talk is a product of I-and-myself experience,
and there are many cases of such experience.   Consider

the following: 'I observed with satisfaction that I
was enduring the pain with composure.' There is the
suffering self which, as suffering, is not in a state
of satisfaction, but there is also the self who can
experience satisfaction with reference to the way the
suffering self is enduring its suffering. The spectator self can respond in a variety of different ways
to the behavior of the observed phenomenal self. 'I
surprised myself, I didn't think I had it in me to make
that witty remark.' 'I was revolted to hear myself
pompously uttering those platitudinous comments.' 'I
was appalled to witness this uprush of vindictive
hatred in myself.' 'I was relieved to observe that I
didn't hesitate to forgo the unfair advantage.' 'I
saw myself awkward and embarrassed in the situation
and felt a certain compassion for that poor unhappy
self.'

Now, to be sure, the use of 'observe,' 'see,'
'witness' in these contexts is not exactly the same as
their use in other contexts. All I wish to claim is
that the use is intelligible *in* context. If remarks
such as those cited above pass as intelligible in
ordinary discourse, the fact that they do is evidence
of something about us as self-conscious beings. As
self-conscious beings we have a capacity to transcend
ourselves and see ourselves as 'other.' If we recognize this, we should also recognize that we have a
capacity to transcend ourselves and enter into the
situation of another.

When we hear the imperative: 'Put yourself in his
place, see the situation as he sees it, realize how he
must feel!' we understand what we are being asked to
do. This is the request for an act of imaginative
projection, imaginative identification. It will not
be considered that we have made any attempt at imaginative identification if we simply reply: 'Well, I
recognize that he feels disappointed, threatened,
humiliated....' Knowing that such and such is the
case is not the same thing as 'realizing what it is
like.' The only way to realize what it is like is to
live vicariously through the experience of the other
person.

To the question: Can we always be sure of doing
this successfully? the answer must be no. 'I thought
I understood just what his experience must have been,
but his subsequent behavior was so discordant with this
as to make me believe that I was mistaken.' How did
I come to misimagine? There might be several answers
to this. For example, I did not have sufficient back-

ground information about the person and his situation to
provide an adequate basis for the act of imaginative
projection. Or, again, I did not, on this occasion,
detach myself from myself sufficiently. I imagined
myself in the situation instead of imagining myself *as
him* in the situation. However, if it be acknowledged,
as I believe it should be, that there is a kind of
understanding to be achieved by this means, an understanding for which mere informational report is no
substitute, we shall be justified in seeking this understanding despite the fact that success in its achievement is not guaranteed.

It is one thing to observe human behavior and accept
what we observe as data for inference; it is another
thing to 'read' the behavior as expressive. If we
recognize this difference we will understand why we can
most readily enter into the experience of fictional
characters and dramatis personae. Artistic talent can
present experience as expressively articulate and, by
exercising control over our imagination, render it
perspicacious. But though, with the not inconsiderable
assistance of Shakespeare and some talented actor, we
can more readily enter into the experience of Lear than
into the experience of many actual persons, our response to literary and dramatic art would not be intelligible except on the basis of the assumption of our
human capacity for imaginative projection and vicarious
experience.

4

My claim is that knowing by living through, whether this
living through be actual or vicarious, is a distinctive
mode of knowing. The only thing that can be known in
this way is what can be lived through, and the only
thing that *we* can live through is some actual or
possible human experience. The kind of knowledge this
mode of knowing affords is knowledge as realization.

There are contexts in which for the word 'realize'
we can substitute 'recognize' without distortion of
meaning. For example, 'I realize that he is certain
to be disappointed,' 'I realize that it would be judicious to postpone decision.' But there are other
contexts in which this substitution is not regarded as
adequate. If someone claims to realize the situation
of a victim of persecution or irrational prejudice, we
can intelligibly question whether, in fact, he does.
It makes sense to say: 'He *recognizes* that the situation

of the victim is unfortunate, but he does not enter into
the situation, there is a failure in imaginative understanding and he does not *realize* it.'

Recognizing that such and such is so with reference
to some kind of human experience is not the same thing
as realizing what this experience might be like as
lived experience.   Confession of failure to understand,
in the sense of realize, is perfectly compatible with
absence of doubt concerning matter-of-fact.   For
example, 'I do not doubt that certain persons enjoy
situations of physical danger, and even seek them out,
but I don't understand it.'   What the speaker does not
understand is the lure, the fascination, of danger.
Again, 'I do not doubt that certain persons believe in
a life after death, believe in the immortality of souls,
and that they believe this with complete conviction,
but I don't understand it.'   What the speaker does not
understand is what it would be like to live in the light
of this conviction.   If we distinguish, as we should,
between the tenability of a belief and the experience of
entertaining the belief, or the experience generated by
that entertainment, we will recognize that anything
that would effect a transition from nonunderstanding to
understanding can properly be said to extend the range
of our humanistic knowledge.

When someone says: 'I know what it's like.   I've
lived through it.   I've experienced it,' we commonly
accept that he does know, even when he cannot convey
this knowledge.   Knowing beyond saying is acceptable in
such a case, not because saying is impossible, but
because the only kind of saying that would be relevant
is a saying that requires some degree of literary
talent.   Mere fluency in the language is adequate for
informational report, but talent is necessary for the
imaginative evocation of vicarious experience.

The notion of knowing by living through, and the
belief that there is a kind of understanding to be
achieved by this means, will not, I think, strike the
ordinary person as in any way odd.   We have all heard
the remark: 'Oh, if only you could experience it, or
something like it, you would understand!'   Even the
philosopher, when not in the grip of epistemological
anxiety about whether he *may* use a cognitive term
without having credentials of verification in his
pocket, will relapse into these assumptions.   The
solicitous father, who must deal with the fear of the
child, will assume that he must enter into his experience and understand it as lived experience.   He will
struggle to achieve this imaginative understanding

regardless of whether such understanding has received acknowledgment in his officially endorsed epistemological theory.

What we need to assume, and do assume, in our personal dealings with persons, ought perhaps to receive recognition in philosophy.

14 On not being judgmental

Ian T. Ramsey

THE PROBLEM

What I hope to do in this lecture is to come to grips
with an issue in the field of Pastoral Care that constantly arises when clergy, ministers, counsellors and
social workers come together.   It is an issue which I
think needs a very great deal of clarification and it
can be easily and seriously misunderstood.   The issue
is this: The attitude of the minister towards human
problems is often condemned as 'judgmental' and then
contrasted to its loss with the attitude of 'acceptance' adopted by the well-trained caseworkers, the
sensitive doctor and so on.   The point is made for
instance in the recent British Council of Churches
Report 'Pastoral Care and Training of Ministers'.   We
read, page 36:

> The aim of the doctor is usually to reduce guilt on
> the grounds that it is a rather useless feeling and
> to palliate anxiety with tranquillisers.   Tradi-
> tionally the minister has made use of guilt to move
> his flock to penitence.   There may even have been
> times in the past when this has come perilously
> close to spiritual blackmail.   There are issues
> here which neither doctors or ministers, have
> squarely faced and surely they should face them
> together.

But the paragraph grants: 'Here however, doctor, caseworker and minister may well find themselves on occasion
in opposite camps and the issues are by no means easy
to resolve'.

It is this tension and opposition which I shall seek
to analyse and clarify as far as I can.   Incidentally,
doctor as well as minister can be deceived by appearances:

290

The factors which are undermining health may not be
obvious on the surface.   Human beings who bear their
sufferings with fortitude often have little idea how
far they are the unconscious architects of their own
misfortunes.   It is fatally easy for even the experienced family doctor to collude with a patient's lack
of insight.   In a series of studies, Dr Michael
Balint and his associates have shown that the doctor
can unwittingly attract to himself a series of
patients who are, by their own choice of this particular doctor, insulated from the risk of getting well.
Or again, still introducing the issue with which we
are going to be concerned, this time as it arises in the
field of Marriage Guidance, we read in the same BBC
report, page 36:

The saintly spouse, husband or wife, may well be
driving the partner to the verge of breakdown and the
children into ill-health yet this spouse may be the
one who stands well with the congregation.   The
minister in dealing with a member of his Church may
not be as clear sighted in the matter as he might be.
He may even resent the suggestion that religious
belief may be used at this point as a means not of
facing but of evading real issues.

The report comments: 'All this is not to suggest
that the minister is intrinsically more likely than anyone else to make this kind of mistake but merely that
up to the present he has often been singularly ill-
prepared to realise his mistakes'.   Another way of
expressing the issues before us in this lecture is to
say that I shall try to clarify what precisely is the
mistake which the minister may be making and which he
may be 'singularly ill-prepared to realise'.

Still continuing to get the problem rather more into
focus let us consider an example of an adolescent girl
which is discussed on pages 37-38 of the Report.   The
girl, who had been sent for a behaviour problem to an
approved school, was illegitimate and had since childhood lived with her grandmother who was now a widow.
The quote from the Report:

The minister was contacted by the Social Case Worker
to see if he could include the girl in parish youth
activities.   On hearing that she was returning to
her grandmother he objected as he thought the old
lady was not a good influence on the girl.   He took
what the social worker considered to be a judgmental
attitude to the grandmother.   [Later the Report,
commenting on the minister's attitude, remarked:]
The Minister thinks in terms of 'defending' - as we

may say 'protecting' - the girl; the social worker
regards this as treating the girl as immature and
thus preventing maturity from being achieved.   There
are times when the minister as a result of his training will look on life from a judgmental point of
view springing perhaps from his own defensiveness,
[though in fairness it adds that] on the other hand
the minister may have felt in this case that there
were too many risks involved in the social worker's
concurrence with the girl's wishes.   [The Report
then continues] There is no easy answer to this
dilemma, both sides of the matter need to be taken
into account.   The ideal way with such a matter is
to begin as far as possible with a full awareness of
one's presuppositions and the safe way to continue is
by constant vigilance without too much interference.
There may be much to learn here about the openness of
faith and the capacity of faith to take risks.

Again I may say that this lecture is concerned precisely
with the background presuppositions of this kind of
learning, with what in fact is involved in 'the openness
of faith and the capacity of faith to take risks'.

Yet again, in discussing the example of a boy's
behaviour and his relationship with his very 'proper'
mother after the death of his delinquent father who had
been strongly addicted to alcohol, the Report comments:

At this point the minister might have been tempted to
speak to the child to warn him, to exhort him to
behave, or to remind him that his mother had enough
worries without his adding to them.   By doing this
he would adopt the role of disciplinarian, and might
even earn merit with his congregation but this would
not touch the real problem.   The solution lay here
in the minister's ability to get the woman to face
her feelings about her (dead) husband.   [Later the
Report adds] The minister by trying to articulate
her real feelings could begin the necessary Grief
work to release tension and avert the breakdown which
would otherwise probably take place.   Perhaps a word
like 'well you really must have loved him a lot at
one time' or some such sentiment may be enough to
get the natural processes working.   The mistake not
to make [the Report continues] would be to commend
her for being brave in the face of death.   This is
not a case for the minister to support the defences
of the woman but gently to encourage grief to work
its way out and support her while this is happening.
Only by placing her true feelings could this woman
find real resources for living and be reconciled to
the boy.

In those remarks about this particular case is implied something of the contrast between the 'judgmental' and the 'acceptance' approach.   Another line on the distinction is given in some remarks by Miss Jean Heywood in her book 'Casework and Pastoral Care'.   She asks, page 72:

> ... are there differences between the way the Priest and the Social Worker look at behaviour [and her answer is] I think there are.   To the Caseworker sin is irrelevant in the context of his work.   He knows and recognises that certain things are morally wrong, irresponsible and evil but he looks at acts of behaviour this way - Why did this person feel he must do this, what did it mean to him, what lies behind it all?   The casework method is designed to find this way out.   Sometimes, as in the case of the suddenly bereaved child who steals something of value to symbolise replacing the treasured mother he has lost, the act is seen as an appeal to compassion, a cry for help; sometimes it is an act of hate against a cruel world.   The worker cannot change the behaviour except by giving to the child a repairing experience of love either through himself, or through providing some closer relationship.

The implication all through is that this is very different indeed from the approach of the Priest or the Minister to such a person.

There then is the issue with which I shall be concerned in this lecture and the kind of context in which it arises and I now propose first to look at what is involved in calling an attitude 'judgmental', and then to follow this by a similar examination of the attitude of 'acceptance' with which 'judgmental' is often contrasted.   Thereafter I shall attempt a critical evaluation of the two terms.   It seems to me that when the word 'judgmental' has been used to express the kind of criticism to which I have referred, we can discover at least seven different contexts for it, and I will try to segregate them as well as I can.

CONTEXTS FOR 'JUDGMENTAL'

1 First, to be judgmental is, in one sense of the word, to make a particular kind of judgment of someone's behaviour namely to condemn that behaviour as sinful or guilty.   For it is claimed that to judge someone's behaviour as, for example, 'sinful' is either as Miss Heywood said, irrelevant or, especially when set in a

condemnatory context, sets up the very conditions which
hinders a caring ministry from being effectively
exercised.   Miss Heywood tells us that even the
Christian caseworker is 'wary about arousing too much
guilt because he knows its paralysing effect and the
serious depression which may follow it'.   There then
is my first sense of judgmental.

2 Broadening that first sense, being 'judgmental'
can next mean imposing some dogmatic interpretation on a
situation.   For instance we may refuse to accept a
divorced person's need for re-marriage on the grounds
that since a metaphysical *vinculum* or bond had been
created at his Wedding Service, that first marriage had
not been broken nor could it ever be broken despite the
fact that now at any rate there seems to be no evidence
whatever for it.   This would be a case of imposing a
dogmatic interpretation on a situation which from the
point of view of every empirical fact seems plainly to
run counter to it.   Or a text from scripture might be
used in isolation to provide a judgment of a universal
kind.   Though I know that this particular text is open
to many misunderstandings, it is good enough for an
example and it might be used by people who have never
known what the scriptures said or didn't say: 'Better
to marry than to burn'.

3 More generally still to be judgmental may be to
work with prior notions.   Notice the way in which the
first three senses become more and more generalised as
we pass from 1 to 3.   To be judgmental in this third
sense then is to work with prior notions and so to make
far too speedy and superficial reactions to the complexities of the human situation whose complexities,
thanks to developments in the Behavioural Sciences, we
are coming increasingly to recognise.   In this way
people who are judgmental would have greater concern
for their conceptual frame than for those to whom they
were supposed to be ministering.   The judgmental would
attempt to impose stereotypes on empirical fact and a
number of these stereotypes come readily to mind.   I
have mentioned one or two already tonight.   The duti-
ful daughter, the saintly spouse, the good for nothing
brother, the lazy scoundrel, the merry widow, are some
of them.

4 Judgmental is sometimes a way of characterising a
disciplinarian, who has strict rules of how people
ought to behave and sees human behaviour at its best as
conformity to such rules and considers that any violation is to be condemned outright.

5 The judgmental need not to register an altogether

condemnatory attitude.   We have seen already that it
can be used of those who seek to protect a person.
You remember the minister in relation to the child he
thought ought not to go to the grandmother.   Closely
related to judgmental as used by those who in a particular way 'protect', is judgmental used of those who
seek to manipulate a person in any particular way.

6 Another example of being judgmental is that of
someone constantly uttering warnings and exhortations
forbidding this and urging that - in this way bringing
harsh and sometimes unfair pressure, authoritarian and
insensitive pressure, to bear on people.

7 Something quite different - a judgmental attitude
has sometimes been associated with the pronouncing of
absolution.   For someone might seek forgiveness in
this way, and absolution be pronounced, in a situation
whose complexities demanded a much more searching and
a much more prolonged exercise.   Penitential exercises,
it would be said in this connection, are altogether too
easy and too superficial for the complexities of human
behaviour and it might be added that ironically enough,
these prescriptions of traditional piety may only conceal what is in fact needing forgiveness, a situation
which needs to be faced frankly and analysed very
carefully.

Those are the seven senses in which so far as I can
gather from the literature, the word judgmental can be
used and has been used by way of criticism.   What
characteristic features do we now find looking back on
these seven senses?   What features do we find a judgmental attitude to display which can account for the
caseworker's suspicion of it?   I think we can group
our answer broadly under two headings.

First the caseworker is suspicious of it because of
the shallow and superficial understanding of human
nature which it often implies.   It represents the
desire, so it would be said, to get by without any of
the knowledge which can be given by techniques or other
ways of knowing human nature.   Second, the caseworker
is suspicious of the judgmental attitude because it
uses methods or concepts which, whether because of
implied hostility or otherwise, inhibit response and
oppress the spirit of man by being embodied in some
authoritarian judgment.   The judgmental attitude often
names or condemns a situation, or both, rather than
reacts creatively to it.   There then are the seven
senses of judgmental, and the caseworker's reasons for
being suspicious, if you like, of them all.

FEATURES OF 'ACCEPTANCE'

Now contrasting with that judgmental attitude is the attitude of acceptance.   What do we make of this?   I think there are three features distinctive of this attitude of acceptance.

First of all it describes an attitude, relatively passive, which helps someone in need to articulate freely feelings which have been hitherto repressed or unacknowledged or undiscriminated and whose repression is proving a danger to health and well-being.   The evidence for such a claim is that when these feelings have been articulated freely there is an obvious growth in health and well-being.   Second, the attitude of acceptance is meant to build up and to develop, as far as knowledge and skills can go, all the empirical particularity of a certain situation.   It is meant to create empathy and sympathy between those who accept and those who are accepted.   Third, it is avowedly non-authoritarian in character, so much so that some have criticised it, I do not say necessarily unfairly, but have criticised it for being an altogether casual attitude - so open-minded as to be empty-minded.

But the claim would be that the caseworker and counsellor working with this approach is never off-putting, wins the confidence of the client and provides a climate and an atmosphere in which men and women can be helped to grow freely to maturity.   Now it might seem that the case is absolutely clear-cut, that there is every need in a caring ministry, whether of priest or caseworker, not to be judgmental but always to develop an attitude of acceptance.   What more could there be to say?   I fear, however, that we have not completed the story.   Let us now see how the edges of that clear-cut judgment begin to be rather blurred. There are some five points for us to consider.

BLURRED EDGES

First, in rightly criticising many judgments expressed in terms of sin and guilt as being either irrelevant or unhelpful we must not go so far as to exclude from our assessment all moral or theological interpretations of human behaviour.   Recalling as an illustration the case of the 'suddenly bereaved child who steals some-thing of value to symbolise replacing the treasured mother he has lost', there are at least three points to make. (i) In regard with this case, first of all the act of stealing as such is wrong. That I hold, we take for granted. (ii) But second, and following very quickly on that first reflection, no-one knowing, by the skills and techniques and knowledge now available to us by the Behavioural Sciences, no-one knowing the whole situation in this way would, I think, ever condemn the child or want to speak of sin or guilt in relation to the full circumstances. Here we may recall an obvious distinction of which, it seems to me, in this whole field we make use far too rarely. This is the distinction between right and wrong, good and evil on the one side and praise and blame on the other. There may be many actions, good and right for which people could and should be blamed; and there are many actions wrong and evil for which people could and should be praised. I think this is a logical possibility that the kind of hard and fast distinction between the judgmental and acceptance attitudes often fails to make. In judging an action wrong or a situation evil, we do not necessarily blame anyone, still less the person or persons who seem to be directly involved. This distinction which G.E. Moore discussed at length in his book on 'Ethics' (Home University Library pp. 187-95) is sometimes entirely lost sight of in the field of social work and yet it is clearly important to make a distinction between right and wrong, good and evil on the one side and praise and blame on the other. There is no reversible entailment between the one set of concepts and another. We have got to be very careful indeed how we move from the one set to the other and no doubt many of the condemnations of the judgmental have resulted from a confusion in this conceptual area. (iii) Third when on some particular occasion a moral judgment is made it must be genuinely moral which ensures in particular that it will not be authoritarian. How do we ensure this? The answer is: when and because the judgment discloses an ideal in relation to which a moral judgment is made. A moral judgment has lost its point and importance, and does not deserve to be called a moral judgment, unless it succeeds in mediating an ideal, a moral obligation which people acknowledge spontaneously and to which they respond freely.

Incidentally it would seem as if Miss Jean Heywood cannot in any way be surprised at this, cannot at all escape moral categories in her discussion of and assessment of social work cases. For instance she remarks, page 73, 'No casework, no caseworker ever knows the struggle which goes on in a person's mind as he wrestles with "want" or "thought", how easy it was to come down on the right side or how difficult'.   I should have thought the implication of this comment was that, while no caseworker would ever know the moral struggle in all its intensity, this was certainly a feature of the situation which anyone concerned with a reliable assessment of it ought to do his best to know and certainly to acknowledge.   Again the only way to change the child's behaviour Miss Heywood would say is to give him 'a repairing experience of love' on which obviously Miss Heywood would set extremely high value and make of that repairing experience of love is the moral level at which she would assess it.   My point is, you see, that the distinction between judgmental and acceptance attitudes begins to be blurred.   We see that the caseworker cannot avoid making moral judgments, or embracing some kind of moral ideal as the very presuppositions of his or her work, can't avoid engaging people in moral exercises.   Yet at the same time we must rightly doubt whether the way to display these presuppositions or to initiate these moral exercises is by means of terms like 'sin' or 'guilt', not least when these are set within an authoritarian context.   For then they fail to mediate the redeeming love which is the Gospel, a love in response to which men find freedom and life and the confidence of ultimate triumph.   I think that one of our greatest needs in theology, as it bears on casework examples, is so to style terms like 'sin' and 'guilt' that they make evidently clear the Gospel the good news which they should be articulating.   So often when I hear sin and guilt discussed in theological contexts they appear to be part of the worst possible news that has ever at any time come to man from anywhere, and they certainly do not initiate appropriate or beneficial moral exercise.

Second, having said all that in relation to the term 'judgmental' let us now note that the term 'acceptance' is not without its ambiguities.   Very often in casework it is said that whether with ourselves or other people we must accept the evil that is in us and them. Now here, it seems to me, are two very important points. Acceptance by itself cannot possibly be a term strong enough to bear all the weight which the caseworker puts on it.   Acceptance by itself is not a term strong enough to avoid being misleading, for it can be far too passive in its overtones.   It can register far too little involvement and concern.   For instance day by day, year in year out I accept the fact that Newcastle

is north of London and south of Edinburgh but there is
never an occasion I get warmed up about it.   I even
accept the fact that we have a two-tier postal structure
and I am not much fussed about that either, and we can
all recall the lady who said she was perfectly prepared
to accept the universe and who prompted the remark
'ma'am, you had better'.   Now it is to meet this difficulty that 'acceptance' is far too weak a term to use,
that it is ambiguous in its context, that very often
you will find in the literature that another word is
added to it.   We have to get people to accept and to
'face' a particular situation.   The word 'face' is
often added.   So far so good and indeed much better.
But now comes my main point.   When we accept and face
the evil around us what is quite clear is that the
alternatives are not denunciation and toleration.   What
is quite clear is that we have not to choose between
denunciation on the one hand which oppresses and imperils
the spirit of man, and toleration on the other if that
is supposed to be, as it often is, a just-couldn't-care-
less attitude.   For Christians at least there is a
third possibility, redemption and loving concern, the
conviction that by the love of God shown forth in
Christ, and reflected at least in true Christians,
there is no evil which cannot in measure be already re-
deemed and have its part in a creative development.
So here there arises a context for 'acceptance' and
'facing' which allows (unless we think that 'denunciation' and 'toleration' are exhaustive alternatives) for
having the third possibility which at once introduces a
theological interpretation even into and associated
with the attitude of acceptance and facing.
    Third, as we try to bring together the judgmental
and acceptance attitudes in a critical evaluation, let
us remember that appearances especially in human nature
are indeed often deceptive.   But judgments are made
on situations even by caseworkers.   Naturally as a
matter of pastoral expediency and professional discretion it is recognised that they will not always call
to be, nor should they be, publicised beyond ourselves.
But that does not mean that they are not made.   The
important point here in an area where appearances can
be very deceptive and misleading and where judgments
are particularly intricate and hazardous would seem to
be this: always keep these judgments which, it seems
to me, that caseworkers as much as priests inevitably
make, always keep these judgments tentative and ready
for reform.   Never let them be dogmatic.   Let them
be open and at risk.   But this is a feature of course

which many people would argue has not enough belonged
to theology and needs to belong to theology, and that
while it has belonged to theology in its most devout
and creative eras, for instance in New Testament times,
that is by no means to say that it always has belonged
to theology, or does largely belong to theology today.

My fourth point concerns this matter of absolution.
Now undoubtedly absolution can describe an activity
which is as empirically naive as it is ritually stereotyped and theologically suspect.   Undoubtedly it can,
it may, tempt a priest to play the God role and in
this way to pretend to an infallibility, an omnipotence
and a divine status which since they are given to no
finite person are inevitably and necessarily parodied
and contorted.   That needs to be said.   But another
interpretation altogether can be given to the act of
absolution.   In relation to sin and wrong-doing, it
can in principle occur as an expression of the Gospel,
just as indeed in relation to a community the Church
occurs as an expression of the Gospel, and as in relation to written words the Bible occurs as an expression
of the Gospel, and just as in relation to food, the
Lord's Supper, the Holy Communion, occurs as an expression of the Gospel.   What I am saying is that in relation to sin and wrong-doing absolution may occur as one
of many legitimate expressions of the Gospel, the
Gospel of God's redeeming love.   In this sense absolution can be a feature of the reconciled community which
in this way shares through its spokesmen in the unsearch-
able riches of Christ.   This I believe to be the true
interpretation of verses 19-23 of the twentieth chapter
of St John's Gospel viz. that absolution is a characteristic feature of the forgiven, reconciled community,
reminding its members of the redeeming love of God in
which they constantly live.   What I am saying is that
absolution may in its rite and ceremony and when justified always will in its rite mediate this redeeming
reconciling love in a disclosure.   Absolution in this
theological context can surely do nothing but good for
it mediates God's redeeming love, in such a way that
men freely and spontaneously accept it, as they respond
to genuine inspiration.   Absolution in this way creates
and mediates that atmosphere which is the context of
the Gospel and it is an atmosphere which we see also
mediated in the word of God and the sacraments, and
indeed by all Christian doctrine when they reliably
express the Christian Gospel.

Which leads me, fifth, back to our talk about guilt.
The BCC Report to which I referred earlier and from

which I quoted some relevant remarks on guilt, comments
in relation to the dilemma over guilt.

The premature removal of guilt and anxiety may be
detrimental to spiritual and mental health while
the perpetuation of either feeling may be equally
detrimental [and it continues] presumably the
answer lies in solely treating guilt as to increase
responsibility [but it concludes] the path which
religious belief should play has yet to be adequately
worked out [and here comes the quotation I made at
the start] Doctor, caseworker and minister may well
find themselves on occasion in opposite camps. The
issues are by no means easy to resolve.

Well, may I make an attempt to resolve them and in this
way to take a little further points which I have made
already? There surely can be no objection to judgments of guilt or sin where, first of all, these are
reliably made by people themselves (and notice that I
inserted the word 'reliably'); and/or second, when
they arise not as superficial or conventional or authoritarian interpretations of certain behaviour but as a
response to the incoherence and the discord which has
been disclosed when certain behaviour is set in the
context of an inspiring ideal which we freely and
spontaneously affirm. We can surely not object to
judgments of guilt when they arise not in some authoritarian or dogmatic context but as a response to our
discerning discord between certain behaviour and an
inspiring ideal which we freely and spontaneously
affirm. For to make such judgments would surely be an
accepting and a facing. But the very accepting and
facing of the situation on the one hand, and of the
ideal on the other, would surely involve making a judgment which itself reveals the hope and possibility of
redemption and initiates a growth to maturity indeed.
Ironically enough it would seem to be judgments of sin
and guilt which when properly articulated and reliably
exercised that must lie at the heart of any growth to
maturity. We all know that terrible agonising cry:
'They don't care enough to say that I am guilty'.

THE MEETING OF JUDGMENT AND ACCEPTANCE

Now all this may seem startling. Does it mean, you
might say, an entire volteface? Is there then no
defence whatever for the caseworker's 'acceptance',
nothing to be said for 'not being judgmental'? No,
to make my own central point quite briefly, criticism

of the judgmental attitude is at its heart a criticism
of an authoritarian theology, and of practices that show
a shallow and superficial understanding of human nature
and men's needs. Yet it often rests also on an inadequate understanding of the character of genuine moral
judgments. In short, it is a devastating criticism
somewhat weakened, however, by being expressed in terms
of a shallow understanding of moral judgments. In
other words, the point is this. For men and women to
grow to maturity they need to respond spontaneously and
freely to something which wins them over, to something
which inspires them. Now in that sense to grow to
maturity demands a response to something taken as
authoritative but not, never, authoritarian. Neither
caseworker nor priest can ever hope to succeed in their
concern for maturity unless somewhere along the line
they can effect some authoritative disclosure in responding to which men and women can find their freedom
and life and fulfilment. The good caseworker and the
good priest will both seek to create the conditions for
such a disclosure to occur. Meanwhile what we have
come to see and what I have implied is that much traditional theology and many traditional Christian practices
so often fail to evoke such a disclosure, whereas ironically enough many of the natural techniques and skills
and understandings of the social workers do. Now
there, it seems to me, is the real tension between
being judgmental and not being judgmental. Here, so
to say, is the rub, the devastating contrast between an
ineffective, harsh theology, a polished cistern which
contains no water, no living water and the knowledge
and skills of the Behavioural Sciences which seem to
minister so obviously and creatively to the spirit of
man. To overcome this tension we need to restyle our
theology and our Christian practices from the one side
and from the other side we must look for the fulfilment
of natural concepts and practices in a Christian framework whose dominant theme is redeeming love. That it
seems to me is the task which the judgmental controversy
sets us.

A true theology that mediates the Gospel will never
be, and can never logically be, authoritarian for it
will always have the power and authority of God which
in Whitehead's phrase is, 'the worship he inspires', or
to give that remark a Christian context we may say that
a true theology will have the power and authority of a
love which never lets us go. Again moral judgments
are worth nothing whatever, indeed they aren't even
moral judgments, unless they mediate a moral ideal which

freely inspires and spontaneously wins our acceptance.
It is perfectly true that no good can ever come from a
judgmental attitude which is hostile, repressive of
the spirit of man, which imposes *a priori* dogmatic
interpretation, which despises or ignores the wealth
of our knowledge about human personalities, about
their needs and hopes and fears, the kind of knowledge
that the psychological and behavioural sciences can
give us. (Incidentally, in case I have misled anybody
when I said 'Behavioural Sciences', I hope that all the
way through the reader will translate this as 'Psychological and Behavioural Sciences' for I always had both
of them in mind.) But once theology has learned that
it is primarily the purveyor of a vision, and that its
authority is that of an inspiring ideal, and that moral
judgments are worth nothing unless they arrive as a
response to a disclosure of obligation around all the
relevant empirical facts, then a judgmental attitude,
so called, loses everything of its harsh, oppressive,
inhibited, ignorant character. Furthermore, the
attitude of acceptance receives in its turn the fuller
setting and explication it must have if it is to be
responsible and creative and point to freedom and
maturity and fulfilment. The truly judgmental and the
truly accepting attitudes come to the same point from
quite opposite directions, the one coming from a theological and a moral direction, the other from a natural
and behavioural direction. They meet together when
they are both genuine at the point of all those who
stand in need of adequate help.

But when we realise that the image of the Church is
often judgmental in the bad sense, and its officers in
that some sense are supposed to be judgmental too; we
also realise what an appallingly difficult task lies
ahead of us, those of us in the Church as Christians
or in the Church as its officers. Not only must we
ensure that the overall image is changed, but that the
character of the Church's caring ministry makes certain
that it will be. Until that happens there will not
only be a lie instead of the Gospel in our right hand,
but we shall have failed to minister God's Grace to the
needs and hopes of humanity, and the cry of judgmental
will be heard and rightly heard in our clinics and in
our streets, not to say at our casework discussions.
Not only will it be heard, but the condemnation it
expresses albeit in a misleading way, will be amply
deserved.

Bibliography

This bibliography includes all those sources referred
to in the Editors' Introduction and others which may be
useful in the study of particular topics raised by the
essays collected.   The topics to which the items
listed are relevant are indicated by their titles, with
the possible exception of Benn and Peters (1959),
Feinberg (1973) and Peters (1966), which have directly
relevant chapters, but are also good general introduc-
tions to moral and social philosophy.   Other references
can be found within the essays or their notes.

ARISTOTLE, 'The Nicomachean Ethics', trans. by Sir
David Ross, Oxford University Press, 1925.
ARROW, K.J. (1972), Gifts and Exchanges, 'Philosophy
and Public Affairs', vol. 1, no. 4.
ATTFIELD, R. (1974), On Being Human, 'Inquiry', vol. 17.
BEALES, H.L. (1945), 'The Making of Social Policy',
Hobhouse Memorial Lecture, no. 15.
BENN, S.I. and PETERS, R.S. (1959), 'Social Principles
and the Democratic State', London, George Allen & Unwin.
BROOKE, R. (1972), Social Administration and Human
Rights in P. Townsend and N. Bosanquet (eds), 'Labour
and Inequality', London, Fabian Society.
CAMPBELL, T.D. (1976), Discretionary 'Rights' in Timms
and Watson (1976).
DOWNIE, R.S. (1971), 'Roles and Values', London,
Methuen.
FEINBERG, J. (1973), 'Social Philosophy', Englewood
Cliffs, Prentice-Hall.
HALL, P. (1952), 'The Social Services of Modern England',
London, Routledge & Kegan Paul.
HARE, R.M. (1952), 'The Language of Morals', Oxford
University Press.
HARRIS, E. (1968), Respect for Persons in R.T. DeGeorge
(ed.), 'Ethics and Society', London, Macmillan.
304

HENDERSON, C.R. (1902), 'Introduction to the Study of the Dependent, Defective, and Delinquent Classes, and of their Social Treatment'.

HNIK, F.R. (1938), 'The Philanthropic Motive in Christianity'.

JONES, O.R. (1971), ed., 'The Private Language Argument', London, Macmillan.

KEITH-LUCAS, A. (1953), The Political Theory Implicit in Social Casework, 'American Political Science Review', vol. 4.

MACLAGAN, W.G. (1960), Respect for Persons as a Moral Principle - I, 'Philosophy', vol. 35, July, and, Respect for Persons as a Moral Principle - II, 'Philosophy', vol. 35, October.

MARSH, D. (1970), 'The Welfare State', London, Longmans.

NAGEL, T. (1975), 'The Possibility of Altruism', Oxford University Press.

PETERS, R. (1958), 'The Concept of Motivation', London, Routledge & Kegan Paul.

PETERS, R. (1966), 'Ethics and Education', London, George Allen & Unwin.

PINKER, R. (1970), Stigma and Social Welfare, 'Social Work', vol. 27, no. 4.

PINKER, R. (1971), 'Social Theory and Social Policy', London, Heinemann.

PINKER, R. (1974), Social Policy and Social Justice, 'Journal of Social Policy', vol. 3, no. 1.

PLANT, R. (1970), 'Social and Moral Theory in Casework', London, Routledge & Kegan Paul.

PLANT, R. (1974), 'Community and Ideology', London, Routledge & Kegan Paul.

RAPHAEL, D. (1967), 'Political Theory and the Rights of Man', London, Macmillan.

RAPHAEL, D. (1970), 'Problems of Political Philosophy', London, Macmillan.

RESCHER, N. (1972), 'Welfare', University of Pittsburgh Press.

ROBSON, W. and CRICK, B. (1970), 'The Future of the Social Services', Harmondsworth, Penguin.

SINGER, P. (1973), Altruism and Commerce: A defense of Titmuss against Arrow, 'Philosophy and Public Affairs', vol. 2, no. 3.

SLACK, K. (1966), 'Social Administration and the Citizen', London, Michael Joseph.

STALLEY, R.F. (1976), Non-Judgmental Attitudes in Timms and Watson (1976).

STRAWSON, P.F. (1959), 'Individuals', London, Methuen.

STRAWSON, P.F. (1962), Freedom and Resentment, British Academy Lecture reprinted in P.F. Strawson (ed.),

'Studies in the Philosophy of Thought and Action',
Oxford University Press, 1968.
STRAWSON, P.F. (1971), Categories, in O.P. Wood and
G. Pitcher (eds), 'Ryle', London, Macmillan.
TELFER, E. (1970), Friendship, 'Proceedings of the
Aristotelian Society', 1970-71.
TIMMS, N. and WATSON, D. (1976) (eds), 'Philosophy in
Social Work', London, Routledge & Kegan Paul.
TITMUSS, R.M. (1968), 'Commitment to Welfare', London,
George Allen & Unwin.
TITMUSS, R.M. (1970), 'The Gift Relationship', London,
George Allen & Unwin.
TITMUSS, R.M. (1971), Welfare 'Rights', law and discre-
tion, 'Political Quarterly', vol. 42.
WATSON, D. (1976), Social Services in a Nutshell, in
Timms and Watson (1976).
WILENSKY, H.L. and LEBEAUX, C.N. (1958), Conceptions of
Social Welfare, ch. 6 of their 'Industrial Society and
Social Welfare', London, Macmillan and New York, Free
Press.
WINCH, P. (1958), 'The Idea of a Social Science', London,
Routledge & Kegan Paul.
WINCH, P. (1964), Understanding a Primitive Society,
'American Philosophical Quarterly', vol. 1.

For Product Safety Concerns and Information please contact our EU
representative GPSR@taylorandfrancis.com
Taylor & Francis Verlag GmbH, Kaufingerstraße 24, 80331 München, Germany